Go, Gwen, Go

Elizabeth Jorgensen | Nancy Jorgensen

Go, Gwen, Go

A Family's Journey to Olympic Gold

Foreword by Bob Babbitt

MEYER & MEYER SPORT

British Library Cataloguing in Publication Data

A catalogue record for this book is available from the British Library

Go, Gwen, Go

Maidenhead: Meyer & Meyer Sport (UK) Ltd., 2020

ISBN: 978-1-78255-191-1

Aachen, Auckland, Beirut, Cairo, Cape Town, Dubai, Hägendorf, Hong Kong, Indianapolis, Maidenhead, Manila, New Delhi, Singapore, Sydney, Tehran, Vienna

Credits
Cover and interior design: Annika Naas
Layout: Amnet

Front cover photos: © dpa
All other photos: © Elizabeth Jorgensen and Nancy Jorgensen, unless otherwise noted
Graphics: © AdobeStock

Managing editor: Elizabeth Evans
Copyeditor: Sarah Pursey

Member of the World Sports Publisher' Association (WSPA), www.w-s-p-a.org

Printed by: C-M Books, Ann Arbor, MI, USA

ISBN: 978-1-78255-191-1

Email: info@m-m-sports.com

www.thesportspublisher.com

CONTENTS

FOREWORD

Imagine this. Your daughter or sister is finishing up her CPA and has already accepted a great job from Ernst & Young as a tax accountant. Then, out of nowhere, she receives a call from someone at USA Triathlon, the governing body for a small sport that was first showcased in the 2000 Olympics. That call will send her life—and yours—on an amazing journey into the unknown and, eventually, to Olympic glory.

Gwen Jorgensen swam for three years at the University of Wisconsin–Madison and ran for three years. During those last two years, while she was finishing up her CPA, she won the 2009 Big 10 Championships at both 3,000 and 5,000 meters.

In 2010, the folks at USA Triathlon asked Gwen if she had any interest in racing for the US and possibly going to the Olympics. The Olympics? Gwen had never ridden a high-performance bicycle before and was just beginning her career at one of the most prestigious accounting firms in the world.

Gwen wasn't willing to walk away from a career at Ernst & Young that was just beginning to take a flier on becoming a world-class triathlete, so she took baby steps. Tom Schuler, a former professional cyclist, was brought in to help Gwen learn how to ride a bike while she attempted to balance both her position at Ernst & Young and learning this new sport.

Early on, she would fall over at stoplights while trying to unclip from her pedals. But Gwen was tenacious and eventually she would learn to not only ride a bike, but also learn how to train for and race a triathlon.

While training on the bike, Tom Schuler introduced Gwen to a friend and professional cyclist who then helped coach and rode with this cyclist-come-lately. His name was Patrick Lemieux, and he and Gwen would eventually marry and become parents to their little boy, Stanley.

This memoir is written by her mother Nancy and her sister Elizabeth. In the pages of this book, you'll be introduced to the Gwen they knew from when she was a little girl. The Jorgensen family was there to support her as she went from CPA to novice triathlete to racing her first professional event.

Less than two years after getting into the sport, Gwen Jorgensen was on the starting line at the 2012 Olympic Triathlon in London. During her triathlon career, she became the first American woman to win a World Triathlon Series event, the first person in history to win 12 consecutive races on the ITU circuit and the first American triathlete, male or female, to win an Olympic Gold Medal, which she did in Rio in 2016.

Gwen Jorgensen became the very best female Olympic-distance triathlete on the planet, and her family was there to cheer her on.

This is their story.

Get ready for one heckuva ride!

–Bob Babbitt
USA Triathlon Hall of Fame Inductee
Ironman Triathlon Hall of Fame Inductee
Competitor Magazine *Co-Founder*
Challenged Athletes Foundation Co-Founder

PROLOGUE

I was born an introvert. Thankfully, my older sister Elizabeth was not. When I learned to talk, I rarely wanted to share with others, so my sister took over, answering questions I was asked. Elizabeth got to know me this way. She could speak my mind just by looking at my expressions. We spent hours together as children with our mom, Nancy, and dad, Joel. We didn't have cable television, cell phones, or PlayStation. Growing up, we talked to each other, played, and fought. Dad made wooden puzzles that we assembled at night; I always wanted to finish the fastest and pulled out a stopwatch as everyone solved Dad's newest invention. Dad, EJ, and I played HORSE at the backyard basketball hoop while Mom cooked snacks inside. My most vivid memories are of my sister and me playing violin with Mom accompanying on piano. I didn't always enjoy the violin, but I did enjoy time with my family.

As the quiet one, I often observed my older sister and mom talk, work, play, and cook. It taught me about overcoming challenges, being in the moment, and expecting to better myself. In this book, my mom and sister give their accounts of what I was like as a child, and how I developed into an Olympic champion. They accurately capture my struggles, aspirations and joys. They include excerpts from my perspective as well, but often my sister and mom capture my thoughts better than I, the introvert, could convey.

My experiences taught me you don't have to be anything special to become successful. I was born into a middle-class family, and no one pushed me to do sports. My sister and I each played at least one instrument and one sport from the age of eight. Our parents allowed us to make choices for ourselves. From an early age, I was taught to take responsibility for my choices. If I decided on basketball camp, I couldn't quit halfway through the season. I learned to make well thought-out decisions and follow through, no matter the outcome.

I am now starting a family of my own and wonder how my children will grow and mature. I hope I will know my child as well as my family knows me. I love going home as an adult because it is like nothing has changed. Mom still spoils me. She turns my laundry right-side out, cooks amazing meals, and shares what's going on in her life, while my sister injects energy and emotion into our family. Elizabeth brings games, knows what she wants (like Mom's homemade pretzels and Dad's choices of cheese presented on his hand-crafted cheese board) and isn't afraid to tell us. Our family is perfectly abnormal. We get along because we are a family based in love, and I hope the same for Patrick and me. I hope you enjoy this book as much as I do. It tells my story, while also showing the emotions and struggles a family goes through when an average daughter goes from CPA to Olympic gold medalist.

–Gwen Jorgensen

Photo courtesy of Talbot Cox.

CHAPTER 1

A Convolution of Circumstances

2009 & 2010

NANCY

In May of 2009, a few weeks before my daughter Gwen's University of Wisconsin commencement, I took a seat at the Fayetteville, Arkansas, NCAA track finals. My husband Joel, older daughter Elizabeth, and I, traveled 700 miles from Waukesha, Wisconsin, for a celebration and farewell. We were saying goodbye to Gwen's collegiate running career. To three years of track stadiums and cross-country courses. To five-kilometer races in sun-baked summers, and six-kilometer ones in snowy Novembers.

The final meet concluded more than a sports season. It capped a life season. For Gwen, it ended competitive sports and for us, it ended cheering, pom-poms, and spring breaks with a college kid at home. We celebrated too: Gwen's record-setting track wins and All-American cross-country victories, her graduation with an accountancy degree, and her first job at a Big Four accounting firm. We reveled in Gwen's accomplishments and hoped for one final triumph. In the battle of emotions, pride shoved nostalgia aside allowing only joy and hope.

ELIZABETH

A few days before the meet, Gwen called me from her apartment. She lived in a rented house on Mifflin Street where hardwood floors moaned in the Wisconsin winters. Charming and perpetually dusty, the two-story structure stood guard each spring during a thirty-thousand-person block party. Uninterested in the bash, Gwen favored its proximity to campus.

She said, "I have a few minutes before class. I'm just on the bed with my feet up. You have time to talk?"

"Yep."

"I'm packed and ready to leave for Arkansas. I have some leg pain still, but it's my last meet so I'm going for it." Gwen rarely admitted to pain, so her mention of injury suggested its significance.

"I'm sure you'll do great, Gwen."

"And after, I'm going to Europe. That will give it time to heal." Gwen had planned a post-graduation backpacking trip, but it seemed unrealistic she could heal while traveling.

"You're okay to run?"

"I want to finish as an All-American. But really, I'll be happy to help the team and get some points."

"Either way, Mom and Dad and I will be there. It should be fun."

"I'm excited to see you guys."

NANCY

Gwen asserted her place on the outdoor track, toe grinding tar at the 5K start line. Five feet, 10 inches tall, 125 pounds—she towered over girls built closer to the ground. Her dark curls bobbed in a ponytail. She looked fatigued in yesterday's preliminary race, but her results qualified her for finals. The previous night, an ice bath flushed lactic acid from her calves, and a therapist massaged her muscles. Today, the best finishers would be All-Americans. And experts called Gwen a favorite. The gun went off. Gwen reacted last. Her slow-motion start allowed competitors to charge forward.

"She's always slow at the beginning." Joel held a thumb on his stopwatch. "She'll be fine."

I wasn't worried yet. A negative-split runner, Gwen saved her speed for the back end of a race.

Elizabeth shielded her eyes from the sun, squinting to see across the track. "She looks tired."

None of us was surprised by Gwen's position, but she didn't have her usual energy. Then a minor hitch became a limp, and Gwen tipped sidelong with each step. After only one kilometer, she stared at the back of 15 jerseys. At the 2.5-kilometer mark, she hobbled to the side and withdrew. It was the first time I saw her drop out of an event—stoic and unemotional in public, she specialized in pain and manufactured miracles to finish every contest.

By the time we saw her an hour later, an orthopedic boot shackled her shin. I mourned the loss of her final race—it seemed a heartsick way to close a career, without even crossing the finish line. I learned later Gwen suspected a stress fracture but refused x-rays for fear of the truth. She willed her way to finals, but the pain won out.

ELIZABETH

As we exited the stadium, Gwen limping in her boot, a woman approached. She looked official, her identification tags on a lanyard. "Gwen, do you have a minute?"

Gwen introduced us to Barb Lindquist from USA Triathlon's collegiate recruitment program. Barb had noticed Gwen's swim and run background as she searched for potential triathletes. "That was a tough race—I'm sorry to see you're injured. Give it some rest and you'll heal quickly."

"Thanks."

In high school, Gwen and I confided in each other about basketball, track, and swimming. Now, she made decisions with college coaches and this was the first I heard about triathlon.

Lindquist, 40ish, fit, and tan, smiled. "You should consider triathlon—swim, bike, run."

12

Gwen shifted the weight of her backpack and seemed ready to leave. "I can't do a 10-hour Ironman."

"This isn't Ironman. It's Olympic distance. Only a two-hour race."

Gwen leaned on her healthy leg. "I don't have a bike."

"We'll find one for you and get you a coach."

I wondered what this recruiter saw in my sister, an injured track athlete with little success on the University of Wisconsin swim team.

"I have a job lined up with Ernst & Young. I'll be doing tax accounting 40 hours a week." Irritation crouched behind Gwen's words.

"You can try it in your free time, and we'll help you get started."

"I'll think about it."

After Gwen shook Lindquist's hand, we continued walking. I wondered why Gwen hadn't mentioned triathlon and what Lindquist's proposal meant for my little sister.

NANCY

After Lindquist offered her business card and retreated, Gwen confirmed her disinterest. "She keeps calling and emailing, but I'm too busy to even think about it." Gwen committed her summer to studying for the 14-hour CPA exam—324 questions in auditing, business concepts, financial accounting, and regulation.

But Lindquist, a former Olympic triathlete, knew about determination and persistence. In phone calls, she suggested Gwen explore triathlon and decide later if she had potential. In emails, she promoted USA Triathlon, coaxing and cajoling. "We need gifted athletes like you in our program."

I knew Gwen was flattered but that she lacked confidence. Passionate about swimming, Gwen joined the University of Wisconsin swim team, confident she would thrive in Division I athletics. But she plunged from high school MVP to collegiate afterthought, not once swimming an NCAA finals meet. Fresher in her mind were three years of collegiate running that ended with a stress fracture.

Gwen told me what she said to Lindquist. "I know how strong you have to be to succeed at the top. I don't have that kind of talent."

Lindquist sweetened the prospect with confidence in Gwen's abilities. "Gwen, on paper, you are stronger than I was. And I was an Olympian."

Gwen began to succumb to the allure of competition, of exploring potential, of pushing limits. She started to believe perhaps she could perfect her swimming, leverage her running, and pick up cycling. Perhaps the whole could be more than the sum of swim, bike, run. Perhaps she could be a world-class athlete. Perhaps triathlon was the winning formula to amalgamate her talents and reveal a champion.

Several weeks after graduation, Gwen said, "Yeah, Mom, I'm thinking about giving triathlon a chance. I always planned to work out in my free time, so if I'm running anyway, I suppose I could add a few swim workouts and pick up the bike."

I understood Gwen's reasoning. Why not gamble a few hours every day? On the income/loss sheet, her gain in fitness would surely justify the hours invested. And I trusted her judgment—always sensible, she would continue working while she trained.

Gwen had one experience with triathlon. It was a bucket list item for eighteen-year-old Gwen and her Waukesha South High School track teammate, Maggie Lach. Neither knew anything about the sport, but in 2004, when a local group sponsored a one-hour super-sprint, Gwen and Maggie registered.

On a hot July morning, Joel, Elizabeth, and I gathered on Wisconsin's Pewaukee Lake beach to cheer. "Good luck, girls."

"Meet us at the finish line?" Gwen pulled a swim cap over her ponytail. "Maggie's going to wait for me after the bike, and then we'll run together. We plan to tie, no matter what place we're in."

They dove in, swallowed up by the mass of competitors, and after 10 minutes, ran up the beach in perfect step. Maggie mounted her road bike and leaned over her drop bars, accelerating easily. Gwen borrowed my mountain bike—a poor choice for pavement and rolling Wisconsin hills—and struggled on the wide tires.

Maggie waited for Gwen in transition, and once in running shoes, they strode in tandem down the chute—tied for first. The 60-minute event was far from the two-hour professional sport Lindquist described.

As Gwen started to buy in, Lindquist found a bike sponsor and arranged coaching. Gwen began training with Milwaukee run groups, bike clubs, and swim programs. But she also worked as a tax accountant for Ernst & Young which sometimes meant 60-hour weeks. Early morning runs and late evening bike rides bookended her days, while at the office she met with clients, computed formulas, and studied tax law. I asked how she was holding up.

"I'm not sleeping, Mom. It's hard to relax after late workouts."

Cramming training sessions into the few free hours of an accountant's day, Gwen lacked time to recover—or to consume enough calories. One morning, she called complaining of stomach pain. She woke up hungry in the middle of the night. "All I had in the apartment was cereal, so I ate the whole box," she said.

"What kind of cereal?"

"Fiber One."

"Did you have any milk with it?"

"No, I was out of milk."

An entire box of dry, fiber cereal? Honey, no wonder your stomach hurts.

For months, she conjured opportunities for swimming, biking, and running. She skipped a movie to clip in for a 50-mile bike ride. She cheated Sunday services for fartleks and hills. She skimmed minutes from sleep to swim before sunup at the Walter Schroeder Aquatic Center—and met program director Dave Anderson, dreamer and visionary.

Some people cast themselves in Olympic stories, while others direct from the wings. Anderson wrote his script long ago, waiting for a superstar to fill the role, and he seized on Gwen's budding triathlon career. Anderson watched Gwen's pool sessions, impressed with her stroke, her competitive instinct, and her unflagging attendance. Like Lindquist, Anderson recognized potential—Olympic potential. He imagined himself a facilitator and promoter.

Even as Gwen committed to triathlon, she harbored doubts about her ability to combine swim, bike, and run into a legitimate Olympic effort. But success in local races boosted her confidence, and she entered an elite development race—as an amateur—in Clermont, Florida.

ELIZABETH

Gwen suggested Mom, Dad, and I travel with her to Florida. Mom and I taught in the same high school, and we both used our personal day to create a long weekend. Dad and Gwen each requested a vacation day from their employers.

I had no idea what to expect, and the Florida triathlon jump-started a learning process for all of us, Gwen included. Still accumulating gear, Gwen lacked equipment, so friends lent her a wetsuit, and she borrowed a bike bag to pack her bicycle, tools, helmet, and a portable trainer. Even with handlebars removed, the bike in its case was an unwieldy monster. *Do the airlines allow a bag this big?* As Dad loaded the Honda Civic for the airport, Gwen panicked. "Dad, my bike doesn't fit in the car."

"Be patient. It might take some adjusting." Dad, ever repairing broken toys and household plumbing, hoisted the bag in and out, finding the precise angle where the door could close. Gwen and I, accustomed to trusting Dad for solutions, handed him suitcases for the trunk.

At the airport, Dad piled the bike bag and luggage on a cart, arousing curiosity as travelers guessed at the hulking black case. "Is that a set of golf clubs?"—"A massage table?"—"A musical instrument?"

Once through check-in, inspectors opened the oversized bag, searched, and hastily reassembled Gwen's equipment—then charged Mom and Dad an extra $150.

NANCY

At the Florida race, triathletes lined up on the beach in neck to ankle neoprene wetsuits. All wore the same color swim cap. Gwen, like the others, jogged in place, swim-stroking the air to stay warm, or perhaps to battle jitters. When the horn sounded, 30 women dashed into the water, initiated dolphin dives, and finally swam freestyle. Heading for orange buoys, the pack morphed into a line, barely visible from shore, as they stroked through the one-mile course. Twenty minutes later, exiting up the beach, competitors tore off caps and goggles and yanked wetsuit zippers while sprinting toward their bikes. The bikes rested on racks in the transition zone, lined up at numbered stations according to ranking. The best-ranked athlete, number one, racked closest to the bike course.

In the transition zone, athletes peeled off wetsuits, donned helmets, and guided their bikes one-handed toward the cycling course. The best competitors switched from swimming to biking in fewer than 30 seconds.

After a flying mount at the yellow line, cyclists pedaled barefoot. Their feet pushed against the top of shoes attached to their pedals; they gained momentum before sliding their feet in for the 40-kilometer ride. Eight times, riders sped around a five-kilometer loop, circling past the crowd once per lap. On each lap, Gwen lagged farther behind, her fear of corners evident as she stalled around curves while experienced cyclists shot past.

In the final meters, the women slid out of their shoes to pedal barefoot again. They dismounted before a designated line and ran back into the transition zone where they racked their bikes, discarded helmets, and put on pre-tied running shoes. Gwen's novice biking skills left her eight minutes behind the leader.

The 10-kilometer run was completed in two loops, and we could see Gwen twice on each lap if we dashed from one viewpoint to another. Stopwatch in hand, Joel clocked Gwen's splits while Elizabeth shouted encouragement. "Gwen, you're only eight minutes down. Go catch those girls!"

With each step, Gwen propelled herself closer to the leaders.

"Go, Gwen, go! You're only down by three minutes now!"

Gwen finished in eighth place, right behind the pros, and earned her professional card—the official license to race as an elite triathlete with entrance to top-level competitions and top-tier prize money. It was March, 2010, only 10 months after she rebuffed Lindquist's first overtures.

With Gwen's rapid rise to elite status, Lindquist revised her playbook. She wanted a public commitment to Olympic pursuit. Anderson needed an Olympic commitment for a car deal he arranged. The word "Olympics" became a persistent theme in their vision of Gwen's future.

But Gwen hesitated to say the word. "I'm just not sure, Mom. What if I say I want to go to the Olympics and I'm not good enough? Once I make that announcement, everything I do is public."

I understood her hesitation—but also the power of her competitive drive. As Gwen worked full-time and trained more seriously, demands increased in both work and sport. Considering a move to part-time accounting (and Olympic pursuit), she asked my opinion.

"Honey, you're only 23 once. If you want to try professional sports, now is the time. Move home if you need to. We can help with finances."

"I'm not doing this if my parents have to help me."

The next time we saw Gwen race, she wore a Timex kit and used their sponsorship for expenses. USA Triathlon supplied her bike and coach, and she was negotiating a car sponsorship with David Hobbs Honda in Milwaukee. But she still worked for Ernst & Young, hashing figures on corporate taxes and bumming rides to workouts while she waited to secure the car.

****

In April 1986, when Gwen was three-days-old, I drew her first bath. As I dribbled water over Gwen's toes, her fetal coil relaxed. Three-year-old Elizabeth dipped a tiny washcloth in the water for me. "Mama, she likes her bath."

In July, Gwen splashed with Elizabeth in Grandma and Grandpa's outdoor pool. In October, Joel and I registered them for winter lessons at the YWCA. While Elizabeth whimpered about chlorine in her nose, six-month-old Gwen laughed when I plunged her head underwater. Wet-dark lashes blinked away drops as her lips bubbled the swells. Even as a baby, Gwen loved water in every form—outdoor pools, cool water beaches, long baths.

Several years later, when Gwen was in grade school, the Waukesha Optimist Club offered third grade students a formal swim meet experience—one Saturday with whistled officials, diving block starts, electronic scoreboards, and ribbons for finishers. Gwen packed her goggles and suit and when the weekend arrived, she stepped from snow-packed streets to sky-high natatorium. The combination of steaming air and chlorine was like flint and steel sparking her eight-year-old proclivity. A craving for water/swim/compete crystallized that day.

After the meet, Gwen climbed in the car. "Dad, look! These papers tell about the swim team. Do you think I could join?"

"Let's see." Joel and I looked for cost and commitment. Since I worked as a high school choral director with evening rehearsals and concerts, I counted on Joel to chauffeur Elizabeth and Gwen. "The schedule looks fine," he said.

"Can I, Mom?"

"Would you enjoy swimming twice a week?" I already knew the answer and swimming offered exercise, competition, and friends.

We indulged Gwen's love of water and swimming, just as we cheered Elizabeth in basketball and running. But so many activities required miles of driving, so one summer, I convinced 12-year-old Gwen to join 15-year-old Elizabeth at track camp. Before doing a backward drill, the coach cautioned against speed. He said the exercise targeted balance, form, and posture, and one year too much hustle broke a girl's arm. Competitive drive can be a perilous virtue. While Elizabeth and the other girls lifted their knees and corrected their slouch, Gwen accelerated. Unable to control her momentum, she slipped and her full weight landed on one forearm—snapping both bones.

While prepping for surgery and an overnight hospital stay, she said to the surgeon, "I've seen kids swimming with a special cast on their arm. Can I have one of those?"

When the surgeon looked from Gwen to me, I saw disbelief and amusement in his face. "It's not that kind of break." Gwen kept her cast dry for eight weeks and spent her time reading Olympic biographies.

Gwen entered high school with one goal—to swim on a Division I university swim team. Each year, she was Waukesha South High School's MVP and earned seeds in the Wisconsin State Swim Meet's distance events. For every meet, Joel and I rooted from the bleachers, unless one of us watched Elizabeth in a basketball game. For some events, all four of us traveled to Minnesota, or Indiana, or just across town.

Although a regular on the Wisconsin State High School podium, Gwen never stood on the top step. But she believed a bronze or silver medal could be converted to gold with 30 more minutes at the pool, 20 more pounds on the weight machine, or 10 more minutes with the club's sports psychologist. Impressed with her devotion, I arranged our schedule to accommodate added workouts.

During her junior year in high school, Gwen booked recruiting trips to Big Ten universities. But swimming in a small Waukesha pond did not prepare her for the collegiate sharks. Every woman loved water as much as Gwen did, but they were six-feet tall, muscular, and buoyant, with strokes that stirred tsunamis. While they sorted through offers, no one wasted paper on Gwen's 120 pounds stretched over a 5'10" frame.

While she could have scored a full ride with a less competitive team, Gwen decided to walk on at the University of Wisconsin–Madison. And I gave up my notion of a tuition-free college kid.

Gwen's dream slowly dissolved in the waters of Indiana University, Notre Dame, and Michigan State. Her seasons ended at the Big Ten Conference Championship while talented swimmers went on to NCAA Finals and Olympic trials. After three seasons, in 2007, her coaches agreed—Gwen had reached her potential.

Lucky for Gwen, her high school track coach, Eric Lehmann, followed her career. Lehmann believed in Gwen's natural talent for running, and he intervened to spin her from the UW pool to the UW track. The transition would propel Gwen's future triathlon career.

****

In March 2010, Gwen returned from Clermont, Florida, an elite triathlete with credentials for top-level races. With the help of USA Triathlon and her coach, Cindi Bannink, she booked eight more triathlons in Valencia, Montreal, San Francisco, British Columbia, Edinburgh, Tuscaloosa, Huatulco, and Puerto Vallarta.

On each trip, Gwen traveled with an Ernst & Young computer, completing corporate tax returns from hotel desks and airport terminals. Over the next year, she pared work hours gradually, reducing from 80% employment to 60% to 40%. Meanwhile, USA Triathlon added her to the National Team, which provided financial assistance including race fees and a travel budget.

Although we helped Gwen travel to Clermont, Florida, job responsibilities kept Joel, Elizabeth, and me in Wisconsin for most of the 2010 season. As Gwen prepared for each trip, I quizzed her about terms I discovered in online articles. "Gwen, what is a World Cup? And Continental Cup?"

"Mostly, I'm entering less competitive races. World Cup is just a little more competitive than Continental Cup."

"Okay. What is the World Triathlon Series?"

"Oh, I'm not ready for that yet. That's the WTS and only the best women can enter. But my next race isn't any of those. It's for university-age women—anyone under 25."

On May 28, in Valencia, Spain, Gwen competed in the World University Triathlon Championships, representing USA on a team of five women. I wondered how she would compare to her international peers, but I was nervous about her solo travel and looked for her first email.

> *can't type long. but i'm here….:)*

> *YAY love it. see you guys soon.*

> *Gw*

With no live coverage, we waited for Gwen to contact us with results.

"How did the race go?" I asked during our international phone call.

"I got second place, but it was a limited field—only people in my age group." She tucked triumph behind self-critique.

"Wow! A silver medal. That's unbelievable!" Proud, and pleasantly surprised with Gwen's success, I felt a pang of regret at missing it.

"Mom, this was just university-age athletes. It doesn't mean I'll stack up great with people who have been doing triathlon for 10 years."

But Bannink, Gwen's coach, sent an enthusiastic email.

Gwen!!! Holy cow, you are amazing!

2nd place and just 7 seconds out of first? I can't wait to hear your full race recap, what a day! Congrats!

Don't worry about getting in a workout tomorrow, just focus on your travel, getting back into a routine once home, and overcoming the time change. Mon and Tues are easy recovery days IF you feel like it.

Let's chat when you have some time, looking forward to it.

Cindi

Gwen responded.

all due to GREAT coaching!!!!

just want to verify i'm going to montreal for sure - parents want to book a flight. i am delayed at airport, trying to get some stuff settled (bags are lost, etc.) but will call soon to talk :)

Gwen had always been humble about race outcomes, even with family. She preferred to analyze her performance, scouring ways to improve, sometimes forgetting to celebrate accomplishments. I recognized the characteristic in other successful people—those rarely satisfied always had a new goal. Despite Gwen's humility, I knew her Valencia race was a significant accomplishment and an accurate gauge of her talent on the world stage. Of 57 women from 27 countries, Gwen placed in the top two.

Joel and I were eager to see one more 2010 event, and I lobbied for Coteau-du-Lac, near Montreal in Canada. "We could get an international experience without the European price tag. And I know a little French."

Joel never turned down a chance to see a race. "All the European races conflict with your teaching schedule anyway—let's do Montreal." Because Elizabeth taught summer school, she skipped this trip.

We flew with Gwen to Montreal for the June 26 race. For travel, Gwen wore an official team warm-up. White letters, eight inches high, blazoned her blue jacket: USA. She toted a USA backpack and wore USA on her red-white-and-blue hat. Always affiliated with some sport, Gwen amassed gear from Waukesha Express Swim Team, Waukesha South High School, and the University of Wisconsin. She rarely wore anything else. But seeing her in Team USA gear stirred a new order of parental pride. When next to her, I walked a little taller, matching her stride. And more than once, I dropped back to see USA on her jacket. I hoped travelers noticed too, and I sneaked a peek to see who might be looking at our not-so-famous-but-important daughter.

Once more, tiny cars balked at so much gear. Overstuffed bike bags bullied their zippers. Airport inspectors, with no interest in caution, ripped through costly equipment. As Joel hucked backpacks and duffle bags onto airport scales, I read relief in Gwen's eyes when she whispered, "Thank you, Dad."

Language also complicated our trip. In French-speaking Montreal, our first snafu occurred en route to the hotel. We arrived on June 24, surprised to find decorations in the streets, marching bands, banners, and costumes. "Gwen, what is this? Is it for the triathlon?"

"No idea."

Confused by the hullabaloo and French road signs, we made a wrong turn into extremely slow traffic. We soon realized a marching band set our pace, and the sight of a giant float behind us confirmed we had driven into a St. Jean Baptiste Day parade. We smiled, fluttered a royal wave, and searched the skyline for our hotel.

"There! I think I see Holiday Inn." Joel zipped into underground parking. After that, we planned routes more carefully.

Race day arrived on June 26, and after years of accompanying Gwen to swim meets, track meets, cross-country meets, and now triathlons, we knew her routine. Rising early, Gwen quietly and methodically prepared. We worked as support team, supplying fuel and carting gear like a motorsport crew in the pit. Performance requires calories, so we supplemented her hotel breakfast with bananas and almond butter from the corner store. Tires must be checked, so Joel spun wheels and adjusted pressures. Concentration must be cultivated, so Joel and I silenced ourselves. Pre-race, Gwen occupied an alternate world that only coaches could invade. We learned years ago not to be offended by her reticence or emotional distance.

Gwen unapologetically insisted on these conditions, and I realized this too was a trait of winners—successful people know what they need and advocate for themselves.

A novice triathlete, Gwen faced fresh challenges with each event. In Montreal, she confronted cold conditions. Before the race, competitors warmed up in the water, stretching muscles while exploring the lake for current and depth. But when Gwen completed drills and scrambled up the water bank, she looked anything but warm. "Oh, she's shivering. Why does she only have that tiny towel?" More sturdy women appeared comfortable as they stretched or relaxed their limbs. It would be years before Gwen engineered a fix.

While the Valencia, Spain, event compared Gwen to university-age peers, Montreal's Coteau-du-Lac Continental Cup set her against a range of athletes, many older and more experienced. As the race began 100 yards away, Joel and I stood on the canal bank. "Do you see Gwen?"

"With all the matching caps, I can't tell where she is." Peering into binoculars, he searched for Gwen's familiar stroke.

Twenty minutes later, swimmers bolted from the lake. "There! She's running up the steps."

When the 28 athletes exited the water, they scooted up a flight of stairs and dashed across a grassy expanse to their bikes. Earlier, Gwen explained the physics of transition. "When I'm swimming, my body is horizontal and I use my arms, but I don't kick much. Then, when I stand up to get on the bike, blood rushes to my legs and they feel super heavy. And my heart starts to pound."

For the hour-long cycling stage, Joel and I jogged back and forth between vantage points. "What do you think?" I asked.

"A lot better than Clermont. She's quicker on the turns, and she looks faster too." Instead of eight minutes, as in Clermont, only three minutes separated her from the front pack when she dismounted.

On the run, as Gwen passed competitors, I called, "Go, Gwen," as though she could use my cheers to make up the deficit.

With only minutes before the race ended, we staked our place at the finish, pushing close to other spectators. I waited nervously, peering down the road.

"Here she comes." Joel counted the women as they finished. "One...two...three...four...Go, Gwen, go!" Gwen took fifth, completing the 10-kilometer run faster than any other competitor.

Once again, I reveled in how well Gwen had done. But that evening, Gwen downplayed the result. "Mom, this was only a Continental Cup. The women are a lot faster in WTS races." Gwen's questioning and self-scrutiny would prove integral to her success. Assuming all elite athletes possess talent and training, winners cultivate an extra-fertile mental territory. Gwen grew her internal space long ago, and I learned to appreciate it as perhaps her best weapon for winning.

While pre-race we supplied Gwen with silence and assistance, post-race our game played on. Our job was not to question or analyze—coaches are paid for that—but to be present. After the race, Joel and I met Gwen at the finish line. I allowed a thousand questions to go unspoken: *How did you get so far behind in the swim? How tough was that uphill bike? Did you feel strong while you passed those girls on the run?* I knew Gwen would reveal herself after she decompressed, refueled, and rehydrated.

After the medal ceremony, we followed Gwen to the transition area where she packed her gear. Joel slung a backpack from each shoulder, and I carried an extra wheel. On the ride to the hotel, Gwen slipped particulars of the race into our conversation. "That swim was really rough today—everyone swimming on top of each other. Mom, can you look at my neck? Is it all scratched up?"

"No, but you might have a bruise on your shoulder. Is it always so dangerous in the water?"

"Oh, Mom, don't worry. It's just part of the race."

At a team dinner that evening, I listened as Gwen talked with Lindquist. "Some of the leaders on the bike were yelling at me."

I saw interaction among runners on a track and some elbowing on a basketball court, but I didn't know cyclists communicated directly.

Lindquist nodded. "They were hoping you would lead. It's grueling to be in the front of the pack, and they wanted you to take your turn."

"So, did I make some enemies today?"

"It's all part of the sport. As you get stronger, you'll play a bigger role."

****

Until her junior year in college, Gwen's only passion was swimming. But Joel and I insisted on a broader experience for both Elizabeth and Gwen, with mandatory violin lessons and optional basketball and track. While Gwen recoiled at any activity that interfered with swimming, she easily fit grade school basketball into her schedule. With Joel coaching and scheduling practices, she never missed a swim workout. She passed the ball in afternoon drills, dribbled in Saturday games, and perfected her layup before evening swim practice. But when she tried out for the high school team and coaches forced her to choose between sports, the basketball squad lost their best free-throw shooter.

Focused only on the pool, Gwen set school records in individual and relay events. But one random workout session rattled her strategy. Preparation for the pool includes dry-land workouts—weights, crunches, stretching, running. It was during a freshman run session that Waukesha South High School track coach, Eric Lehmann, noticed Gwen's natural stride, her long legs, her light frame ideal for running, and her absolute alignment ankle to knee to hip. Lehmann walked into Gwen's perfectly painted scene and scribbled all over her plan.

ELIZABETH

As a senior on the track and field team, I enjoyed socializing more than competing and used practice for gossip instead of improving my personal bests. Lehmann recognized my talents as better suited for the yearbook and orchestra and entered my name on junior varsity heat sheets. But he saw something different in Gwen.

At an outdoor workout, the sun reflecting off asphalt, I staked a position near the hose, sipping water, delaying my next interval.

Lehmann, broad and stocky, with short hair that never lay straight, walked over and splashed water into his cup. "Your sister, she's a great athlete, hey?"

"She does love swimming."

"Bet she'd be really good at track." Athletes shot past us, Lehmann shouting encouragement and times.

"I don't know. She's probably not interested."

"Well, I could keep her in junior varsity meets for the season. You'd be okay with her on the team?"

"Sure." I didn't think Lehmann stood a chance at convincing Gwen to exit the pool in favor of looping the track.

After swim and track practice, Lehmann approached us. "You've got talent, Gwen. I think you could be one of our top runners. You should join your sister on the track team."

"Yeah, that's Elizabeth's thing. And I swim every day. I don't have time."

"What about cross training? With all that aerobic work in the water, I bet you could just step on the track and run." Lehmann suggested she skip workouts and only compete.

It was the only scenario Gwen would consider, so Lehmann signed her up for the 800-meter run and his 3,200-meter relay team. In her first season, she graduated to varsity and was on the podium at the Wisconsin State Track Meet. My times never qualified me for varsity events, much less State, but I didn't mind. We each did what we were best at—Gwen competed while I decorated the car and shook pom-poms.

NANCY

In spite of her running success, Gwen remained committed to swimming. When conflicts arose, she sided with her favorite. Lehmann remained steadfast too, trying to convince Gwen her true talent lay on dry land. When Gwen was on the Wisconsin State High School Track podium as a freshman, Lehmann chided her. "Hey, Gwen, you did better at State Track than you did at State Swimming."

Gwen shot arrows of contempt at him and ignored the truth. But Lehmann refused to give up. He followed Gwen's college career, and when she struggled on the University of Wisconsin–Madison swim team, he suggested she return to track.

Quoted later by the press, Gwen said, "We have a little tiny break where we have a couple weeks off, and I was doing some running. My high school coach talked to me about trying out for the [UW women's] track team and called Coach Stintzi about me."

Gwen ran a time trial for Stintzi and found herself a rookie junior on the track team.

During holiday break, Gwen explained, "I wanted to do both swimming and running, but the coaches think it will be too much for my body. So, now, I'm just going out for track."

I worried how Gwen would cope without her lifelong passion, but I knew my daughter well. Dedicated and emotionally attached to swimming, she was also analytical, practical, and bold. She expected effort to yield results—and when necessary, she would shift her focus to achieve success.

Lehmann's assessment was accurate from the start. He recognized Gwen's gift for running but diagnosed her swim obsession as nearly insurmountable. He persisted—and then chose the right moment to steer her to the track. It took six years.

Given opportunity and training, Gwen's running led to success, including Big 10 Championship victories. She earned 2009 Division I Great Lakes Track Athlete of the Year. On the University of Wisconsin scoreboard, her times ranked in the top five for 5,000 meters and top ten for 3,000 meters and 10,000 meters. After years of devotion to swimming, Gwen started to explore her true talent and began her love affair with running, competing...and winning.

ELIZABETH

While working at Ernst & Young, Gwen settled into her Milwaukee apartment. As we chatted on the phone and sent text messages, I appreciated having my sister closer to home. Often, Gwen convinced me to join her downtown. Sometimes, I drove to Milwaukee just to cart her to Mom and Dad's house for dinner. At one meal, Gwen shoveled salad and meat and between mouthfuls said she met Tom Schuler, a former professional cyclist. Like Anderson at the aquatic center, Schuler recognized Gwen's talent and volunteered to coach her.

On one of their rides, Schuler introduced Gwen to Patrick Lemieux, a twenty-something professional cyclist from Minnesota. "He's tall, tan, with dishwater blonde hair." During a three-hour trek, Patrick coached her in shifting, descending, and powering through hills. But Gwen said they found more in common than aero bars and derailleurs. She smiled and blushed. "Patrick suggested we exchange contact info. While he was cycling, he took both hands off his handlebars and typed my number in his phone. I couldn't believe it."

Gwen said she agreed to dinner and during the next few months, Patrick traveled to Milwaukee for additional bike races—and late-night dinner dates.

Patrick knew road cycling would improve Gwen's triathlon performance, so he encouraged her to race competitively, and Gwen entered criteriums (crits) in the Tour of America's Dairyland series. Set in towns across Wisconsin, the tour offered Mom, Dad, and me a chance to see Gwen, learn more about cycling, and figure out how serious she was about this new guy.

We discovered crits comprised laps around a closed circuit.

"Let's watch from here—we can see the last corner and the finish line," Dad said.

Race organizers shut down streets, forming a course around several blocks. The tight course demanded repeated 90-degree turns on each loop. Mom agreed. "Sure. It's crowded, but we can hear the announcers. Maybe we can figure out how this works."

As riders repeated the one-kilometer loop for an hour, a formula of time and laps determined the winner. Crits allowed the same draft-legal format as International Triathlon Union (ITU) races—riders pedaled in congested groups and those in the back of a pack benefited from the leaders' work. Only inches from each other, riders risked crashes from wheel-to-wheel contact and chanced disaster if another cyclist went down.

We applauded attacks where cyclists broke from the group to establish a lead. We admired team strategies that leveraged an individual win. We averted our gaze as riders leaned so far on a corner we thought they would tip. And between races, we studied Patrick—his athletic frame, his doting attitude, his ever-smiling face.

In men's races, Patrick rode in the highest category, controlling pack dynamics to maximize his team's opportunity. Mom, Dad, Gwen, and I stood on the side of the road, cheering. The male cyclists whizzed by so fast, Gwen had to point him out in the blur.

Gwen entered lower category races. She improved (but never graduated to the top level) and by the end of the summer, she attacked hills and read race dynamics. But she still feared descents—a challenge in becoming a proficient cyclist.

NANCY

Between pre-race preparations, hour-long races, and post-race cool-downs, Gwen and Patrick had little time for socializing. I got acquainted with Patrick through quick chats. "So, what are your days like, Patrick?"

"Well, a lot of days I travel for my team—Kenda 5-Hour Energy." Like Gwen, he relished competition and pushing limits. "But it doesn't pay all the bills, so when I'm not on the road, I live above the bike shop and make a few extra dollars doing repairs."

Patrick won me with his personality and hard work. Committed to coaching Gwen, he arranged his schedule to accommodate hers. He bettered her cycling skills, avoiding criticism and applauding progress.

In training, Gwen and Patrick played student and coach. But off the trail, they equaled each other, Patrick towering over Gwen in height only—never in attitude or bearing. They enjoyed a balance of Gwen's restraint and Patrick's loquaciousness; Gwen's driven temperament and Patrick's laid-back nature; and Gwen's realistic mindset and Patrick's romantic side.

I welcomed Patrick's partnership in Gwen's career, but dismissed thoughts of a serious relationship. In the past, Gwen eschewed high school flirtation in favor of her true love: the pool. In college, she prioritized studies over courtship. Although she dated an accountant while working at Ernst & Young, the demands of training and competition killed the relationship. How could a long-distance Milwaukee-to-Minnesota romance possibly survive?

****

In the eight ITU triathlons of her 2010 debut season, Gwen finished top ten in every race except Edinburgh (which was actually a hilly duathlon of biking and running). In six of the races, she scored in the top five. She capped her season with a runner-up finish in Puerto Vallarta and earned USA Triathlon's Rookie of the Year award. Accolades flooded her Facebook, Twitter, and email. It was an auspicious beginning with results some athletes work years (or decades) for.

CHAPTER 2

Off to the Races

2011

NANCY

With improving skills, Gwen launched a 2011 season that included 12 triathlons across North America, Europe, and Australia. Her first and last races ranked as ITU Continental Cups and World Cups, while the middle of her season featured four World Triathlon Series (WTS) events—the most competitive. Since national federations enter a limited number in each WTS event, USA's choice to include Gwen affirmed their confidence in her.

The season's first race took Gwen once more to Clermont. After February's three-day, 19-inch Wisconsin snowstorm, I was ready for Florida sun. Elizabeth joined us.

One year ago, in 2010, Gwen competed in Clermont, vying for her professional card. She returned this year a rookie pro facing some of the best in the world, including Great Britain's Helen Jenkins—2008 ITU World Champion—and USA's Sarah Haskins—2008 Olympian.

I noticed the 2011 event billed as a sprint triathlon and quizzed Gwen. "How is a sprint different from Olympic distance?"

"Everything is shorter by half. So the swim is a half-mile instead of a mile. And the bike is 20K instead of 40K. And we run 5K instead of 10K."

"And it takes one hour instead of two?"

"Right."

In college, Gwen specialized in long events for swimming and running, so I wondered if the shorter distance would create a disadvantage. On the other hand, I hoped the brief bike stage would favor her novice cycling.

We headed to the beach. While athletes warmed up and checked bikes, I roasted in the sun, tilting toward its warmth as I perched atop a picnic table. I memorized the scorch on my shoulders, the grit between my toes, and the light glinting off Lake Louisa. I tried to forget about Wisconsin's snow and cold.

Athletes selected start line positions on the shore, strategizing the shortest distance to the buoys. Based on a points system, highest ranked athletes chose first. When the horn blasted, the women bolted toward the water, knees high to maximize their efforts against the water's drag, running as far as possible.

The eight-minute lap kept swimmers in a tight group, and although Gwen exited the water 19th of 29, she was only 23 seconds from the leader. As athletes sprinted toward their bikes, we headed toward transition too, hoping to see Gwen discard her swim gear and mount her bike. While the women skimmed the sandy beach, flying above the squishy surface, I seemed to move in slow motion, each step sinking into sand. By the time Joel, Elizabeth, and I arrived at transition zone, Gwen was in her saddle, pedaling.

ELIZABETH

As Gwen set off for the first bike lap, Dad clicked his stopwatch. Mom and I pushed through heat-thick air and waited for the whirring buzz of tires on pavement.

Analyzing the pack of cyclists, anyone could see Jenkins, Haskins (and most of the field) bested Gwen in form.

"Should Gwen be low like Jenkins? Down close to her drop bars?" Mom said. Jenkins's position reduced wind resistance, while Gwen's arched back prevented effective aerodynamics.

The 20-kilometer ride allowed the leaders only 30 minutes to establish a gap, but at transition, Gwen trailed by 50 seconds. Still, 50 seconds seemed minor compared to Gwen's previous deficits and I knew running was her strength. But with the short run—only about 16 minutes for a 5K—could she catch the leaders?

"Well, Lyza Jo, can Gwen do this?" In family vacation mode, Mom reverted to my nickname.

"Heck, yeah! She just needs us to cheer louder." Gwen said she heard us during races. I figured the louder we shouted, the faster Gwen would run. "Dad? Can she make up that much time?"

"I wish it were a 10K. With only five kilometers, she might run out of road."

Gwen, in 15th place as she started the run, used her natural stride to spur herself toward the front. We dashed into a grove of orange trees where athletes u-turned around a set of road cones. Lining the route, volunteers extended bottles of water into the runners' path. Most athletes snatched one, took a sip, dumped the rest on their head, and threw the empty bottle toward the ditch. Gwen explained earlier: "In certain areas of the course, we can throw water bottles or gel packs. That's the litter zone. If you drop something outside the zone, you get a penalty."

Despite my shouts, "Come on, Gwen!"—"You look good!"—"Catch that girl ahead of you!" Jenkins dominated, running solo into the finish. Forty-five seconds passed before Gwen's teammate, Sarah Haskins, finished second. Gwen followed five seconds later to claim bronze.

We met her at the finish line. "Good job, Gwenevere," Mom said—another childhood nickname.

I gave her a hug. "You looked great! I'm so happy for you."

Dad added praise, too. "Gwenevere! Great race!"

Since elementary school, I told Gwen, *If only you went faster, you would have won,* but thought this not the right time to joke. Gwen breezed past to the athletes' tent. "Thanks, guys. I have to find water and food, and then get to drug testing. See you in a little bit."

I knew "a little bit" could mean 30 minutes or hours. Podium finishers expected routine drug testing, and the process was unpredictable. If a urine sample was satisfactory, the test was quick. But if the sample proved too dilute, the athlete remained until they produced another. More commonly, dehydration prevented athletes from producing the required 90 milliliters. I hoped for a speedy return and early dinner.

NANCY

Gwen joined us after a quick drug test, and then Joel and I toted gear to the rental car while Gwen and Elizabeth walked ahead.

After we dressed for dinner, I asked Elizabeth, "What did Gwen say about the race?"

"She needs to swim faster in order to make the first bike pack." This seemed obvious when Elizabeth said it, but I often forgot, in focusing on Gwen's attempts to learn cycling, she also needed to improve her swim.

"What about the run?"

"She heard me yelling at the corner, but the 5K was too short to make up much time."

Social media responded with acclaim about Gwen's third-place finish. I, too, was optimistic about upcoming WTS events that featured the best triathletes in the world. But first, Gwen would compete in lower category triathlons. Her reduced work schedule, approved by Ernst & Young, allowed time to race in Mexico and Australia.

While Gwen traveled for the next three races, we stayed home. When available, tweets or a live timing system supplied updates, our imaginations spooling the video. Gwen's top-20 results (3rd in Clermont; 5th in Mazatlan, Mexico; 5th in Monterrey, Mexico; and 16th in Mooloolaba, Australia) forecasted a promising debut at the live-streamed WTS Madrid event.

Eager to follow action with both stats and video, Joel and I set up our computer on June 1 for coverage from Spain.

Athletes entered each race with a ranking based on points earned in competition. With her minimal points, Gwen ranked 35th of 65. The low ranking meant her bike rested far back in transition zone, and she had little chance to choose an advantageous swim start position.

Geography and climate dictated conditions on each triathlon course. Depending on location, competitors faced frigid water, oppressive heat, high altitude, driving rain, or cobblestone streets. In Madrid, they suffered Spanish terrain. While some triathlon courses were flat and technical, with sharp curves and 180-degree turns, the Madrid course goaded athletes with mountainous hills. Eight times, riders faced an uphill grade—a 12% incline over 400 meters—that tested their legs and endurance.

As the event began, cameras zoomed in on top-ranked women setting up their bikes while announcers predicted winners.

Then, overhead cameras focused on the lake in Casa de Campo Park as women lined up for the start. Given Madrid's warm June temperatures, official rules prohibited a wetsuit. Gwen would miss its warmth and buoyancy, but she would be spared the struggle to wrestle it off.

Even in person, it is difficult to identify swimmers in the pack of swirling arms. On a computer screen, it was impossible. Occasionally, announcers identified the leader, but we waited for the swim exit to see results. Timing chips strapped to each woman's ankle triggered the screen to post splits as they ran from water to bike. By the time Gwen ran out of the water, coverage already focused on the lead cyclists. We never saw her exit the lake, but the chart revealed Gwen in 46th place.

During the one-hour bike stage, commentators reviewed the field of athletes, discussing USA's contingent. "Hey! They mentioned Gwen!" Joel said.

"Shhh. Maybe they'll talk about her again."

We monitored the leader board to find her not in the lead bike pack, or even a strong chase pack, as she fell further and further behind. Mid-bike stage, the cameras showed her out of her pack and riding solo. She wore full-body fatigue.

"What do you think?" I asked.

"She looks pretty tired."

Once a rider loses contact with a group, they cede the benefit of drafting and fall irrecoverably behind. "Is she trying to catch the next group? Or is she giving up?"

Joel is reliably optimistic, but even he recognized Gwen's failing efforts. "It doesn't look good. If the leaders lap her, she'll be disqualified."

The camera zoomed in as she pushed through an ascent and commentators speculated. "I think her day is done. She will probably pull out." They were right. In the contest of hills, Spain won and Gwen dropped out. So did 12 others.

I worried Gwen might have sustained an injury or crash. Or was she dehydrated? Or had something happened in the water? I wanted to call, but assumed she was busy with post-race activity. I knew she checked email after each race. In my message, I focused on the positive and hoped Gwen's reply would explain what happened.

Hi Gwen,

We got to watch the race today, and it sounded like the bike course was rough. The announcers kept saying how the best athletes in the world were getting beat up by the 12% incline on every lap of the bike course.

You got mentioned a bunch of times as an up-and-coming triathlete. They said the USA is lucky to have 5 great athletes (mentioned your name here along with Bennett, Groff, Peterson, Haskins) when they go to choose 3 for the Olympics.

When do you fly home?

M & D

Hello everyone,

Not my day today...Swim wasn't great (not horrible either)...fell on run to T1 [transition one]*, dropped my cap and had to go back for it in T1...but also got on my bike and had a pack there...then got dropped...another pack came...dropped again...repeat...repeat...legs were just not there today. I've had an awesome time out here in Madrid, and Sarah and Laura did phenomenal!*

Some days it just isn't your day...but you know what? I've had worse days!

Gw

Gwen's deficit was obvious. In spite of her work with cycling groups and private tutoring from Patrick, when faced with a mountainous course, she lacked power and endurance. But if Madrid exposed Gwen's weakness, it also revealed her resolve. She made no excuses and increased workouts to build her legs. As Gwen learned in accounting, investments yield rewards, and she'd already committed assets. She was slowly giving up an accounting career that cost five years of tuition, study, a CPA exam, and work. The ante grew each month as she invested in travel, coaching, equipment, and training. Returns came in with top-10 finishes, but losses intruded too—and Gwen undertook to correct those. She returned to Wisconsin with five weeks to prepare for WTS races in Hamburg, London, and Lausanne, and a World Cup race in Hungary.

ELIZABETH

One day, when bad weather cancelled her outdoor cycling session, Gwen enlisted our help. In her Milwaukee apartment, she slipped into a racing singlet and padded pants, wheeled her bike from the basement, and laid a roller in the hallway. I had seen stationary bike trainers where the bike is fastened down for indoor training, but on Gwen's device, she was supposed to pedal over rolling metal cylinders, maintaining her balance. Three feet long by two feet wide, the roller sat six inches off the floor. Gwen placed her bike on top of it, resting her rear tire between two parallel rolling cylinders that spanned the width of the apparatus. The cylinders were about three inches in diameter with a two-inch space between them. Her front wheel floated on a single rolling cylinder. She claimed balance came from something called "the gyroscopic effect," and the faster she pedaled, the more stable she'd be.

"But each time I get the bike on the rollers, I lose my balance." Preparing to try again, she braced her arms on the hallway walls.

Dad balanced the bike as Mom played spotter—ready to break Gwen's fall. I thought Gwen was insane. There was no way to balance a bike on spinning cylinders. I took a seat on the couch.

When (or if) Gwen produced momentum, Mom and Dad would move away. It reminded me of a kid first learning to ride while her parent holds on. Gwen clipped in her pedals and bobbled, teetering and tottering, one side to the next, as

I played on my phone, wondering how long she wanted to try this impossible task. Hungry, I scoured a restaurant's webpage for dinner options.

Mom and Dad assisted Gwen for close to an hour without much progress. A few times, Gwen established control and they stepped away. Black marks spoiled the walls where her tire skidded on failed attempts. Gwen eventually surrendered, showered off sweat, and dressed for dinner.

At the Ethiopian restaurant, Gwen said, "So I did something stupid the other day. I got a traffic ticket."

We sat in a circle around the woven basket that served as a table. Tearing off chunks of injera—soft, flat, spongy bread—we scooped vegetables and meat from the communal plate. No forks or spoons were provided in this authentic African restaurant.

"What did you do?" I was not used to Gwen breaking the law.

"I ran through a stop sign on my bike. I had no idea bikes had to follow stop signs too. I still have so much to learn."

I laughed and asked how much this error cost, and then transitioned to her race schedule. "What's up next?"

"I'll be riding in a crit, if you want to come."

A few days later, I harnessed my caramel-colored cockapoo, Branji, as Dad loaded Gwen's bike into the trunk. On our way to the Milwaukee park, Gwen reviewed what she knew about biking: "Rubber-side up. I really want to stay rubber-side up."

Dad and I—not thinking or dissecting Gwen's words—just agreed. "Okay, so you want us to yell 'rubber-side up' and cheer?" I asked.

Gwen nodded and went back to her pre-race peanut butter covered banana.

Dad and I made a plan for viewing. We would run back and forth with Branji, darting between loops. Dad, stopwatch in hand, planned to time each lap.

To include Mom, who had a school choir event, I would record the crit and upload it to YouTube. Trying to keep the mood light, we joked about Gwen taking my dog with her in a basket.

"I need to work on my bike handling skills," she said. She didn't mention winning the first place prize: a box of Cliff bars.

"What else should we know about this race?" I asked.

"I don't like being videotaped," Gwen said. But I already promised Mom.

The race started—no fanfare, no gun—and each time Gwen passed, we screamed, "WAY TO STAY RUBBER-SIDE UP!" The race ended—Gwen unaware she was in the final lap—as experienced riders sprinted. She finished in the top ten.

After the event, when I uploaded the video, I realized Gwen was as mixed up as our screams. Her bike should (and thankfully did) remain rubber-side *down*.

Embarrassed, but not surprised, I attributed Gwen's error to a tendency, inherited from Dad, to muddle words and phrases. Whether he's saying *Oconomowoc* when he means Mukwonago or *congersation* when he means conversation, we try to hear what Dad means and not what he says.

Dad comes from a family with nine brothers and sisters and loads of aunts and uncles. One year, as we planned a family function, Dad told me of my grandma's 10 sisters and mentioned the ones still in Wisconsin: Florence, Mae, Agnes. I wanted to invite as many as I could. I asked Grandma, "Should we invite Aunt Mae?"

Tears filling her eyes, she said, "I wish we could."

"Why can't we, Grandma?"

"Because she's dead."

I realized then Dad meant Marie, not Mae.

Gwen, hearing too many of Dad's criss-crossed sayings, picked up a few of her own. In early interviews, Gwen fumbled "get-go" and said, "It was great from the get-gun." She missed the stone reference and said, "I killed two birds with one bullet." And at the end of her crit on that April day, Gwen said, "We loafed it. There were places we didn't even pedal." I didn't question her. But I wondered what loafed meant. Or had Gwen bungled that term too?

NANCY

Several months earlier, eager to see a WTS event, Gwen's 2011 European itinerary enticed me. I dreamed about the trip of a lifetime—my first to Europe. During January's cold days, Joel and I studied Gwen's summer schedule and discussed a two-week trip, starting with the London WTS race and ending with the World Cup in Hungary.

We hesitated. Could we afford two weeks in Europe? What about the language barrier? The eight-hour transatlantic flight? Would we rent a car or use buses and trains? "Gwen, Dad and I are thinking about seeing some races in Europe. What do you think?"

Gwen was enthusiastic. "Go for it! Who knows when there will be a chance like this again?"

I thought it would be nice to have the whole family together and asked Elizabeth to join us.

"You and Dad should definitely do it, but I've traveled enough this year. And it's too expensive for me right now."

"What about seeing Gwen in a WTS race? All the big names will be in London."

"Yeah, I talked to Gwen. She said it's not a big deal."

So Joel and I planned our itinerary. As we discussed filling the days between races, Gwen suggested we connect with family history. For years, Joel talked about his immigrant grandparents. Along with their Danish names—Walborg and Oliver—they crossed the sea with recipes for aebelskivers and raspberry jam and the skills to cut stone.

"Dad always talked about seeing Denmark," Gwen said. "Since we're so close, I'd like to go."

We checked prices for the added flight and confirmed plans for an August departure to Heathrow, followed by four days in Copenhagen and a final stop in Hungary.

Then, Barb Lindquist heard of our plans.

"I talked with Barb and she doesn't like me going to Denmark," Gwen said.

"Really? Why not?"

"She thinks I'll be distracted and she wants me to concentrate on training for the race in Hungary."

"What should we do?"

Gwen was accustomed to a busy, diverse schedule, training for three sports while fulfilling her corporate duties. She remained confident in her ability to focus, unwilling to give up time in Denmark. "I'm not changing my plans. We're all set. It'll be fine."

****

In March, five months before our departure, Joel's chronic leg pain sent him to an orthopedic surgeon. I went along to hear the doctor's options. Joel sat close to the surgeon, palming his hip as though he could polish out the pain. The promise of smooth, oiled joints hung in the exam room. The doctor recommended a total hip replacement and Joel agreed to surgery.

We scheduled the operation for my April spring break—vacation from my high school teaching job—so I could care for Joel. I wondered if this was the right decision. What is the recovery? Would Joel be ready for an eight-hour flight in four months? Would he be up to hitting three countries in two weeks?

Joel's return home from surgery was stressful for both him and me. In my job as a high school choir director, I dealt with 100 adolescents at a time, disciplining, teaching, conducting, and accompanying. I saw 400 students daily and often worked 12-hour days. I moved quickly, catered to an array of personalities, and produced 25 performances each year. But none of that prepared me for nursing one 210-pound man and his new hip.

The first time Joel maneuvered up the stairway, I nervously followed behind, hands on his belt like the physical therapist modeled.

"I'll be fine," he said.

Let's hope so, because if your 210 pounds fall backward, we're both going down.

By August, Joel progressed from wheelchair to walker to cane. We boarded our international flight in Milwaukee, and once in Great Britain, Joel's cane became a magic wand. On the Tube, old ladies tottered against a grab rail so he could have a seat. In restaurants, a hostess concocted seating for Joel while the reservation line stood idle. I was ignored—as were other able-bodied citizens—while even sullen London teenagers deferred to the man with a cane. *If we ever travel again, maybe you should get the other hip replaced?*

In London, Gwen and her coach, Cindi Bannink, booked accommodations near Hyde Park's race site. Since our travel agent placed us several miles away, we chased the subway map's multicolored lines to the park. We surveyed the course, making plans for the next day's event.

Race day arrived on August 6, 2011—my 57th birthday. Joel paced the hotel room, adjusting his USA Triathlon baseball cap while memorizing the course map. "Let's get to the course early and look it over."

"We did that yesterday—and we have four hours until the start."

"Yeah, but the weather's good. We could walk around."

We rode the subway to Hyde Park and again scrutinized pontoon start, buoy placement, penalty tent, and 180-degree turns, looking for vantage points. Joel adjusted his brim to shield the sun. "Do you want to watch the swim up close?" he asked. Some spectators would watch from the shore of the Serpentine, London's recreational lake in Hyde Park. "But then we'd have to sprint to the grandstand for transition."

I looked at Joel leaning on his cane—*sprint to the grandstand?*

We decided to watch from the grandstand where we would see swimmers on the jumbotron. The transition would happen in front of us, and then riders would speed past us eight times on the bike—once per lap—and four times on the run.

Joel and I mounted the grandstand, climbing almost to the top. We claimed a spot within sight of bike rack 54—Gwen's number—which meant of 65 competitors, she ranked one of the lowest, with her bike far back in transition zone.

A chummy Brit introduced himself. "I'm just an average age-group racer myself."

"And who are you rooting for?" I asked.

"Like the rest of London, I'm cheering for Helen Jenkins, Jodie Stimpson and Vicky Holland. What about you?"

"Oh, our daughter, Gwen Jorgensen, is just a rookie. There, her bike is in front of us. But the best women for USA are Laura Bennett, Sarah Groff, Sarah Haskins, and Jillian Petersen."

"I'll cheer for your daughter then, too."

At the end of the swim, Gwen clambered up the lake's ramp in 27th place, 22 seconds behind the leader. Once on the bike, the women formed packs, with Gwen at the back of a chase group. While riders develop a unique style and personality, I learned packs assumed an identity too. When riders worked efficiently and took turns pulling at the front, a pack gained time. When riders failed to organize or forced one woman to do most of the work, they lost ground. London's lead pack allowed the chasers to gain advantage, and by the end of the one-hour 40K ride, the entire field entered transition together. The race came down to a 10K run.

But race dynamics created disparity. Those who rode at the back, forcing others to work up front, saved energy. The leaders, battling the wind, expended calories and leg muscle.

Gwen never intended to avoid work on the bike. With her lack of confidence and skill, she hung in the back, just trying to remain in the race. I doubt she was any less tired because of where she rode. In fact, she probably expended more energy than most through poor decisions on shifting, cornering and accelerating.

"Well, what do you think?" I asked.

"I know she can outrun some of these women. I'm saying top 20."

Our British friend overheard Joel's predictions. "So, your daughter is a strong runner?"

"She's really new to biking," I said, "but running should be the best part of her race."

Gwen started in the back of the field and bolted, passing several athletes. Built for running, with long legs and a light frame, her muscles rippled under just an inkling of fat. We spotted her drawn-out stride across the Serpentine. As a rookie, Gwen was unknown to her competitors and not recognized as a legitimate threat. As she whizzed by, they probably thought, *No one can keep up that pace. Stupid to wear yourself out in the first 5K.*

The scenario reminded me of Gwen's first high school track meet. Coach Eric Lehmann entered her in the 800-meter—a medium distance to gauge her abilities. At the halfway point, Gwen led as she stormed past Lehmann. Thinking she set an unsustainable pace, he yelled, "Gwen, slow down."

A stranger to track strategy, Gwen refused the counter-intuitive advice and blasted forward, winning her heat. She told us later what Lehmann said. She had been incredulous. "No coach ever told me to slow down."

In both that high school race and this London triathlon, Gwen and her capacity were unknown and disregarded. As she looped between orange cones, through streets and park, Gwen passed world-ranked runners. During the first lap, she moved from 45th to 17th. When I saw her run past the grandstand, my excitement soared—she was in the top 20. But positions can change quickly in the final stages of a race, as those with a strong sprint surge ahead.

In laps two and three, Gwen maintained her momentum, positioning herself in the top 10—and she wasn't wearing out.

At this point, I remembered top finishers would automatically qualify for the London 2012 Olympics. Most countries sent their prime competitors—this race offered experience on the same course they would confront one year later. USA could qualify up to two athletes who finished in the top nine. I knew the other four USA women harbored Olympic aspirations, but that Gwen only aimed to show up, learn, and finish the event. We had not hoped for—or even considered—an Olympic berth. In a few minutes, the inconceivable became possible.

At one point, Gwen came up behind USA favorite Laura Bennett, who placed fourth in Beijing 2008. Gwen described it later in her race report:

> *...never have I had a better moment in ANY race: I was passing Laura Bennett :(and I said, "come on Laura, we can do this!" and she just looked at me, slapped me on the butt and said "Go get 'em girl!" WOW WOW WOW. What a team player – what an awesome, encouraging thing to hear. She spent energy helping me. Seriously, so grateful.*

Sometime in the final lap, I looked at Joel and said, "Can she do this?"

He mumbled something, but when the crowd cheered and I didn't hear what he said, I turned to him. He pressed his eyelids together a few times and spoke as though he were choking. "I think she can."

I reached over and squeezed his hand.

With one lap to go, Gwen positioned herself in second place behind Great Britain's Jenkins. The crowd leapt to their feet, cheering the hometown favorite. Joel and I stood too, craning to see around fans waving the Union Jack. Noise for Jenkins swallowed up our, "Go, Gweeeeeen, go!"

"I can't believe it!" I said as I spied Gwen. "She's going to take second!" I focused only on Gwen—her lean torso, muscular legs, confident stride—noting her comfortable margin ahead of third place. As she bounded toward the finish line, someone reached over a barricade and handed her a USA flag. She stretched it in front of her chest, smiled as she ran the last few steps, and crossed the line.

I reached for Joel. We hugged. I dropped my arms, and then grabbed him again. I searched for one more glimpse of Gwen before hugging Joel for a third time.

Our British friend stared at us, apparently as surprised as we were, and offered his hand. "Congratulations—the silver medal!"

Gwen's performance was a victory for her as well as Team USA—Gwen finished better than any American woman in the history of the World Triathlon

Series. And more astonishing, she earned qualification for the 2012 London Olympic Games.

ELIZABETH

I woke up the morning after the London race to a buzzing phone. "Your sister did it."—"She qualified!"—"What a great race." But I slept through it. I hadn't bothered to figure out the time difference, find the race online or follow tweets. I anticipated this race would be the typical run-from-behind, best-case scenario, top-20 finish. After all, it's what Gwen led me to believe.

Gwen's athletics are as integral to our family as Dad's woodworking or Mom's music. It's just what Gwen does. As Gwen's sister, I tolerated family trips to stinging-cold cross-country meets, sopping track meets and steaming pools. Instead of reading books on the beach, snorkeling and tanning, I spent vacations in stuffy, chlorine-drenched, suffocating pools.

Instead of resenting and lamenting, I unleashed my outgoing personality as Gwen's personal superfan. In high school, I decorated the car for the Wisconsin State Track and Field meet. In college, I scoured new cities for quirky coffee shops and talked with baristas about events. Once I started teaching, I used examples of Gwen's athletic determination to motivate my students. Gwen's success gave me an opportunity to cheer loudly, to embarrass her with signs, and to throw her off with wacky questions at press conferences.

Superfan was a role I played rather well. I got nervous at the right moments. I knew Gwen's times and achievements, and I loved being loud. I didn't care what she was competing in or how well she was doing. Gwen was my sister. And I was proud.

But still, when Mom and Dad mentioned London, I didn't consider it. Working full time, I couldn't go to every race. My teacher salary didn't cover world travel, and with our two-personal-day rule, I carefully selected which races to attend and which to skip. I'd just been to Florida to see her race, and watching Gwen maneuver her bike reminded me of the witch in the Wizard of Oz, upright and stiff, and moving at granny speed. Granted, Gwen earned her pro-card, but she looked anything but professional.

Ranked 54th, Mom said Gwen needed top nine to earn Olympic qualification. Gwen never mentioned Olympic qualification. *It's such a long shot*, I thought. *Gwen would have mentioned it if she thought she'd qualify.*

So, the morning after, I scolded her. "Why didn't you tell me I should go? Why didn't you explain what a big deal this was?" Had I just missed the biggest race of my sister's life? All the hours counting down races until Gwen swam her 500 meters. All the traveling across the Midwest. All the minutes waiting for Gwen to finish her cool-downs. It all led to this—my sister an Olympic qualifier—and I missed it.

Gwen, still shocked, claimed she didn't expect it. She said I shouldn't expect big things at the Olympics either. But I was disappointed. My role was cheerleader. My specialty a hoarse voice, cowbells, and attention-seeking outfits. I missed the grandest stage for my cheering—and Gwen's grandest win. I missed celebrating and congratulating. I missed Dad crying. I missed the moment where Mom's birthday present was an Olympic qualification. Forever etched in stories to our grandchildren and told in the book we would write, my presence remained absent. I was angry. And I resolved to not miss another important race.

Gwen downplays accomplishments, making it hard to put achievements into perspective. Forever focused on improvement, Gwen would talk of the next workout, the next race, the next personal best. What I saw as a win, Gwen criticized: minutes to shave, splits to improve, form to perfect. Although I saw those things too, I also saw moments, milestones, and (when I wasn't there) a family memory. Minus me.

At the end of our conversation, whether Gwen admitted it was a big deal or not, I was determined to be at the London 2012 Olympics—and I thought matching t-shirts, a handmade red-white-and-blue headband, and stars-and-stripes pants could make up for missing the qualifying event.

NANCY

Immediately after the London 2011 Olympic qualifying race, media bombarded podium finishers. Shouldering behemoth cameras or palming mini-recorders, reporters charged the platform. Lingering in a medals ceremony afterglow, Great Britain's Helen Jenkins (1st) and Germany's Anja Dittmer (3rd) wore their victory attitudes, while Gwen's smile wavered as though she were astounded.

The throng of cameras circled within inches. I watched nervously, rooting for Gwen to overcome her shyness. She must have wondered how to answer questions with both honesty and humility. How to accept praise, but also give credit. How to explain her sudden rise to the top when she was more surprised than anyone. Gracious and accommodating (also brief, stilted, and uncomfortable), at one point she remembered it was my birthday—providing reporters with a story angle.

Attention didn't end at the race site. Word spread about the rookie American who stole second place from a field of experienced triathletes, and wherever Gwen went—in Hyde Park, at the Paddington Hilton, eating bangers and mash in a pub—fans requested autographs and photos. Gwen entered London an unknown, but a silver medal and Olympic qualification ended her anonymity.

We joined Gwen and her coach as they celebrated in their hotel room. Smiles and laughter filled the room, but this win generated another range of emotion. Tears appeared. Gwen rarely cries, and I recognized her emotion as a sign of stress.

"I don't get this obsession. Everyone I meet wants one thing—to talk triathlon," she said.

You should understand obsession. For 20 years, you lived in a water bubble. "Everyone is excited for you. And they're intrigued by how fast you learned triathlon." It was too soon for Gwen to formulate thought into words. Later, she would sort out elation, amazement, shock, thrill, and guilt.

The media bazaar had just begun. Added to a schedule of part-time work, training, and recovery would now be internet stories, TV appearances, photo shoots, magazine interviews, United States Olympic Committee promotions, sponsor billboards, podcast conversations, and radio talks. Although interest from the London press seemed oppressive, those questions and photo requests were piddling—managing the media would be one of the most challenging aspects of the next year.

Twenty-four hours after the race, Gwen, Joel, and I flew to Denmark, landing in Copenhagen to August's chilly sea winds, bicycling commuters, and not one person who recognized the newest personality in ITU triathlon. With a World Cup race one week away, Gwen trained with runs in the city and swims at an indoor community pool, but she also toured with us.

Online research revealed a bike tour of Copenhagen that takes riders to historic sites. We set out to find the bike shop, and although baffled by Danish street signs, found the group assembling. Mike (of Bike with Mike Tours) inquired about Joel's cane. "Have you ridden a bike lately?"

"I'll be fine," Joel said. "I only need the cane for walking." Although true, I realized how ridiculous that sounded.

Mike reserved comment, but I read anxiety in his movements as he checked Joel's brakes. Joel balanced his cane on the handlebars and rode confidently, oblivious to the guide's concern.

We followed Mike up and down narrow streets, to the harbor, and through the city, stopping for tales of Denmark's industry and history. Mike apparently worried so much about Joel navigating the cobblestones, he never noticed the world-class triathlete who just qualified for the Olympics. Gwen shot me looks that said, *Don't embarrass me by saying anything about triathlon.* I didn't say a word, and Gwen remained blissfully anonymous.

After our bike tour, as we studied a dinner menu, Gwen took charge. "Let's order a bunch of different things and share. I want what the Danes eat—food we can't get at home."

Gwen studied Spanish, and I spoke a little French, but none of us knew Danish, so we quizzed the waiter. When he couldn't offer a translation, we took our chances and waited to discover what we ordered. We devoured smørrebrød (open-faced rye-bread sandwiches), liver paste, herring, and who knows what else.

"We have to try the Carlsberg beer," Joel said.

"None for me," Gwen said, and then tasted mine. "But I hope you guys save room for dessert."

While in Denmark, Gwen connected via phone with USA Triathlon's Barb Lindquist. As Gwen decompressed from the attention and shock of Olympic qualification, Lindquist told her, "This was a great idea for you to have a few days with your family. You needed to recover and regroup." *Who knew?*

Following our days in Denmark, Gwen would race a World Cup in Tiszaújváros, Hungary, so we flew from Copenhagen to Budapest and waited two days for our rail connection to Tiszaújváros (Tizzy).

We composed a see-do-eat list, heavy on the eats, and after checking in at Sofitel Budapest, hit the streets. Seeing Gwen's lithe physique, one might think she restricted calories, but she is an adventurous—and voracious—eater.

"Oooo, Dad. Let's stop for lángos," Gwen said. Hungarian food carts specialized in the deep-fried dough. Their street-side preparation spewed vapors into the air, laden with onion, spice, or sugar; each haze compelled us to sample.

"What kind of filling should we get?" Joel asked. We examined the Hungarian sign and found an English translation.

"Mmmm. Garlic? With sauerkraut?" Gwen suggested.

Waiting for our order, we watched bakers prepare the plate-sized treat, and when our circle of puffy dough came out, hot and greasy, I passed it to Gwen.

She sank her teeth into the edge and tore away a chunk. "Here, Mom. Have a bite. It's great!" She handed me the steaming pillow in its white paper wrapper. I took a bite and gave it to Joel, who passed it back to Gwen. As we shared the savory dough, Gwen craved another. "Sweet cheese for the next one?"

Almost as appealing as street foods were Budapest's thermal baths, and given Gwen's fascination with water, I resolved to find one. Toting suits and towels, we set out on foot as I synced street signs with a paper map, steering us to Szechenyi Baths. I recognized the century-old spa by its massive pillared facade and domed roof. Lines formed at the entrance where I attempted to ask about the queues. While I survived in the hotel, where personnel spoke English, on the streets, I wore my ignorance like an extra layer of clothes. Between my non-existent Hungarian and the locals' rudimentary English, I received no answer and chose a random line.

Within minutes, a uniformed guard approached. "American?" *Oh my god, is it that obvious?* "Come with me," the official said. *Did we do something wrong?* He hustled us to a new line. "For you." He smiled, indicating the shorter wait time.

I never figured out why tourists received special privilege but appreciated the courtesy. We successfully communicated with the desk about lockers and a key and headed for Szechenyi Baths' 18 pools.

"Where should we start, Gwen?" The scent of chlorine permeated the air, wafting up from three outdoor pools—a lap pool, a thermal sitting pool, and an adventure pool filled with noisy children playing games.

"The sun feels great—let's stay outside." Gwen dove into lap lanes while Joel and I alternated between sunning and dipping in the adventure pool. The warm water (27 to 38°C—81 to 100°F) supplied by geothermal springs was once touted for its ability to treat joint diseases and contains sulphate, calcium, magnesium, and bicarbonate. *Hey, Joel, this should be great for your hip.* While Gwen executed her daily stroke-kick requirements, we hovered around pool-bottom jets, waiting our turn for the mild massage. With her workout complete, Gwen said, "Okay, let's see what they have inside."

First, we found a hot spa nestled in the pillared halls. We tempered our toes, gradually slipping into the scalding tub, and I could have steeped all day in the torture. But Gwen won the lottery with so many pools, and she resolved to cash in. "C'mon, Mom. There're 18 pools. How many have we seen?"

We fevered inside a sauna, and then shocked ourselves with an icy dip. We waded through a basin where old men played chess. We sampled a water fitness pool. Like Goldilocks, we went room to room and tried each one. "So, which is your favorite?" I asked.

"I liked the lap pool," Gwen said. "I could be outside without little kids in my way, and the sun warmed my back."

"Joel?"

"I know you like the hot tub, but that was too warm for me. I guess I like the big family pool."

Back at the hotel, thinking about my difficulty with the language, I felt nervous about our trip to Tiszaújváros. Our travel agent secured train tickets, but somewhere in the middle of Hungary, they required a transfer. I approached the desk clerk. "Could you help me with these documents please?"

"What do you need to know?" Her command of English reassured me. She could surely help us navigate the journey.

"Can you tell me where the train station is? And then, I'm having trouble translating the timetable."

The clerk studied our tickets, checked her computer, and then raised her hands as though confused. Timetables contradicted each other, making our travel chancy—but we had no choice if we wanted to get to Tiszaújváros.

Travel to Tizzy was not a problem for Gwen. Since hosting organizations provide athletes with transportation, Gwen would arrive via private van.

I pictured Joel and me on a deserted train platform in the middle of the Hungarian forest. I imagined howling winds and a driving rain, the two of us huddled against a dilapidated station house, searching the horizon for the next train.

Gwen interrupted my depressing daytime nightmare. "Mom, there's room for two more in the private van. Do you and Dad want to join us?"

Choice: Use the train tickets we paid for? Or lose money on the tickets and actually make it to Tiszaújváros? We rode the private van.

ELIZABETH

On the two-hour ride to Tizzy, Mom called and told me of their travel issues. I recalled a 2009 transport problem Gwen experienced in Mexico City. Dressed in shorts and a t-shirt, she befriended a Mexican on the seven-hour flight from Milwaukee. Gwen told me she and the woman conversed, filling time until their midnight landing.

Despite the late hour, Gwen expected a driver to pick her up, and when he wasn't there, a phone call revealed the misunderstanding. Instead of midnight, he planned for noon.

At baggage claim, Gwen encountered her seatmate again. "Did you find your driver?" the woman asked. "He should have your name on a sign."

"He was confused about the time, but it's okay. I'll grab a taxi." Exhausted and uncertain, Gwen feigned confidence.

"Honey, you can't get a taxi in Mexico City dressed like that. It's not safe. You need to be in long pants—covered up!" Unknown to Gwen, Mexico City experienced a spate of taxi-related crimes, and travel required additional precautions. "You come with me. We'll travel together to your hotel."

The woman accompanied Gwen, confirmed her reservations at the front desk, and slipped her a phone number in case of emergency.

When Gwen called me at two in the morning, unease pinched her words. She exhaled through sentences as though she might cry.

Stunned, yet thankful for the stranger's generosity, I worried about my little sister traveling the world solo. And I wondered if this predicament replayed itself with other professional athletes.

I was glad Mom and Dad traveled with Gwen on the Tizzy trip and told Mom to keep me updated.

NANCY

As we traveled in the van to Tizzy, I was grateful for the safety and knowledge of a private driver. Within two hours, we arrived in Tiszaújváros, its lush green hills a foil to the town's meager resources. It was obvious from broken-down cars, the forint's poor exchange rate, and residents scavenging in dumpsters that Tizzy suffered a sluggish economy. Triathlon, however, was strong and thriving.

Tiszaújváros mounted an annual week-long festival for amateur triathletes—from elementary school to adult masters—that culminated in an ITU World Cup. Vendors created a fair, hawking food, beer, and trinkets. Locals wandered the tents and kiosks, stepping over sound-system cables to gather sausages, lángos, and ice cream. Old men clutching plastic beer cups moseyed toward park benches, mothers pushing strollers shopped the peddler tables, and purple-haired teenagers danced at the rock band tent.

After Gwen's daily training, we met at a tavern for potatoes, pickles, beets, and stew. In the evenings, we joined Hungarians at the festival.

On the final day of racing at Tizzy, we arrived at the grandstand. Families sat in groups, and teenagers congregated in packs. Girls wore freshly manicured nails, short skirts, and sunglasses; guys looked casual in extra-long shorts. In the shade-deprived bleachers, I applied a layer of sunscreen and bought bottled water. "So, no jumbotron?"

"I guess only WTS races have a screen," Joel said. From the grandstand, we would see Gwen once per lap—eight times on the bike, four times on the run. But the swim took place at a remote location.

In the spirit of the week, live musicians alternated with an announcer who paraded the blue carpet while a mascot in a crocodile suit danced and mimed.

When the race began, the announcer reported on the swim portion—but only in Hungarian.

We waited for the 40-kilometer bike stage to see Gwen. As riders approached the grandstand, the announcer's antics transformed the crowd from excited to electrified. Fans shook noisemakers, clanged cowbells, and shouted hurrahs.

"Gwen's in the first chase pack—not bad, right?" I said.

When riders cycled out of view, the announcer called Hungarian updates, fast and loud. Gwen wore number one—she jumped ahead in the rankings with her silver medal in London—and he tracked her. His Hungarian words were occasionally interrupted by, "...Gweeeeen Yyyyyorgensen..." and we knew she rode rubber-side down.

Each lap, we searched for Gwen, buried in her 43-woman chase pack. Scanning the group, I stopped breathing and searched for her helmet in the conglomeration of arms and aero bars. "Do you see her?"

"I think so...wait...yes, that's her. Middle of the pack. About 20th."

I exhaled. "How do you think she looked?"

"Yeah, good. On the last lap, she was at the back of her pack, and now she's in the middle."

At the end of the bike leg, as women dismounted for the 10K run, Gwen trailed by more than a minute. The lead pack featured Russian Irina Abysova and Italian Annamaria Mazzetti, both World Cup medalists.

Gwen later described her thoughts in a race report:

> *I got off my bike...just thinking I needed to run down as many as I could. An AUS girl from our chase pack was pushing the pace, and I just stuck w/ her for the first 2 laps.*

As Gwen drilled her run pace, race dynamics changed and, louder and more frequently, we heard, "...Gweeeeen Yyyyyorgensen." After the first lap, Mazzetti led, with Gwen steadily advancing.

> *I heard that we were gaining a lot on the leaders... Pretty soon I was in top 6 and could see 3rd place. The CAN coach was so awesome – he was [shouting] splits as to how far back I was from the leader.*

After the second lap, Mazzetti still led. "Look! Here they come! Is that Gwen? In second place!"

We stood and shouted "Go, Gwen" and "You got this," our words buried under deafening Hungarian chants. Nearby spectators stared at the strange words coming from our lips, but then ignored us in the frenzy.

"I can't believe it! Another silver medal," I said.

> *...I could see 1st place and just tried to slowly creep up. On the last lap, I ran behind Annamaria until about 600 [meters] to go, then I put in a surge...*

Joel and I stood on the bleachers, shouting. We yelled, "Gooooooo, Gweneveeeeere!" and watched Gwen accelerate toward Mazzetti.

Mazzetti seemed to stall.

Then, with only a few meters left, Gwen strode past Mazzetti toward the finish line. In first place.

Once Gwen grabbed the tape, I forgot to watch the rest of the race. My eyes followed only her, afraid she might collapse. I saw too many athletes sprint full speed to the end, and then keel over, medics wheeling them away.

Later, we read Gwen clocked 33:49 for the 10-kilometer run—42 seconds faster than any other competitor. We also read Gwen's recollection:

> *Some Tizzy official handed me a flag, I took it and*
> *again was baffled by the flag :(*

In London, she was surprised by the flag's bulk and how to hold it while running—should the stars be upper left or upper right? Should it wave behind her head or in front of her body? After her Tizzy confusion, USA clarified protocol.

> *SO SO SO glad [USA Triathlon program director]*
> *Andy [Schmitz has now] sent me an email on flag and*
> *podium expectations/etiquette…*

For the second time in two weeks, Joel and I repeatedly hugged in the grandstand. Anxiety that built during the race—about danger in the water, and potential for a crash on the bike—still buzzed. But with a podium finish, that energy morphed into elation. Liberated from race worry, I felt charged and proud. I hoped Gwen did too.

We stayed in our seats for the ceremony as Gwen marked her first World Cup win. She climbed to the top step of the awards platform and searched for us in the grandstand. We waved to attract her attention, and she acknowledged us with a smile and her own small wave. And for the first time that day, I heard a familiar sound—*The Star-Spangled Banner.*

Following the 1 p.m. race, Gwen joined us to watch the elite men. After, there were lotteries, prizes, a fashion show, street dance, and finally at 9 p.m. (Gwen's usual bedtime), a medals ceremony on the rock band stage.

Never anticipating the results of the week, Gwen packed bikes, swim gear, running shoes, and workout clothes, but no skirt or dress. Unprepared for Tizzy's gala, she accepted her award in jeans and a t-shirt next to a festive Mazzetti and Abysova, both in party dresses and heels. In a continuation of the street dance, lights focused on the medal winners to highlight their victory dance— uncomfortably executed by all, especially the girl in jeans.

The week's victories launched Gwen into the spotlight. She left the United States an unknown rookie and returned an ITU World Cup champion and Olympic qualifier. I didn't think about details—Gwen's job, Olympic training, media, travel, sponsorship, an agent, funding. For weeks, I lived on pride and a little disbelief—*is Gwen really an Olympian or did I dream this?*

CHAPTER 3

Tires and Tribulations

LONDON 2012

NANCY

With Olympic qualification secured, Gwen analyzed her weaknesses:

> *MUST get in FIRST bike pack…need to 1) make me*
> *an AWESOME swimmer and 2) be able to hammer w/*
> *feet out of shoes for first 5 minutes…need that power/*
> *quick speed at the beginning…*

She noted shortcomings in swim, bike, run, and added transitions to her list. Transition one: strip wetsuit while sprinting; deposit goggles, cap, and wetsuit in basket; fasten helmet; unrack bike; and execute a flying mount. Transition two: while cycling, remove feet from shoes; pedal with feet on top of shoes; dismount before the line; rack bike; and slide sweaty feet into running shoes.

London 2012 was a certainty. But how to prepare was not. An early morning swim could be squeezed in before work, but professional athletes require a nutrient-dense breakfast and recovery—not a morning of tax forms and team meetings. An evening run after work would supply miles, but also dangers—dark streets, rush-hour traffic. With the Olympic Games her immediate focus, Gwen met with her Ernst & Young supervisor. She called me later that day. "So, I met with Mark Helmer. I was afraid to ask for more time off, but he was really supportive." I sensed relief in her voice. "He thinks I should take a leave of absence."

To me, a leave seemed the only option and I was grateful for Helmer's encouragement. "Is that what you'll do?"

"He says I can have my job back whenever I'm ready, and there is no pressure to return soon. And he wasn't specific, but it sounds like Ernst & Young might support my Olympic journey."

****

Even before Olympic qualification, Gwen garnered fans at Ernst & Young. During 2009 and 2010, Gwen ran to stay in shape and earn cash in road races, the magnet of athletics yanking her back again and again. She won a few hundred dollars in Milwaukee and a frozen turkey in northern Wisconsin. When race results appeared in the *Milwaukee Journal Sentinel*, Ernst & Young staff offered email congratulations or a shout out at the water cooler.

Gwen raced the Samson Stomp, a 5K January run to benefit the Milwaukee County Zoo. Joel, Elizabeth, and I layered on undershirts, t-shirts, sweaters, wool socks, insulated boots, hats, scarves, and ear warmers. We prepared for slapping winds and icy roads on a 15°F Sunday morning. Per usual, Joel demanded an early arrival.

"Let's stay here in the warm-up area until race time." I preferred the heated gathering room where athletes milled about.

"It's not that cold. Let's get a good place to watch. Lyza Jo, you coming?"

Outside, competitors dotted the course, sprinting, lunging, and stretching, apparently oblivious to the freezing conditions. Most dressed in leggings, running shoes, a thin top, and headband. I stomped my feet to see if I could feel my toes and breathed into a wool scarf, exhaling to warm my face. I curled my hands inside my mittens, giving my fingers a chance to warm.

"Here we go. They're lining up," Joel said.

I noticed Gwen chatting with some men. On her honor to choose a fair place within the starting wave, I assumed she asked how fast the guys expected to run. She remained next to them.

When runners dashed onto the zoo's winding path, Joel, Elizabeth, and I bolted for the race midpoint. We arrived just in time to see Gwen still with the leaders. As runners completed the final half, we took a shortcut to the finish, sidestepping icy patches, holding each other to keep from falling. Waiting at the curb, hands under my armpits, I jostled my frozen feet and peered down the road. A few men charged toward us. I counted them as they finished...1...2...3...4... and saw Gwen trailing the fifth runner. I yelled encouragement, shouts muffled by my scarf. Gwen finished sixth overall (ahead of 534 men) and earned first place among 610 women. She began a standard for road races with first place the norm.

ELIZABETH

In 2010, as Gwen fit road races into her corporate schedule, I faced a life crisis. Gwen's search for a race provided distraction. When divorce ended my marriage, I dreaded holiday dinners and questions from extended family. I sought diversion, a get-away, and something to create a new family memory. I wanted to feel safe and coddled, far from any reminder of my failure.

When Mom discussed Thanksgiving plans, I suggested a Wisconsin Dells water park weekend. No one—not even Gwen—looked thrilled. Divorce left me fragile, so they obliged. But if this trip was about escape, it was also—like all family trips—about sport.

We packed into the Honda Civic in our assigned spots. Gwen, years ago, placed a University of Wisconsin Bucky Badger sticker inside her window. As a kid, Gwen obsessed over sports. On her childhood bedroom ceiling, glow-in-the-dark stars spelled out 5:15—her goal for the 500-yard freestyle. On her arm, faded Sharpie marks recalled swim heats. Taped inside her high school locker, decorations anticipated her trip to state.

As we drove two hours northwest, I wanted to be out of town. But Gwen wanted to win something, and I wasn't surprised when she found a Turkey Trot en route to the water park.

Barely awake, pillow pushed against the window, I sensed the car slow and exit the freeway. Gwen shuffled belongings and added a layer of clothes. Dad parked and Gwen ran strides. Mom and I, bundled in layers of wool and fleece, waited for her at the registration tent where competitors gathered in turkey hats and tutus. Gwen ran. We cheered. She won. And then, we piled her first-place turkey in the trunk, confident the 25°F temperature would keep it frozen for the weekend.

Accustomed to summer days at outdoor water parks, we lamented our indoor stay with its humidity, truncated rides, and lazy river filled with babies in diapers. But at the vegetarian restaurant, we talked about money I found in the wave pool, the rides Gwen and Dad enjoyed, and our foray into the outdoor hot tub. We laughed, we poked fun at each other, and we talked about everything but my divorce.

NANCY

Already supportive of Gwen's road races, Ernst & Young colleagues responded enthusiastically to Gwen's Olympic qualification. Accountant Nancy Flagg suggested an Olympic fundraiser and, with corporate encouragement, organized the event. She booked a hall at her family-owned restaurant and invited Ernst & Young employees, television stations, and Gwen's fans and supporters.

I was surprised and grateful that Flagg, a veteran accountant, invested time and resources to benefit Gwen, a new hire about to take a leave of absence. A week before the party, I drove past the venue where a marquee read, "GO, GWEN, GO." So much of the past few months seemed surreal, but seeing Gwen's name above the restaurant underscored reality—my daughter would be an Olympian.

For Flagg's event, Gwen dressed at our home while Elizabeth got ready at hers. But the doorbell interrupted us—a surprise visit from the United States Anti-Doping Agency (USADA). USADA demanded 24/7 notification of elite athletes' whereabouts. Each week, online, Gwen documented her hour-by-hour location, subject to athletic suspension if not present when agents arrived.

The two-person USADA team, one man and one woman, unloaded kits, vials, and paperwork onto my kitchen table. Gwen selected a collection vessel, verified it was tamper-free, and disappeared into the bathroom with the female chaperone to secure a sample. Back at the table, Gwen poured it into containers—*you are pouring urine back and forth on our dinner table*—but it was too dilute and they needed another. Gwen had 45 minutes to produce a second sample before she was due at the fundraiser.

"Mom, I need food to help me pee."

"Look in the fridge. There's leftover lasagna...and maybe broccoli."

"No bananas?" Gwen drank water and ate peanut butter with a spoon.

Once the process began, the female chaperone shadowed Gwen. Unperturbed, Gwen dressed for the fundraiser. Joel and I visited with the agent. "So, how many athletes do you cover?" I asked.

"We handle the Midwest and get to Chicago and Minneapolis. But Waukesha is convenient, so when Gwen is home, we like to stop here."

"And the two of you travel together?"

"Actually, this is my mother. We work well together—we've known each other a long time." The agent's mother served as chaperone (pee witness) for female athletes.

I knew firsthand about combining family and work—Elizabeth and I taught in the same high school and often met for lunch, a welcome break in my days of choir rehearsals and dance sessions.

Years later, Gwen told us of other USADA encounters. Agents tracked her in Madison and Milwaukee. They found her in Spain and Australia. They knocked on her door at night, at dawn, and at work. One morning at Ernst & Young, a USADA official attended her corporate tax meetings. *Hello everyone, please meet the lady who will collect my urine.*

Gwen moved between her bedroom, doing makeup and hair, and the kitchen, eating and drinking. She waited as long as possible, giving her body time to metabolize the food, and at the last minute, produced a second sample. After it was pronounced satisfactory, Gwen bottled and labeled the sample, verified information, and signed papers. We arrived at the fundraiser only a few minutes late. *Mental note to self—wash that kitchen table again.*

****

To prepare for the 2012 Olympics, Gwen took her Ernst & Young leave of absence in the fall of 2011. Meanwhile, Joel and I planned our London 2012 trip. This time, Elizabeth would join us.

"You know prices go up during an Olympic year, right?"

Joel shrugged. "I guess so, but there's no way we're missing this."

We budgeted carefully, and then a few surprises made the trip more affordable.

"Mom, I was talking to Ernst & Young about ideas for sponsorship. They might help finance the family's trip to London." Ernst & Young was not an official sponsor, but much of Nancy Flagg's fundraising helped with our expenses. Then, I got a letter from Proctor & Gamble (P&G).

"What's that? It looks official," Joel said.

I ripped through the envelope, glancing at a plastic card attached to the letter. It appeared to be a credit card advertisement. A second look confirmed a legitimate gift card. "There's a $1,000 Visa card—with my name on it. It says P&G has a *Thank you, Mom* campaign for mothers of Olympians." Along with congratulations for raising an Olympian and the $1,000 gift, the letter described a P&G London Family Home. "We're invited for complimentary food, drinks, haircuts, game rooms, just to relax...the whole time we're in London." A few days later, P&G followed up with a gift basket of travel items—toothpaste, mouthwash, makeup.

Although flattered, I knew my role was secondary. Lots of moms raised great kids, and I was lucky to have two motivated, hard-working daughters. I wasn't sure I had much to do with Olympic qualification, but I appreciated the perks.

A lifetime of frugality supplied the rest of our travel budget. Choosing a modest home, economy cars, and home-cooked meals allowed for violin lessons, swim fees, and college tuition. Our thrifty lifestyle continued after the girls left home as we saved for retirement and banked extra funds. We delayed gratification for 35 years, not knowing what we waited for. Now, Gwen's sacrifices paid off with Olympic qualification. And our sacrifices allowed us to join her at the Games.

But first, Gwen's lineup featured two U.S. races, so Joel and I arranged a weekend trip to California. Media hyped the May San Diego event with Gwen at the center of the blitz. Her silver medal in London 2011 was USA's best finish in World Triathlon Series history—and fans expected a repeat performance on home soil.

"Mom, when are you getting to San Diego?"

"I only took one day off work, so we arrive the day before your race. Can we do dinner that night?"

"Sorry, I'm booked solid." Gwen scheduled a week of pre-race photo shoots, appearances, interviews, radio spots, and TV features. Pressured to accommodate media, she spent whole days promoting triathlon, neglecting her own race preparation. "But after the race, for sure." When we arrived in San Diego, we met Gwen in her hotel room, and then had dinner on our own.

The next day's race celebrated 40 years of triathlon in its city of origin, and the event was another 2012 Olympic qualifier. With Gwen and Sarah Groff already qualified, a third spot could go to a USA athlete in the top nine. International contenders hunted for qualification through each country's process. With so many Olympic hopefuls, the lineup showcased the world's best.

Gwen documented races in a report she shared with her coaches and with USA Triathlon's Barb Lindquist. Lindquist posed questions to spur Gwen's self-assessment.

Lindquist: "Pre-race timeline, what went well, what didn't?"

> *Woke up, did a 20 min jog and felt pretty good. Went over to race site about 2 hours before the start...waited around a bit before going on a two-lap preview on the bike course. Then got my stuff ready, did a short run, and did almost one full loop of the swim in my wetsuit (even though it was non-wetsuit swim) to keep warm. I practiced some run-ins and stepped in a big hole, and twisted my ankle which hurt really really bad, but it wasn't so bad that I couldn't run, and it actually felt better when I was moving full speed. I was feeling very full—I had a lot of nuts, oatmeal, fruit, etc. before the race and in the morning I had eggs, fruit, oats, yogurt, etc. Right after my swim warm up, my stomach wasn't feeling good, but I felt I needed to get some calories in, so I ate two GU Chomps.*

As the women lined up for a beach-run start, we watched the grandstand jumbotron. I couldn't find Gwen in the horde of athletes sprinting toward the water, but announcers heralded the leaders. Brit Helen Jenkins led. Sarah Haskins and Laura Bennett, USA favorites, also swam in the front pack. As the swim concluded, Gwen exited the water 24th of 70. I searched for her on the screen but couldn't find her in the hustle of bodies and bikes.

A few minutes into the bike stage, as I scoured the screen, riders crashed around a corner. I held my breath and looked away, afraid to confirm who went down. "Can you see who crashed?"

"No. They're all on top of each other," Joel said.

I panicked, scared about the consequences of a crash. Broken collarbone. Fractured arm. Skin scraped raw.

"The cameras have gone to the front bike pack now," Joel said.

I wanted to know what happened. *Was anyone hurt? Did Gwen go down? Where was she?* Eventually, announcers named those who crashed, and although I was relieved it wasn't Gwen, adrenaline left me with jittery fingers and tingling feet.

Cameras followed the leaders and we heard little about the chase group Gwen joined. But they rode past the grandstand once per lap and each time we saw her, she lost more ground.

"Did you time that?" I said.

"Yeah, they're down by two minutes and 19 seconds. The lead pack is working together, and Gwen's chase pack looks really unorganized."

I had seen Gwen recoup time lost on the bike with a speedy run, but this deficit seemed enormous. Gwen dismounted with the slowest ride of the field.

I remained optimistic she could at least reduce the shortfall—she posted the best run of the day in both Hungary and the London qualifying event. Surely, she could do the same today.

As Gwen slipped into her shoes and took her first strides, she held her shoulders high and tight and appeared fatigued. "What's wrong?"

"She's fine. She'll loosen up in a minute."

But rather than dominate like I envisioned, Gwen lost ground as others surged. Instead of passing runners, they passed her.

USA's Bennett took bronze, securing the third Olympic spot, while Gwen recorded the 44th slowest run time and finished 51st of 58—hardly the silver medal repeat fans expected.

Although I never knew what to say after a loss, I knew she appreciated our presence. We met at the finish line, as we usually did, with generic words and a hug.

I noticed a pattern in Gwen's wins and defeats. For her, wins confirmed potential, but never guaranteed future success. Loss was a prodding, poking, jabbing thing. It vexed Gwen until she responded with a plan.

She revealed her thoughts in the San Diego race report.

Lindquist: "Describe the bike."

> ...then it was just me and the other girl for a bit of the bike...she was making pulls, and then yelling at me, saying, "Come on, this isn't practice"...I'm not sure if I was mentally not in it or if it was physical that I couldn't go faster...

Lindquist: "What opportunities for improvement were identified?"

> Wow! Every area. Mentally it was bad, and I think that played a role in how I was feeling physically. Not sure what went wrong, but I'm hoping to use it as motivation going forward.

****

When Gwen celebrated her Olympic qualification in 2011, along with victory came guilt. Naysayers discredited her efforts, belittled her attempts, and attributed her victory more to luck than skill. Competitors called her qualification a fluke. Because the London 2011 bike leg culminated in one large run pack, Gwen told me teammate Sarah Groff said, "It wasn't a real triathlon, just a running race." Triathletes resented an unskilled cyclist who could win with a stellar run. Intellectually, Gwen knew she trained hard, albeit unconventionally, and that her years in the pool and on the track were legitimate preparation. Emotionally, however, she succumbed to doubts about her Olympic worthiness, especially when faced with a poor performance like the one in San Diego.

It was not the first time Gwen encountered resentment from competitors. Disgruntled Waukesha South High School track athletes sniped when Gwen nabbed a relay spot. Where was Gwen while they ran laps? Why could Gwen swim every day and then show up to win a track event?

On the University of Wisconsin–Madison cross-country team, Gwen joined athletes who felt entitled to more than scholarship money—they boldly expressed their intent (and inherent right) to finish first.

One brisk fall day, during Gwen's first collegiate cross-country season, we shuffled through a layer of sere leaves, canvassing a fields-and-forest Wisconsin course. "Is that the map? How much of the race can we see?"

Joel adjusted the visor on his hat as he squinted into the low October glare. "They zigzag here." He pointed from map to land. "If we stand between the two paths, we can jog back and forth to see each pass."

When the race began, we ran too—scurrying to watch athletes charge up hills, bolt around trees, and attack straightaways. During the 30-minute race, we saw the runners four times.

As competitors entered the chute, Gwen and another Wisconsin athlete ran side by side as though they might tie. But in the final meters, Gwen lengthened her stride to inch out the win. Victory is not always sweet. The scholarship athlete expressed disdain. Resentful that a swimmer with no cross-country experience usurped her win, she smoldered. Her fire, intended to ignite a spark of guilt, succeeded. I sensed something amiss and whispered to Joel, "What's up?"

"I think one of the Badger girls is mad Gwen beat her." The women celebrated their team success, but tension photobombed every picture.

Gwen spent three years on her university swim team, her talent never a threat. When running placed her at the top, she discovered winning involved more than the fastest time. Along with course strategy, she learned lessons in squad chemistry as egos—of friend or foe—also competed. She told us about her training. "My coach says I have to work on my mental game."

"How do you do that?" I knew Gwen saw a sports psychologist, but the process remained mysterious.

"I have to feel like I deserve to win. I wanted to win for the team, but I felt bad when a teammate came in second."

Although Gwen won that day, other days, insecurities produced defeat. Did Gwen deserve to win? On paper, in workouts, on the course, yes. But her inner self lacked confidence. Her mental fitness needed a workout along with her physical game.

****

The triathlon equation is solved over months and years, as athletes decipher and analyze variables—road conditions, pack mentality, training blocks, transitions, bike fit, wetsuit rules, mounts, dismounts. As Gwen submitted race reports, Lindquist told her, "Gwen, the process is about fixing your mistakes. Each race, you should learn something new."

Analyzing her San Diego race, Gwen said to me, "It was a mistake to do all those interviews. I lost my focus."

"Can you say no to some of that next time?"

"It's hard because I'm expected to do promotion." But to ensure a better outcome, Gwen postponed future media until after each race. Not a popular decision, and not one for every athlete, she learned from her error and corrected it.

As she prepared for the London Olympics, Gwen followed her San Diego disaster with improved results. She scored a World Cup win in Banyoles, Spain, and an 11th place WTS finish in Kitzbuehel, Austria. The calendar showed six weeks until her Olympic race.

As part of her year-long preparation for London 2012, Gwen participated in a United States Olympic Committee photo shoot. "Mom, they want me to bring props to California—something to show my non-sport hobbies."

I thought it an inspired idea to show athletes doing more than sport.

"Where's my violin? And my Suzuki books?"

"Are they going to have you play? Or is it just a still shot?"

"No idea, but I better practice." Gwen tuned her violin as I set my accompaniment score on the piano, and together we rehearsed Bach's Minuet from Book 3.

"Gwenevere, your vibrato is great! I can't believe you can do that after six years."

"I'm not sure I remember the fingering." In high school, Gwen finished Book 6, but would choose this easy-to-resurrect piece if asked to perform.

She polished the Bach piece, but at the California event only played a few measures. The photo shoot featured Gwen with her props—wheel, goggles, and shoes in one picture; violin and bow in the next. And then she taped a bit for the *Late Show with David Letterman* and completed a round of interviews.

Our days, too, were filled with preparations. I wrote an Olympic blog for the *Milwaukee Journal Sentinel*, and Joel and I answered questions for a cable TV spot.

When August arrived, Elizabeth said, "Let's have an Opening Ceremony party at my house." Gwen was already in Great Britain, training in a rural town.

"Are the t-shirts ready?" I asked. Elizabeth had designed shirts for friends and family.

"Yup. They're delivered. Can you bring dessert for 30?"

The day of the party, I added red-white-and-blue cake pops to Elizabeth's appetizers, drinks, and take-out pizzas. After dinner, we gathered in front of the television. Along with 900 million worldwide viewers, we watched speeches, flag-raising, and a tribute to Great Britain's culture. We talked through the festivities, quieting to watch Queen Elizabeth's cameo. Once the parade of athletes began, I impatiently waited for USA.

"Do we know where Gwen is?" Joel asked.

"She must be lining up." I didn't realize athletes waited outside the venue, while those in $2,000 seats enjoyed the spectacle.

"There they are! The USA athletes." Elizabeth leaned toward the screen. "Does anyone see her?"

"Is she behind the track team?" Joel thought maybe he saw her, but the cameras focused only on big-name athletes. "Tell her next time she should stand next to LeBron James."

At the end of the evening, when Gwen sent her own photo via email, we finally saw her in USA apparel.

The next day, I asked Gwen about the experience.

"I didn't get to see much of the program because USA was so far back in the line, but the best part was taking pictures and hanging out with other athletes. And I could tell who had been part of the Ceremony before—they brought stools to sit on while we waited."

A few days later, we arrived at the airport in our blue TEAM GWEN shirts. Answering stares, Elizabeth explained our mission to passengers and crew—despite Olympic qualification, neither Gwen nor triathlon were well known.

Our 2012 itinerary included more than the Olympics, as once again we considered our trip a rare opportunity. Following the London race, we scheduled two days in Paris, and then a four-day cooking homestay at an Italian villa. But first, and most important, was the Olympic race.

ELIZABETH

I missed the qualifying race that placed my sister on the podium, a silver medal around her neck. One year later, as I braced for the eight-hour transatlantic flight, I dreamed of a repeat performance...one I could experience. I thought there was a legitimate shot at a medal. I told my high school English students Gwen was the one to watch. I read *Sports Illustrated* articles proclaiming Gwen the underdog favorite. I researched prizes for gold medal winners and claimed the one I wanted—a Nike gold-plated watch—while Gwen downplayed the Olympics.

"It won't be like the qualifying race. Only come if you want to," she said. *Only come if I want to?* My sister is going to the Olympics—the games that riveted us as kids when Kristi Yamaguchi and Dominique Moceanu claimed victories of their own. I cried at Bob Costas specials—moved by stories of triumph and defeat—and at strains of the national anthem, celebrating American achievement, honor and freedom. It was possible. Gwen Jorgensen: gold medal winner. Olympic champion. I thought a podium finish, a come-from-behind sprint to the Wheaties box was at least likely. And I would see it—celebrate it—with my family.

We arrived in London a few days before the race and spent our time at tourist sites—London Eye, Buckingham Palace, the Tower of London. As we looked for attractions, fish and chips or a pub, Olympic ambassadors guided us. Dressed in pink vests or shirts, the volunteers meted out directions and recommendations. When they weren't available, I quizzed the nearest bobby. To document our trip, I kept my phone in hand. "Can I take a photo of you?" I asked. The London officer, unhurried and accommodating, posed with a smile. "How about one with my dad? And could the two of you switch hats?" Dad and the bobby eyed each other while I smiled encouragement. "Ready?" They exchanged headwear and posed arm in arm—Dad in a tall wool hat with a shiny badge and the officer in a USA Triathlon baseball cap. "One...two..."

While Mom, Dad, and I toured London, Gwen trained with her coach, Cindi Bannink, in Guildford, 27 miles outside the city. Bannink, who worked with Gwen since 2010, didn't attend every event but spent a week in London preparing Gwen for the Olympics. Patrick, who Gwen still dated, joined them as cycling coach, bike mechanic, and support system.

Just before the race, they all transferred to a London hotel and suggested we meet for dinner. Gwen, maintaining her focus, said the evening would be short. Patrick made reservations, and we adjusted our schedule to accommodate theirs.

NANCY

At dinner, I knew better than to quiz Gwen on the upcoming event. But in race-focus mode, I violated my own rule. "Have you had good weather for training?"

Gwen seemed comfortable talking about the week's work. "Yeah, kind of drizzling...but it may rain on the day, so it's good practice." She said athletes from Wales or England, where the climate is wet and cold, would have an advantage if race day proved chilly and damp. Those who trained in the heat could be at a disadvantage.

"Patrick, how's the week been for you?" Elizabeth asked.

"I'm just keeping up with Gwen's needs...checking tires and cleaning her bike. Most of the meals are provided, but if she needs water or bananas, I look for those."

"You found some chocolate for me one day, too." Gwen smiled and touched Patrick's arm.

"Gwen, will you get out to see anything while you're here?"

"It's crazy...I've been to all these famous cities, but I don't see anything except the water and the bike course. We just fly in, work out, and compete, and then we're gone."

We ended the evening with hugs and arranged to meet up after tomorrow's race.

The next morning, anxiety woke me long before my alarm. A nervousness I felt for weeks churned full throttle. I worried about rain-soaked roads, about physical contact in the swim, about sharp corners on the bike.

At the course, Joel and I claimed the two family-allotted grandstand seats where we would watch athletes move through the transition zone—seven times on the bike and four times on the run. The jumbotron would feed remote video from helicopters and motorcycles, and an announcer would provide updates. Elizabeth and Patrick looked for a vantage point on the street while USA Triathlon personnel and Gwen's coach found places to communicate with Gwen as she raced. Most of Gwen's USA fans stayed home to watch live, at 2:00 a.m. Milwaukee time, but some of Gwen's friends traveled to London. High school teammates Hannah MacDougal, Maggie Lach, and Kate Fahje; and college cross-country friends Sara McKinley and Sarah Hurley would stand somewhere along the route.

ELIZABETH

The day of the race, nerves dominated. Mom, Dad, and I didn't want to say anything ominous or unlucky. It was cold and gloomy, but Patrick assured us his tire adjustments would help Gwen navigate the course.

While Mom and Dad sat in the grandstand, Patrick and I joined spectators on the street. Serendipitously, as we staked our place, I stumbled upon Gwen's friends. It felt like fate. Perhaps, a full circle moment awaited, and I would celebrate Gwen's come-from-behind win with her high school teammates. Behind us—hundreds of yards away—we could barely pick out where the swimmers would exit the water.

NANCY

London dripped its typical damp, creating potentially dangerous conditions on the road.

Although nervous, I felt optimistic. Anything was possible—just one year ago, we watched Gwen earn a silver medal on this course. I dreamed of a repeat.

When the horn sounded for the swim, 55 athletes in wetsuits and bright green caps dove into the calm waters of Hyde Park's recreational lake. Air temperature was 17°C (62.6°F) with the water at 19°C (66.2°F). Gwen missed the lead swim pack, and I knew that meant she wouldn't be in the first bike pack either—but I believed if Gwen was within a minute of the leaders at the start of the run, she had a chance to medal.

The front swimmers quickly formed a six-woman bike group that included USA's Laura Bennett and Sarah Groff. Gwen and the rest coalesced into chase packs as they cycled over a bridge and through the streets of London, looping past Buckingham Palace.

ELIZABETH

Our view of the race spanned 100 meters of road where bikes zoomed past at 20-plus miles per hour. We saw short spurts, and then waited eight minutes for the next lap. Between laps, I made friends with a local. "Who are you rooting for?"

About 40, she held the hand of her six-year-old son. "We're just here to see an Olympic event. You?"

"My sister Gwen is competing. We're from the US."

"We'd love to cheer for her. Can you point her out?"

I alerted them to Gwen as a pack whooshed past.

"She looks good."

"I hope she can get this pack to work together and catch the leaders."

Before the next lap, my new friend said, "Would you like one of my earrings?" She unclasped a star from her left ear, placing it in my palm. Athletes and spectators exchanged Olympic pins and her earring served a similar purpose.

"That's so nice of you!" I put the earring in my ear. "I'll send you a USA headband when I get home." She gave me her address. Meanwhile, Patrick's phone vibrated and chimed as people stateside sent messages. It was our lifeline to the race. Those at home had a far better view—and they had an announcer and color commentary; we had only cowbells and screaming fans.

NANCY

The rain created peril. As riders negotiated lap one of the water-logged course, Pamella Oliveira of Brazil crashed on a slick corner. As the jumbotron replayed her loss of control, I hoped it was the day's only mishap.

British fans surrounded us, rooting for hometown favorite Helen Jenkins, who won the 2011 test event. At the end of lap one, the crowd spied her and roared, waving British flags and clanging miniature cowbells. Sixty seconds later, the crowd cheered the first chase pack. Thirty seconds after that, they encouraged the second chase group where Gwen rode. I had seen bike packs merge and hoped strong cyclists in Gwen's pack could propel her group forward.

During the second lap, Maria Czesnik of Poland crashed on the same corner as Oliveira, and then Italian Annamaria Mazzetti went down, followed by Australian Emma Moffat (2008 Olympic bronze medalist) whose injuries forced her to pull out of the race. The jumbotron replayed each crash, showing belly-down bodies sliding across pavement, and as I watched the video, my throat closed and my heart rate soared. But at least for now, Gwen remained rubber-side down.

Another crash eliminated Canadian Kathy Tremblay, while Hungary's Zsófia Kovács survived a tumble and remounted her bike. I wondered how many more would lose their grip. Then, as riders circled through transition for lap three, Gwen went missing. "Did you see her? She should be in that pack." But Joel didn't respond and I knew he missed her too.

70

Finally, he said, "She must have been dropped." He didn't verbalize the possibility of a crash.

For several minutes, announcers offered no information and I imagined the worst. Then, riding solo, Gwen pedaled past the grandstand. I looked for road rash, but she didn't appear injured. At first relieved to see her still in the race, my spirits shifted when I realized she was six minutes down.

Gwen later told us she felt her momentum change and asked the woman riding next to her, "Do I have a flat?"

"Yes."

She was desperate for a different answer. "Are you sure?"

"Yes. Your tire is flat."

In her short triathlon career, Gwen never experienced a race-day puncture and had minimal knowledge of changing wheels—especially in the heat of Olympic competition. In her effort to learn the mechanics of racing, she remained unfamiliar with the mechanics of her bike. She was barely acquainted with the exchange station—when asked what wheel she needed, Gwen had no answer. "The back one?"

Years later, she would prepare for mechanical failures. Years later, she would learn which wheel to request at the exchange. Years later, she would know how to salvage an interrupted race. But in 2012, determination, rather than knowledge, guided her. She replaced the wheel, but only two women recorded slower bike times.

The jumbotron featured delayed footage of Gwen as she pulled out of the wheel station. She struggled to clip her shoes into the pedals, and seconds seemed like minutes before she accelerated.

As live coverage resumed, we saw street crowds wave flags and encourage the leaders. We assumed they cheered chase packs too, but the cameras never featured those groups.

In the grandstand, spectators surged to greet the women as they circled through four more times. Around us, fans applauded their favorites. I shouted, too, but realized Gwen's flat tire dashed any opportunity for a podium finish. At the start of the race, I hoped for a medal. Now, I hoped Gwen would finish without a crash. I wondered what she thought. Did she know how much time she lost? Did she believe she could run to 20th place? Or 10th? How much physical, psychological, and emotional energy did she lose changing her flat?

I answered text messages from home, my family wondering why Gwen disappeared from live coverage.

As the 43-kilometer bike stage ended, Gwen dismounted and set off as though running for gold. She passed competitors, working her way forward. But even with the 10th-fastest run split, her bike deficit proved insurmountable.

Waiting for her to finish, Joel and I witnessed the sprint for gold between Switzerland's Nicola Spirig and Sweden's Lisa Norden. In a photo finish, officials examined camera footage to award Spirig the win. I applauded USA's Sarah Groff, who just missed the podium, placing fourth.

Then, we waited and waited another long five minutes until, in the final stretches of the race, Gwen bounded down the blue carpet in a sprint with Japan's Ai Ueda...for 38th place.

ELIZABETH

We found Gwen, teary, at the finish line—the first time I saw her cry after an event. Her distress evident, she hugged us and when her high school and college friends appeared, she put on a smile. She posed for pictures and agreed to brunch the next day.

As we carted Gwen's equipment, she walked ahead with Patrick and Cindi. I noticed them quietly reviewing the day's events, obviously resigned and subdued by the outcome. Dad, Mom, and I were quiet too.

I spent months anticipating the race. I felt let down and disillusioned. But as a sister, my ultimate heartbreak was not for myself, but for Gwen. I was frustrated that Gwen's hard work was overthrown by bad luck. I was sad she sacrificed so much and was denied the opportunity to do her best. We were all downcast for Gwen, but she forced a smile and so we imitated her efforts.

NANCY

I was proud, disappointed, frustrated. But mostly proud. Of 55 starting athletes, Gwen suffered a flat tire and still came in 38th. Of 52 who finished the race, she ran faster than 42 of them. And my daughter was an Olympian!

After the race, Gwen posted her thoughts in a blog.

To be honest, I didn't have my best day, and the flat was unfortunate. But it's part of racing. I was determined to race hard to the end...

London 2012 was about "inspiring a generation." I finished my race and realized I inspired myself. I inspired myself to come up with a four-year plan for Rio. A lot can happen in four years, and I know my plan will change, but for the next four years, I'll have one main, long-term goal: qualify for Rio.

The next morning, we joined Gwen, Patrick, and their friends for brunch. We sat around a long, rectangular table, eating eggs, sausage, and tomatoes, sharing smiles and laughter, the mood restrained. I wished Gwen could have a do-over. I thought how much happier we'd all be if she wore a medal.

Pre-competition, Gwen avoided the distractions of the Olympic Village, but after the race she moved into one of 2,818 apartments that housed 16,000 athletes. On the rare occasion when we both found time and Wi-Fi, we video messaged.

"Mom, it is so cool! Every meal I eat with someone from a different country."

"Who have you met?"

"Oh, people from all over. And the food—from every country. No matter what you want to eat, you can find it." I wasn't surprised world cuisines or the 24-hour dining room for 5,000 fascinated her. "I know it's a cliché, but the Olympics bring people together. I met a rower and a cyclist and then this long jumper joined us and I had lunch with people from Colombia. Every person is the same...just trying their best for their country and sport."

As Gwen concluded her stay with team dinners, complimentary tickets to Olympic events, and socializing in the Olympic Village, Joel, Elizabeth, and I attended events too. With tickets expensive and difficult to secure without a London address, we watched the marathon free from the streets. We crowded behind barricades in the pouring rain, shivering under our plastic ponchos and umbrellas. While we buttoned up sweaters and jackets, women in sleeveless jerseys and shorts charged past. Soused with sweat and rain, runners persevered in the drizzle for 26.2 miles, each face a mask of focus and pain. Although the poor weather tempted us to leave, we remained captivated by the parade of world class runners and defended our front-of-the-crowd position.

The next day, Joel and I attended a women's beach volleyball match where the crowd put on a show as entertaining as the sport. Athletes, wearing only inches of fabric, jumped and lunged in sand pits. Crazed fans in patriotic costumes shouted with each point. A few rows behind us, a trio of Americans, dressed as red-white-and-blue coneheads, waved a full-size flag to celebrate each score; rival fans in green-and-yellow jester hats answered with taunts and jibes. During commercial breaks, when the action subsided, dancers reignited fans by gyrating to a pounding beat.

These head-to-head competitions were unlike endurance events. Where the triathlon featured 60 athletes in mutating patterns of strategy, the sand court displayed four women swirling into cyclones of bump-set-spike. Fans adapted to each style. At triathlon, the crowd erupted in bursts as athletes whizzed past and then ebbed for several minutes; in volleyball, a continual tempest brewed, storming up with each serve, penalty, or point.

After our days in London, I mourned the end of our Olympic journey. But with the disappointment of Gwen's flat tire, I welcomed the next diversion.

We boarded the Eurostar at London St Pancras International station for our two-and-a-half-hour journey to Paris. The train traversed land from London to Kent, and then continued underwater via the Channel Tunnel (Chunnel) where, for 31.4 miles, it took us underneath the English Channel, at times plunging 250 feet deep and traveling 186 miles per hour. Near Calais in northern France, the train emerged from the sea and continued on land to Paris.

During our two-day stay in the City of Love, we climbed the Eiffel Tower, cruised the Seine, and joined walking tours of Notre Dame and Montmartre. Then, we bunked in sleeping compartments as our rail journey continued to Italy. We arrived in Florence and rented a car for the two-hour drive to our cooking homestay in Perugia. I wished Gwen could experience the adventure with us. Fascinated with flavors and authentic dishes, she would have relished the classes and cuisine.

ELIZABETH

While Gwen enjoyed international meals in the Olympic Village, Mom and Dad, and I traveled to our own culinary adventure at a bed and breakfast tucked into the Italian countryside.

Food and Jorgensens are synonymous. In high school, my house was renowned for afternoon snacks of homemade bread and fresh cookies, Mom ready to whip up whatever we hankered. Gwen, rushing in the door with wet bags and hair dripping chlorine, needed food fast, so Mom interrupted her piano practice to fill the kitchen table. Gwen, although perpetually thin, funneled, shoveled, and threw food into her mouth. But, not only did Mom prepare huge quantities, she also challenged our palates. Naan, sardines, pizelles, pickled eggs, pickled herring, home-grown sprouts—always something different, unique, strange. Encouraged to explore, we dissected dishes: Was that cinnamon in the chili? Which spice made homemade pickles zip? What's the best way to feature rosemary in eggs? For Jorgensens, food equaled adventure, with trips to the apple orchard, the strawberry fields or UW Madison's creamery.

When we arrived at our destination in Italy's Umbrian province, Cristina, a short, hunched matriarch, welcomed us. In her three-story stone villa, sandwiched between sunflower fields, she lessoned us in homemade orecchiette, the correct way to sauce pasta, and how much wine was appropriate in Italy (turns out much less than in Wisconsin).

"I see you have your bread boards already. Buono!" Cristina measured flour and showed us how to make a well in the middle. "Use your hands to work the water into the flour."

"Dad, I think you have a little too much water." I tracked Dad's efforts.

"Very good, ladies. You know how to knead." Cristina used her own crippled fingers, bent from arthritis, to rhythmically push and fold the dough. She told us she recently sold her own restaurant because of her ailing joints.

"Uh-oh, Dad. Now it looks a little dry."

"It's fine. Just wait till I'm done—it will be perfect."

While we kneaded, Cristina helped us plan the next few days.

"We're interested in what you like to do," I said.

"My two good friends run an olive orchard, but they only make small quantities—top quality oil. Would you like to see?" We did, so Cristina scheduled a private tasting paired with cheeses and meats. "I have a wine tour for you too. My friends will take you through the vineyard on their all-terrain vehicles."

Cristina planned an excursion for us each morning—a local market, the ancient underground city of Perugia, an alfresco lunch at her friend's establishment—and then in the afternoon, under her tutelage, we cooked dinner.

We absorbed the culture, we asked questions, we ate, ate, and ate...and we missed Gwen.

I was used to filling vacation time with Mom and Dad while Gwen scheduled workouts, massages, or meetings. But something about this trip—about being in someone's home, together as a family—made Gwen's absence more apparent. I imagined how she might sneak bites before the meal was served. I envisioned her crazy about the paté and four-course veranda meals. She would have devoured the homemade ice cream topped with strawberries from the garden.

NANCY

Post-race obligations, celebrations, and Olympic Village activity monopolized Gwen's time. With few opportunities for phone calls, we exchanged emails.

> *Mom,*
>
> *wish you would have been at celebration last night... we were able to go up and thank everyone and i wish i could have given you a proper thank you with you and dad and ej there...but know i love and appreciate you!*
>
> *Love* .
>
> *Gw*

> *Gwen,*
>
> *It would have been nice to be there but I am sure it was great to have some time with your friends too. You are so thoughtful to want to say thank you but we know you are always appreciative. And we appreciate*

everything you do to make time in your life for us. We are VERY proud of you! Such an accomplishment to be an Olympian. And very proud of your unfailing determination and dedication. We love you very much. Hope we can see you soon.

Love

Mom and Dad

Mom and Dad,

How was your vacation? are you back? Loved the pictures - looked so fun!

I stayed extra days to do an Ernst & Young event and will be in Closing [Ceremony] tonight and will fly home tomorrow.

Gwen

At the end of the Games, as fans moved to other interests, athletes continued their workouts, promotions, and communications. Returning to Wisconsin, Gwen trained, negotiated new sponsorships, and wrote a keynote speech for incoming freshmen at Carroll University in Waukesha. She concluded her 2012 competitive season with an 8th place finish in Yokohama and a silver medal at the Auckland Grand Final.

Elizabeth, Joel, and I returned to work where we fielded questions about the Olympics, repeatedly reliving Gwen's flat tire. Each colleague's interest reminded me that Gwen represented more than herself or her family. She represented Team USA—and especially Wisconsin—and she made many people proud.

2012 Race Results

6th: Clermont Challenge, Clermont, Florida, United States of America (3 March)
4th: ITU WTS Sydney, Australia (14 April)
51st: ITU WTS San Diego, California, United States of America (12 May)
1st: ITU World Cup Banyoles, Spain (17 June)
11th: ITU WTS Kitzbühel, Austria (23 June)
38th: Summer Olympics, London, United Kingdom (4 August)
8th: ITU WTS Yokohama, Japan (29 September)
2nd: ITU WTS Grand Final, Auckland, New Zealand (20 October)

CHAPTER 4

A Quest to Improve

2013

NANCY

Determined to qualify for Rio 2016, Gwen aspired to win gold. She dedicated every minute of the next four years to her goal. Analytical by nature, Gwen assessed her skills, training, and location. "I can do what I've been doing and place top-ten. But I think with some changes, I can earn podiums." She believed daily hands-on coaching would produce results.

Since 2010, Cindi Bannink, a petite blonde who competed nationally with the best of her age, communicated workouts and advice from Madison while Gwen lived and trained in Milwaukee. They met occasionally but usually connected via phone or computer. With Bannink's expertise, Gwen qualified for London 2012. The relationship was successful, and the results extraordinary. They shared the exhilaration (and disappointment) of the Olympics. I questioned Gwen about how Bannink felt.

"Cindi knows she can't be at every practice and that top-level women work in performance groups—they meet seven days a week with a coach who analyzes fitness, monitors exertion, and adjusts workouts."

"So what happens now?" I wondered how she would find the right fit.

"I've worked with coaches at training camps, and I know what I'm looking for." Put off by threat or intimidation, Gwen sought a collaborator—a mentor and partner—in her career.

"Is it expensive to have a personal coach?"

"Yeah, I need to ask about fees." Gwen's research revealed varying approaches, costs, and locations.

Remembering New Zealander Jamie Turner from a training camp, Gwen recalled his respect for athletes. Jamie encouraged personal responsibility. He advised, but never demanded. Leading a daily performance group in Australia, he attended every workout—three per day—for his cadre of international athletes. Gwen requested an interview and prepared questions: How do athletes pay you? Do you require performance-based bonuses? Would you assist in finding lodging? With so many athletes, will you have time for me? How many countries do you work for? Do you think I can win gold in Rio?

Jamie answered her questions and flipped the conversation. "Gwen, what would you bring to my group?" He only collaborated with those who facilitated progress in others.

I asked Gwen about the interview.

"Jamie said I can pay him what I think he is worth, and bonuses are up to me. And he has apartments lined up in Spain, but everyone is on their own in Australia."

I was surprised Jamie didn't have a prescribed fee. "So, how many countries are in the group?"

"He said it changes, but four right now."

"And what does he think about you winning in Rio?"

"He says I need to swim faster, bike faster, and run a sub-33-minute 10K. And he wasn't happy I let others go first in the swim lanes. He wants me to be a leader."

Gwen felt optimistic about the interview, but training with Jamie would require relocation and Gwen never lived more than 90 miles from Waukesha, Wisconsin. She spent five years in Madison for college and a few years in Milwaukee for work; athletic competitions took her worldwide and she backpacked in Europe—but she always returned to Wisconsin. The hometown girl was daunted by a 9,000-mile relocation.

Gwen also considered the National Training Center in Clermont, Florida. She had spent several weeks there, rooming with triathlete Sara McLarty. When Joel and I met Sara, she said, "USA Triathlon needs people like Gwen—she's helping grow the program." If Gwen moved to Florida, Sara would be a valuable training partner.

A few weeks later, Gwen said, "I made my decision."

Although sad she would be moving, I knew the Midwest's cold and ice hampered her training. Already, I imagined myself exchanging Wisconsin's snow drifts for Florida's sunshine.

"I'm going to work with Jamie Turner."

I was unprepared. "Isn't Jamie in Australia?"

"And in April, he moves his group to the Basque Region in Spain."

For weeks at a time, I didn't see Gwen or Elizabeth, but their proximity comforted me. "How long would you be gone?"

"I'll fly to Australia around New Year's Day, then move to Spain in April and come back in October."

"Nine months abroad?" I struggled to envision the separation and wondered about cell service and whether FaceTime worked internationally.

"I know. I've thought about that. It's a long time to be gone, but I think I can make it work." To move from friends and family, Gwen required a bit of home—something familiar amid foreign languages, peculiar customs, and unreliable Wi-Fi. "Patrick decided to come with me. And I think if he's there, I'll be okay."

Wow. One surprise after another. With her announcement, I understood she was as serious about Patrick as she was about triathlon.

Until now, I didn't consider Gwen's relationship with Patrick a decisive one, but I should have noticed signs of romance. I recalled the fall of 2011 when Gwen lived at home. She typically ate a quick dinner and retired to her room. Running a white-noise fan, she prioritized sleep, often in bed before sunset. But Gwen began to postpone bedtime for late-night conversations. An undertone of whispers and laughs hummed past dark. Spurred by an interest in cycling, Gwen's relationship with Patrick surpassed athletics and thrived via Skype. Then, Patrick started matching Gwen's schedule, joining her in Milwaukee, or Florida, or London.

I trusted Gwen's decision, but Elizabeth's divorce remained a fresh grief, reminding me of love's potential for pain. My protective instinct created hesitance, but my reservations remained unspoken: Gwen, are you sure? This is huge to move across the world. And how old is Patrick? Didn't he just graduate from college? In a few years, will he be happy he gave up his cycling career for you? What do his parents think? Will he find work or are you going to support him? I knew Gwen considered these questions and more. I also knew she was bold enough to take a risk if it meant exploring her potential.

Gwen and Patrick moved to Australia in January 2013. They bought an international phone plan for talk and text but cautioned that sending photos would be expensive. They spent a few weeks at altitude in Falls Creek, and then transferred to Wollongong where Gwen joined the Wollongong Wizards—Jamie Turner's international group from Australia, Hungary, Canada, and Chile. After races in Australia and New Zealand, the Wizards would move to Vitoria-Gasteiz in Spain's Basque Region, convenient for European races.

With a new coach and training group, Gwen aimed to improve the processes of swimming, biking, and running, with no aspirations for stellar results. To begin the season, she entered a February 23, 2013, Continental Cup in Devonport, Australia, and scored a second-place finish. It proved a solid start, with six weeks to prepare for a more challenging event—a World Triathlon Series race in Auckland, New Zealand.

Body type affects sport, but triathlon demands three disciplines, so athletes come in all shapes and sizes. Some are suited to open water swims, with strong shoulders and a buoyant frame. Others wield powerful thighs to muscle through cycling. Gwen's tall, lean frame and long legs bestowed an advantage in running, but her lack of body fat crippled her in cold water.

Gwen's slender build always challenged her athletic aspirations. When she was in high school, Gwen asked her Waukesha Express Swim Team coach, Blaine Carlson, for training advice. "Blaine, what should I do next? Do you think I need longer workouts?" She asked about stretches, massages, weights, ice baths.

Carlson looked at her from nose to toes and said, "Go home and eat a steak."

I wanted to tell him we weren't starving this girl. I served breakfast twice a day (before and after morning swim), hearty lunches with homemade bread and protein, after school snacks, a dinner of meat and carbs, and bedtime treats.

Naturally lean, with a taste for healthy foods, she never struggled with weight, except for how to put it on.

On April 6, 2013, Gwen plunged into the 20.6°C (69.1°F) water alongside Auckland's Queen's Wharf, and lagged; while competitors forged ahead, Gwen labored into transition with the last six women. Her ultrathin body suffered in the chill, and once on the bike she spent so much energy warming up that she had nothing left for cycling. Lap after lap, she lost time and eventually pulled out of the race.

"That was a really bad race, Mom."

"So, what happened?" I worried when Gwen didn't finish—circumstances must be extreme for her to give up.

"The water was freezing. And I couldn't adjust." The air temperature, at 18.5°C (65.3°F), registered colder than the water. "It felt like I was going backwards, and then at one point I thought I got turned around and was riding the wrong way." The confusion and hallucination indicated hypothermia, her loss of body heat sabotaging weeks of preparation.

Gwen's severe reaction prompted her and Jamie to brainstorm solutions. They negotiated with Mobile Warming to build a customized, battery-operated warming jacket that Gwen could wear up to the minute she dove in the water; they designed dry-land exercises to replace race day water warm-ups; and they devised a schedule that excluded ultra-cold waters.

ELIZABETH

Gwen viewed every race as an opportunity to win. And when she didn't win, she analyzed mistakes, made a plan for improvement, and executed her strategy. Meticulous and detail-driven, Gwen ended each training day with a list of three things she did well and three she needed to correct—dissecting, analyzing, and reflecting her means to improvement and championships.

But I did not share Gwen's athletic determination. In high school, afraid of losing, or failing, or disappointing, nerves sabotaged my efforts. Dad—before cross-country and track meets, and even local 5Ks—calmed me: "You won't be the best. You won't be the worst. But if you try your best, you'll be in the top half. Guaranteed." And somehow, he was always right...at least about me. So, I'd board the bus ready to battle my nerves for a top-half performance. No blue ribbons—other than participation ones—filled my memory boxes. I never dreamed of them and so I was never disappointed when they didn't come. But Gwen, following three years behind me, saw first place ribbons as possible—as the prize she wanted—and she kept trying, working, and improving until she earned them.

For Gwen's sixth-grade cross-country meet, Mom, Dad, and I went to Waukesha's Minooka Park, expecting her to do well. We didn't necessarily expect her to win, but we did expect disappointment. In some aspect of the race, in some ritual, or in some achievement, Gwen would be unhappy. At the sixth-grade cross-country meet, Gwen was unhappy with Mom.

In the wind and cold, snow frosting the grass, Gwen competed in her school-issued uniform. The winner (dressed in the same school-issued t-shirt and shorts) ran with tight, black, winter gloves. And in Gwen's head, that was the difference. Gwen's 12-year-old mind thought, *I am as good as she is. What did she do that I didn't? Why did she beat me?* The less than logical answer: the only visible difference between Gwen and the first-place contestant. Her gloves. So, for years, Gwen blamed the loss (her second-place finish) on the gloves. And she blamed Mom: *Why didn't Mom bring gloves for me? Didn't Mom know that was the difference between winning and losing?*

As Gwen matured, so did her analytical skills. She trusted coaches to evaluate her progress; she made changes based on statistics instead of feelings; she used science, research, and evidence to guide her.

NANCY

Although Gwen and Jamie solved some problems, challenges remained. Her single WTS result showed DNF (Did Not Finish), with the next race only two weeks away—in San Diego, where Gwen placed 51st the year before. Since most of Gwen's races would be abroad, Joel and I planned a trip to Austria and Germany. With San Diego the only USA event, we added a California weekend to our itinerary. Elizabeth joined us.

One year ago, at the 2012 San Diego race, Gwen drew attention for her quick rise to elite status, her Olympic qualification, and silver medal in London 2011. But in April 2013, media focused on American Sarah Groff, who placed fourth at the London Olympics and entered the San Diego race a medal contender. Fans speculated about a USA victory on home soil. If Groff won, it would be the first USA gold medal in the history of the World Triathlon Series.

While Groff fielded reporters' questions, smiled for cameras, and appeared at press conferences, Gwen prepared for the triathlon. She and Jamie composed a to-do list: improve swim performance, avoid media distraction, and find redemption after last year's San Diego disaster.

ELIZABETH

When Gwen's next race brought her to San Diego, I dreamed of the beach and Golden State sun. Years ago, our cousin, Kaitlin, moved to California. We hadn't seen each other in a decade and we welcomed the opportunity to connect. Online, Kaitlin looked like a California girl, blonde and blue-eyed, her hair in a braid pulled to one side. She lived two lives: one of makeup and dance clubs, the other of bandanas and dirt bikes. Modeling at car shows, she touted her cleavage with bikinis and crop tops. I was eager to compare her California Dream to my Wisconsin day-to-day.

Mom researched activities (a local taqueria featured on *Diners, Drive-Ins, and Dives*, the San Diego Zoo and La Jolla Cove) and booked our hotel and plane tickets.

Arriving early to assess race accommodations, we found the hometown of triathlon abuzz. The blue carpet. A jumbotron and announcer. Thousands of spectators and age-group participants. Like an NBA or MLB game, this was a professional event. Katy Perry's "Firework" blared. "Dad, where should we sit?"

"I'm not sure. Let's check out the swim start."

Dad gauged the swim start too far from the main action. "The grandstand is our best bet," he said. "We can see the entire race on the screen."

Mom and Dad attended far more triathlons than I did, and I trusted his judgment. "Okay, but let's sit up high." We climbed twenty rows, the hot metal railing stinging my fingers. "This will be fine," I said to Mom. I detected anxiety in her sighs and the way she clutched the railing. Behind the bleachers, athletes warmed up, turning and tucking between the medical tent, the mechanical area, and city streets. I looked for Gwen.

Shortly after settling in, I spotted her frizzy hair and gazelle gait as she walked her bike to transition. I ran down the bleachers, screaming. "GOOOOO, GWEN!"

She waved to quiet me. "Hi, Elizabeth."

"You pumped? You excited? Ready to do this?"

"Yes." Focused, she remained calmer than I did.

Not wanting to intrude on pre-race rituals, I said goodbye—"Have fun! Go get 'em!"—and found a vendor tent where I could eat away my nerves. Roasted nuts salting my tongue, I spied Kaitlin, her arm sporting a peacock sleeve tattoo. We caught up (she now sold dog toys and treats) and I envied her mountain hikes and lazy afternoons.

Kaitlin and I joined Mom and Dad in the bleachers for lineup announcements. I adjusted my headband and sunglasses and repeated positive thoughts about staying safe, racing fast, and winning. *She can do it. She will do it. She will.* Sweat glistened my palms. Nerves tickled my tongue. And then there was nothing left to do but scream, "LET'S GOOOOOOOOOO, GWENNNN!"

NANCY

Despite warm air, water temperatures below 20°C (68°F) required a wetsuit swim. The suit would give Gwen buoyancy and warmth, but cold water could still ambush her strength. Wetsuit removal in transition could also pose problems.

Wearing number 20, Gwen ran the beachfront start with 39 other women. International competitors included Anne Haug (gold medalist at the 2012 Grand Final), Emma Moffat (2008 Olympic medalist), Non Stanford (U-23 World Champion), and USA teammate Groff.

Gwen exited the first of two swim laps in 10th place; she dove back for the second lap and improved to 8th. Her position wasn't enough to put her in the first bike pack. Four leaders—Moffat, Groff, Carolina Routier, and Pamella Oliveira—established themselves ahead of the field, while Gwen rode in the first chase pack.

"Only 30 seconds behind—that's doable, right?" I said.

"Yeah, if the pack can hang on, Gwen's got a shot," Joel said.

For several laps, I maintained hope that Gwen would enter the run leg close to the leaders. But in the last two laps, they surged.

"Not good," Joel said. "The leaders are ahead by a minute."

"You don't think she can do it?" Elizabeth said.

"I'm saying she can," he said.

Elizabeth, just inches from my ear, screamed, "GO, GWEN! GET UP THERE! YOU CAN DO IT!"

I knew every race was important, but one on home soil was especially significant.

Moffat and Groff dismounted. Trailing them, Gwen's group of six (including Stanford, Haug and Jodie Stimpson) reduced the gap to 44 seconds behind Moffat, and 30 seconds behind Groff. "Joel—do you think she can catch Groff?"

"Gwen runs faster in the second half...just when Groff gets tired."

"GOOOOOOO, GWEEEENN!" Elizabeth shouted.

As Joel anticipated, Gwen gained speed and established herself in third behind Moffat and Groff. I made a silent wish she could hold off the other runners and win bronze. Gwen continued to look strong and, better than holding her own, advanced. Elizabeth gave Kaitlin a high five.

Just before the bell lap, Gwen looked poised to pass Groff. "There—she's almost got her. She'll take second for sure," Joel said.

Gwen passed Groff, and I started to believe she might do even more—but to overtake Moffat, she needed to make up 30 seconds in 3,000 meters. "Any chance for gold?"

"I'm saying she can do it." He and I routinely forecasted Gwen's results. We each wanted to call a win. "Go, Gweeeeeen! EJ, she's got this, right?"

"She can do it. Yes. Yes. Yes," Elizabeth said. "GOOOOOO, GWENNNNN!"

As Gwen approached the grandstand for the final lap, Elizabeth bolted from the top of the bleachers to the first row. I knew she hoped to encourage Gwen with her familiar voice. "COME ON, GW! GO GET 'EM. YOU GOT THIS!"

Joel and I, a backup chorus, shouted and rang cowbells.

Spectators turned to us. "Are you her parents? Congratulations! We've been following your daughter's career. She's a real talent—she's going to win today!" The distraction relieved my anxiety, and the strangers' confidence boosted my optimism.

Although with every step Gwen moved closer to the lead, announcer and triathlon guru Barrie Shepley anticipated Moffat's victory. He projected Gwen in second place, short by about 10 seconds. Around me, fans shouted louder and leaned in closer. I hoped hometown cheers would propel her.

Gwen moved closer to Moffat—and Shepley hedged. Now he called Gwen a "rocket on fire," and the fans a "crowd going nuts." Apparently realizing the potential for an American victory, the crowd leapt to their feet. Grandstand decibels exploded.

"This is really possible, isn't it?" I didn't consider any historic significance, only this one win on this one day.

Announcers shouted updates, speaking louder and louder. Elizabeth returned to the top of the bleachers. She banged on the bench and shouted, "Go, Gwen!"

With 1,000 meters remaining, Gwen faced an eight-second deficit. On the jumbotron, she looked powerful and determined, her gait even, her stride long. "Oh, my gosh. She could do this!" I said.

Approaching the finish line, Gwen trailed by four seconds. She positioned herself on Moffat's heel. Looking over her shoulder, Gwen saw Stanford, Stimpson, and Haug looming. She moved to Moffat's shoulder. Joel, Elizabeth, and I were already on our feet—now we stepped on the bench.

Then, on a corner turn, Gwen shot ahead of Moffat.

"Yeah! She caught her!" Joel said. His words faded in the uproar.

"Go, Gwen!" I sent telepathic messages. *Good girl! Hang on!* All around me, thousands of fans cheered—for my daughter. In the moment, that didn't register. I spun attention toward Gwen's final push.

Joel and Elizabeth shouted. "She's got it! Yeaaaahhhh!"—"No question! Gooooooo, Gweneveeeeere!"—"GOOOOOOOOOO, GWEEENNNNNN!"

Gwen charged to the finish and with one last check over her shoulder, accompanied by a roar from the crowd, broke the tape. The next three competitors followed within seven seconds.

I hugged Joel, careful not to fall off the bench, turned to hug Elizabeth and Kaitlin, and then grabbed Joel one more time. I tracked Gwen, watching her congratulate the next finishers. And then I remembered her win was the first USA gold in the history of the World Triathlon Series.

For a few minutes, I tried to absorb what happened, but then the screen featured post-race interviews. I squinted into the sun, riveted by Gwen's face. About her win, she said, "I was just focusing on my race, trying to remain calm." I was impressed that with an historic win, Gwen simply acknowledged her hard work.

On her DNF in Auckland, and whether that provided motivation, she said, "A lot of people had better races than me that day...[today] I just came out and executed on the processes." Gwen used the word "processes" frequently, reflecting

Jamie's focus not on winning but on the mechanics of each discipline. "I just wanted to do my best," she said.

Exiting the interview platform, Gwen took three steps toward Patrick where he waited behind a fence and fell into his arms. He circled her in a hug and, just as the camera swiveled away, kissed her.

After another few minutes, the awards began. I alternated between watching the jumbotron, then peering into the sun toward the far end of the blue carpet to see Gwen live. I watched her ascend to the top step, accept a bouquet of flowers, and lean to receive a gold medal. Then, as we stood—hands over hearts for the *Star Spangled Banner*—Gwen's face filled the jumbotron, layered among billowing images of the stars and stripes. I tried to memorize the feeling, the setting, the image on the screen.

At ceremony's end, the women sprayed each other with champagne. When Gwen gestured for the others to join her on the top step, I was proud of my daughter, who shared the acclaim. Not only had Gwen won a World Triathlon Series race, but she was the first American woman to do so. And she accomplished it in the USA, in the birthplace of triathlon. And we were there to see it.

After the ceremony, we found Patrick in the USA tent where he hucked backpacks and wheels. Gwen, water and banana in hand, walked toward drug testing. "What a race, Gwenevere." Nothing I said could match the magnitude of her accomplishment.

"Thanks, Mom and Dad. Thanks, EJ." Gwen gave us each a hug.

"I'm so happy for you," Elizabeth said.

"Mom, Dad, Elizabeth—this is Jamie," Gwen said and then disappeared with the volunteer who supervised her walk to drug testing.

Jamie extended his hand for a greeting. I expected him to be taller. Built like Joel, stocky and muscular, with dark hair, he stood about my height.

"Hello, Mum. Hello, Ded. Ya're net as tall as I thet ya'd bay." I ran his words through my head again, and thought he said we were short. Interesting how we each pictured the other taller. "Gween is so tall, and neither of ya air. Hmmm. Sis isn't either." He spoke quickly, with a heavy New Zealand accent.

"How was your flight?" I tried to make conversation, hoping to understand his answer.

"Yih, yih, foine."

Jamie seemed eager to get on with the day's work. Or maybe he was skittish around an athlete's parents, not sure if they were the hovering, helicopter type. I felt the same when meeting my choir students' parents. It was best to keep a professional distance, at least at first. "Patrick is planning a dinner for Gwen's family and friends. Will we see you there?"

"Yih. I'll bay thear."

After Gwen completed drug testing, we followed her to the hotel, and I asked about Jamie.

"I can't understand him either. And he speaks in riddles. He told me at the pool I should swim like a Ferrari. What does that mean?"

I used metaphors with my choir students and wondered if they found my analogies indecipherable too.

"I'm starting to get his sense of humor, though," Gwen said. "And you should have something in common—he taught phys ed before coaching."

I decided to ask Jamie about that at dinner and hoped the restaurant would be quiet enough for me to unpuzzle his pronunciations.

At dinner, 15 of us sat around a rectangular table. Patrick's dad, who flew in from Fargo, sat close to me. "Craig, what did you think of the race?" I wondered if he liked Gwen and what he thought about the romantic and professional arrangement between our children.

"What a great day! Patrick and I rode our bikes, following back and forth. It's a perfect way to see the race." Craig raced crits and cyclocross with Patrick and rarely traveled without a bicycle.

As we talked, I noticed Patrick resembled his dad. Both tall, lean, and fair, they smiled and conversed easily. "So, what are your plans?"

"I got in a few long bike rides, but now it's back to work." Craig managed one of Fargo's grocery stores.

During dinner, I found Patrick attentive to Gwen. Arm around her chair, he checked with her frequently. Once in a while, he kissed her on the cheek. I caught up with my niece, Kaitlin, who wore her California tan as if she never heard of a Wisconsin blizzard. I was disappointed Jamie sat too far away for conversation.

As the evening ended, Patrick whispered to Gwen, and I realized, when the bill was paid, they covered the tab. It was their thank you—for coaching, for traveling, for running errands, for cheering and supporting.

With early morning flights the next day, we said goodbye in the restaurant. I hadn't seen Gwen in four months, and it would be another three until I saw her again. Because of the time difference—noon in the USA was 3 a.m. in Australia—texting and emailing would cover most of our communication.

On the flight home, in an *Associated Press* interview, I found Gwen's comments on her win: "It's a huge honor, and I think it's only going to increase our athletes in the U.S. It's going to motivate and push other U.S. athletes as well. It's really exciting because it was on U.S. soil."

The article quoted Jamie too: "Early success, instant gratification on a little bit of work—those things are hard to deal with...Hard work only beats talent when talent doesn't work hard. Gwen was probably a talent that wasn't working to her capacity." I read his comments a few times to understand what he meant.

Before dozing on Joel's shoulder, I said, "Can you believe it? Gwen made history this weekend."

"I know. It's crazy."

A few days later, Gwen posted to Facebook:

> At a loss for words after winning my first WTS. Took a lot of hard work, but even more, support from my fans, sponsors, training partners, family, friends, coach. Thank you for your help. I'm truly honored. Looking forward to the rest of the year.

****

Joel and I watched the next two races at home, streaming from computer to television. Tuning in to the Yokohama, Japan, race on May 11, we searched for Gwen's signature dive—always a fraction of a second late. We hunted for her stroke—right arm, left arm, pause...right arm, left arm, pause...but when we thought we spied her, the camera shifted. I relaxed only when her swim split appeared.

When Gwen started triathlon, I didn't understand the dangers. Now, after witnessing bike crashes, I knew what to fear. My anxiety increased when I watched from home—if there was a crash, I could do nothing from 6,000 miles away. Afraid to watch riders lean into curves or draft within inches, I turned up the volume but avoided the screen. Listening to Barrie Shepley and Trevor Harris, I scrubbed the kitchen sink, sponged the stove, swept and mopped the floor—anything to pass 60 long minutes of the most dangerous part of the race. "Aren't you nervous?" I said to Joel.

"No. Are you?"

Oh, my goodness. Have you noticed me cleaning the kitchen? I can't relax until she gets off that bike.

"She's doing fine. Her biking is better all the time."

As the Yokohama cycling progressed, cool temperatures—21°C (69.8°F)—prevailed and a steady rain created peril. But Gwen avoided multiple crashes and completed the ride with the first pack. Confident in Gwen's running, I returned to the television for the 10-kilometer run.

Gwen began the run in 15th place as Emma Moffat and Jodie Stimpson created a 14-second gap. At the end of lap one, Gwen trailed by 10 seconds. At the mid-point, she lagged by six. Announcers described the "floating...efficiency" in her stride.

"Well, what do you think?" I asked Joel.

"For sure. She's gonna win."

"A few seconds can be a lot to make up."

"I'm not worried. She'll negative split—go faster in the second half like she always does."

Shepley speculated about Gwen's recent dominance in the run. "This streak is belonging to Gwen Jorgensen." He reviewed Gwen's strong runs—in London, the 2012 Grand Final, San Diego, and now Yokohama—and said consecutive wins were exceptional.

"They're talking like she's won already," I said.

With one lap to go, as the camera's rain-spotted lens followed her, Gwen advanced to the lead.

Shepley continued his praise—"One of the best runners I have seen in the sport"—as he predicted a "...monster string of wins." I was accustomed to coaches and teachers complimenting

Gwen, but it was thrilling to hear these words broadcast globally.

Gwen approached the finish. Looking over her shoulder, she saw no one as her toes skimmed blue carpet and, with time to spare, high-fived fans crowding the chute. In some sports, a pre-win celebration is considered poor sportsmanship, but triathletes with a comfortable margin routinely place sunglasses atop their heads, grab their country's flag, and acknowledge fans. Gwen won the race by 15 seconds.

After briefly holding the tape for pictures, Gwen congratulated Moffat—in second—and Stimpson—in third—and then wrapped herself in a Mylar blanket. On the podium, she accepted gold, once again inviting her competitors to the top step for pictures. She remained there for one more ceremony. The series leader now, Gwen posed with the International Triathlon Union trophy that signified her number one world ranking.

Joel and I spent the rest of the day in awe. "I can't believe she just won San Diego and now Yokohama. First USA woman to win a race, and all of a sudden she's got two in a row," I said.

"And ranked number one in the world. Let's watch the replay."

That sounded like a good idea. I could watch the cycling without fear. "I really wish we were there." It was impossible to see every race. We did that when Gwen was in high school and college, but now Asia and New Zealand were on her schedule.

A few hours later, during a video chat with Gwen, who was 6,000 miles away, she described an upset stomach the night before. She downplayed its importance, but when I read her race report, I wondered how she managed to compete, let alone win:

> *I'm not sure what I ate (I think it was a rice dish I had that had some seaweed in it maybe?) - anyway, it upset my stomach. I went to bed, fell asleep, and about an hour later I woke up in night sweats and running to the bathroom. I went to the bathroom, back to bed, and couldn't sleep as my stomach was going crazy. I laid there for a few hours, going to the bathroom a few more emergency times before texting Pat. I really didn't want to tell anyone what was going on. Pat insisted I must call Jamie or Andy [Schmitz from USA Triathlon] that instant, but Vinnie [Czech roommate, Vendula Frintova] was in my room, and I didn't want to wake her. Pat said I must hydrate and replenish food, but nothing sounded good except*

water. I downed about 1 liter of water and some of a
chocolate bar. I then, around 2 a.m., managed to fall
asleep before waking up to my alarm at 4:27 a.m. I
woke up and felt so much better - no longer felt like
I had a fever, etc. I went for a 10 min jog, ate plain
oats, banana, Bonk Breaker, and lots of water and
some coffee.

Her concluding thoughts revealed why she raced.

[It] was a day I didn't want to race, but knew I'd
have days like these...so a great opportunity to race
feeling rubbish.

Three weeks later, on June 1, Gwen took fourth in Madrid as we followed once more from the family room (and kitchen).

Meanwhile, Joel and I confirmed plans to spend two weeks with Gwen and Patrick in Spain's Basque Region. While in Europe, we would see WTS races in Kitzbühel, Austria, and Hamburg, Germany. Elizabeth would stay home to teach summer school.

****

With each international visit, I noticed locals' language skills. In Montreal, resolute Francophiles spoke excellent English. In Hungary, Gwen's massage therapist communicated in Hungarian, German, and English. In Italy, our cooking tutor conversed in four languages. With adjoining borders, Europeans mastered their neighbors' languages—a practical life skill. I felt embarrassed for myself and other Americans who spoke only English. Although I studied French in high school, it crouched in my brain, refusing to be useful. In Montreal, I mangled the words—*je ne parle pas bien français*—then smiled and hoped for the waiter's help. In Paris, I said *bonjour*—a primitive attempt at courtesy.

Years ago, hoping to inspire Elizabeth and Gwen to learn a language, I modeled an elementary knowledge of French. But being typical teenagers, they rebuffed my efforts.

In the car after Christmas Midnight Mass, Catholic motifs remained fresh—candle, wreath, tree, wise men, manger. "Mom, I bet you don't know what the word manger means," Elizabeth said.

"Actually, I do. The word *manger,* from the French, means 'to eat'. The manger was where they fed the animals in the stable. Mary used it for Jesus because that's all they had."

"Ooo la laaaa! Listen to Mom!" Elizabeth poked Gwen and laughed. "She gives us the entire French history of the word."

Even though I had the right answer, they laughed and teased me for expounding on *manger*. My basic knowledge of French is now a family hilarity. If I utter a word of French—*bon appétit, à la mode, faux pas, adieu, voilà*—the girls whoop out, "From zee Frrrrench."

****

On the airplane to Kitzbühel, Austria, I reviewed basic German on my iPhone app and hoped I wouldn't need more than *hallo und danke und auf wiedersehen.*

The International Triathlon Union billed Kitzbühel 2013 one of the most demanding triathlons. The race began in a lake and progressed up Kitzbühel's famous mountain, the Horn. In a typical ITU competition, athletes complete several laps, circling through transition each time. But no part of Kitzbühel's course repeated, as athletes cycled straight up the Horn. Standard triathlon distances were adjusted to allow for the rigorous climb. Instead of a 40-kilometer bike course, athletes cycled 11.5 kilometers on an 867-meter ascent. Instead of 10 kilometers, they ran 2.5 and ascended another 135 meters. The ITU promoted it as historic.

Although Gwen and Jamie worked all three disciplines, they focused 2013 training on swim technique. Jamie would later tell us, "Ya woisted your meney on swem leessons. Gween didn't learn a thing." Although I struggled to decipher his New Zealand accent, I understood enough to be offended. I couldn't craft an answer in the moment, but later I wished I had explained: If the goal were training Gwen for elite triathlon competition, he was right. But I paid splash fees to keep Gwen fit and active, offer a group of friends, and introduce her to competition, teamwork, and dedication. I never dreamed Gwen would be competing in international open water races.

Gwen had told me about her workouts. "Jamie wants me to concentrate on swimming this season, but to do Kitzbühel I need to train more on the bike so I may not compete there."

I knew she felt obliged to race because Joel and I booked flights for the event. "Gwen, don't worry about us. We're happy to watch, even if you don't compete."

"Jamie said the choice is up to me, but that I can't be mad about a bad result. He says the best I can expect is around eighth, and if I train more on the bike, my swimming could suffer. But I really want to be in this race. Everyone says it's one of a kind, and it'll be in the history books. I want to be part of it."

Gwen kept Kitzbühel on her schedule and trained for the uphill bike course. She pedaled the Basque mountains. She practiced Patrick's cycling exercises. She challenged her physical and mental limits.

On July 5, Joel and I checked in at the official Kitzbühel hotel, snug within the Alps. In our chalet-style room, down comforters—tall and fluffy inside creamy white cotton—promised a luxurious sleep. A rustic pine wall served as headboard. "So much spruce on the floors, the furniture..." Joel dabbles in woodworking and notices craftsmanship.

"Look—French doors to a patio." I stepped outside where evergreens wrapped the hills; midway up, red-roofed cottages dotted the slopes; below, cows roamed a meadow. "Let's take a walk along the road. We can follow the fence toward the water." I knew Joel wanted to see the swim course.

At the inland Schwarzsee Lake, competitors in wetsuits tested the current while coaches measured from entry to buoy. It was our only chance to see swimmers in the water; on race day we would be at the top of the Horn, 2,000 meters above sea level.

The next day, prepared for cold conditions, we packed layers. After purchasing cable car tickets, we rocked and swayed in the glass enclosure as it inched up the mountain. I watched the lake shrink. The motorized car seemed to buck at gravity, and even on its straight path, took over 20 minutes to reach the top. I wondered how Gwen could possibly bike the relentless incline.

As we exited, a breeze brushed my shoulders and I tugged a sweatshirt over my head. With the sun shining, I was comfortable, but when clouds blew in, I added a coat. Although the air registered 21°C (69.8°F) at the swim start, temperatures at the top of the mountain seemed much cooler.

With no grandstand, fans gathered inside the lodge or at tables on the outdoor deck. We joined coaches, athletes, and families who stood in a grassy area. I peered toward the lake where swimmers mimicked bubbles in the water. Experts predicted little impact from the swim—cycling performance would determine the winner—but after the short 750 meters, Gwen lagged 20 seconds behind, in 18th. I remembered Jamie's concern about sacrificing swim progress to concentrate on biking.

To follow the race, we relied on announcers and a jumbotron, but the screen was perched several hundred yards away up a steep incline and across an expanse of knee-high grass. A few spectators ventured up, but we stayed on level ground. We squinted first at the screen and then down the mountain as ants morphed into cyclists, zig-zagging up the Horn.

The most frightening factors—huge packs, tight corners, fast descents—didn't exist. And although Gwen ranked number one, no one expected her to win—she didn't have the biking skills. German cycling powerhouse Anne Haug, second in the rankings, was the favorite.

We ordered a beer on the outdoor deck. Sipping from a stein at the picnic table, I overheard two young men mention Gwen. I introduced Joel and myself, and the guys seemed as happy to meet Gwen's parents as they were to see her race.

"She is my favorite female today."—"I've been following her since she started."—"She's the prettiest athlete here, too." German consonants colored their English.

I saw Twitter comments—some not meant for a mother's eyes—about Gwen's looks. These boys, however, seemed innocent and sincere. They added us to their list of celebrity parents, right behind the Brownlees (parents of British superstar triathletes Alistair and Jonathan) sitting at the next table.

When the guys moved on, I returned my attention to the loudspeakers. Announcers barked clipped consonants and umlauts as I waited to hear English translations. For 40 minutes, robust cyclists commanded the race while Gwen waned.

When riders dismounted, Britain's Jodie Stimpson was 40 seconds ahead of a five-woman chase pack, while Gwen rode more than three minutes behind. Of 38 competitors, Gwen posted the 24th fastest bike split. Could she recoup time with her signature run speed? Probably not—the two and a half kilometers offered little chance for redemption.

A 20% grade on the last bike kilometer slammed every athlete, but Gwen's superior run legs survived the trauma. As most runners labored to lift their feet, Gwen put athletes behind her. She ran 20 seconds faster than any woman in the field—but finished in 18th. She relinquished her number one world ranking to Haug, who took bronze behind second-place Emma Jackson (Australia) and the winner, Stimpson.

After the race, Gwen seemed resigned. "I knew these hills would kill me. How did it look from up here?"

"Even the strong cyclists seemed to be barely moving."

"I know. Girls passed me and they were just crawling up the hills." Gwen shivered as temperatures dropped. "I want to watch the men's race later. Could you see much?"

"It was hard to see details, but we could follow who was ahead," Joel said. "You must be hungry. They have sausages inside." He led us to limited food choices, all accompanied by sauerkraut.

At day's end, Patrick rode Gwen's bike down the mountain while she rested in the cable car. That evening, we celebrated with Jamie, Gwen, and Patrick in a Tudor-style restaurant where we sampled local brews—except Gwen, who requested her usual: "Water, no ice please." We studied the menu of frankfurter, krainer wurst, blunz'n, fish and Austrian beef. "Patrick, you studied German. What is blunz'n?" Gwen asked.

"I think that's like morcilla in Spain."

"I'm not sure what that is either," I said.

Jamie confirmed the translation. "Patrick's right. It's blood sausage."

"Perfect. Did you see the sausage platter, Mom? It has some blunz'n. Want to split with me? You pick the second dish." We ordered, and before the waiter left, Gwen added soup and salad. "We can choose dessert later."

Jamie offered no critique that day, allowing Gwen to assess her choices and results. She told me, "I'm glad I was part of the race, but did you see my swim split? It was horrible. I just hope I can get my swimming in shape for Hamburg."

The next day, we flew to Vitoria-Gasteiz in Spain's Basque Region. We would spend two weeks there.

Our room with kitchenette sat a few miles from Gwen and Patrick's place, and after our own breakfast, we drove to their apartment. As Gwen grabbed a banana and headed to paths in the nearby wetland park, Patrick boiled oats. I watched as he dumped several cups into a quart of water. When I made oats at home, I used a quarter cup oats and half cup water. Patrick's portions reminded me of the calories Gwen burned. Almonds and dried fruit sat next to bowls. "Can we help?"

"Not right now. The oats will get creamy as they boil, and when Gwen gets here, I'll poach an egg for the top. You can add nuts, peanut butter, and raisins later. And she likes coconut oil." Patrick answered emails, scratched out a shopping list, and when Gwen returned, whirred into motion, scooping breakfast into their bowls. "What is your schedule today, honey?"

"Swim at 10:30, so lunch at 12:30?"

"Perfect. And then I think I'll join you for the ride this afternoon. Your mom and dad offered to roast vegetables, and if I buy a quick-cooking meat we can do dinner at 7:00."

"Patrick, can you get some cheese today?"

"Sure. Anything special at the butcher's?"

"Mom and Dad, you're staying for supper, right? Get a little extra protein for my dad, but Mom eats like a bird."

I always ate as much as I liked, but compared to a professional athlete's, my portions apparently looked sparse.

Gwen rode her commuter bike to the pool while Patrick jumped on his own for daily shopping: butcher shop that day, but sometimes Aldi or, less frequently, the big-box store, Eroski.

Joel and I tackled chores. After an apartment-sized washing machine tumbled bike kits, t-shirts, shorts, casual clothes, and a million socks, we hung each item on drying racks outside the sliding patio doors. The Spanish sun substituted for an electric dryer, and within an hour the arid breeze and blazing rays lifted moisture. Joel and I went back to work, folding and stacking.

Just before lunch, Patrick returned with groceries. He boiled rice and sautéed chicken. "Gwen likes to eat as soon as she gets back from swimming. Nancy, can you cut up veggies?" With a rotating selection of protein, carbs, and vegetables, Patrick was perfecting his one-pot rice dish.

When Gwen returned, he assembled a monster salad—lettuce and spinach, punctuated by onion, carrot, and feta, dressed with balsamic vinegar—that vanished in minutes. Next, he brought out the one pot wonder. I asked for one cup and Joel scooped out a little more. Forgoing plates, Gwen and Patrick dug directly into the serving bowl and devoured 14 cups of sautéed chicken, white rice, roasted sweet potatoes, onions, peppers, and broccoli, all doused in olive oil.

"So, what happens now?" I asked.

"Naptime," Gwen said. I wasn't surprised. Just watching her eat that much made me tired. "Then after our bike session and dinner, I have a massage."

"Does Beata have time for me?" Joel asked.

"Yup, she put you on the schedule. Mom, she has time for you too, if you want."

"My back is a little tight...sure, let's do it." I hesitated, massages not part of my regimen.

After dinner, Beata arrived with her personal blend of oils and soon peppermint infused the air. Beata was slight, but I could tell her years as an athlete built strength. Dark curly hair framed her symmetrical features and warm smile, and I thought, if she got bored with massage, she could be a model.

For an hour, Gwen lay on the portable table. First, Beata attacked her calves, thighs, and feet. I knew massage aided muscle recovery, and I could tell when Gwen moaned, it wasn't from pleasure. Far from stereotypes of a relaxing session accompanied by music and candles, sports massage realigned fibers and flushed toxins. When Beata finished the lower extremities, she moved to Gwen's back.

"What are you doing now?" I asked. Beata attached a half-dozen plastic cups to Gwen's back, expelling air so they sucked Gwen's skin.

"The cups pull blood to an area. It helps healing." I detected her Hungarian accent as she explained. "It helps tissue develop blood flow." Gwen's expression told me it wasn't comfortable. After giving the cups minutes to work—lifting skin off muscle, allowing blood vessels to expand—Beata released the suction, leaving circular red marks.

I shared second thoughts about my massage. "Oh, don't worry," Beata said. "I will be gentle. Pain is only for athletes. Unless you worked out for six hours today, you don't need anything extreme."

Beata massaged Joel's hip, and then my back which months later remained pain-free.

With Gwen and Patrick's time devoted to training, recovery, and eating, Joel and I planned day trips. We prioritized San Sebastian's La Concha Beach and chose a hot, sunny day to enjoy the seashore. Fifteen-hundred meters of white sand waited on the far side of a 90-minute bus ride. Although we had rented a car, Gwen warned that parking in San Sebastian would be difficult. She mentioned the bus, and I was drawn to mixing with locals.

With sunscreen, towels, and a map in my tote bag, Joel and I walked to the bus station. We entered the open-air space, and I was immediately confused. Before leaving home, I researched Spanish phrases, but in northeast Spain, Basques spoke Euskara. I knew Spanish for street—*calle*—but Basque signs read *kalean*. Hello was not *hola* but *kaixo*. Every word exploited x, k and z. I approached a friendly-looking traveler. "Which window for San Sebastian?" Although I got an answer, I didn't understand it and asked another, "Ticket for San Sebastian?" Blank stare.

Gambling, I chose the longest line, assuming on a tropical day, most travelers would also be headed to cool waters. After waiting 20 minutes, I said, "San Sebastian," and offered my credit card. The ticket seller poked at an English sign—*Cash Only*—and waved me away.

At an ATM, I fumbled finding English directions, but eventually withdrew enough to cover the 12€ fare. I returned to the line. This time, I showed my cash, held up two fingers, said, "San Sebastian," and the seller nabbed my euros.

Behind the terminal, rows of buses occupied a narrow street, waiting for drivers to arrive and collect tickets. When a crowd gathered at a blue-striped ALSA bus, I checked the front—it scrolled *Vitoria-Gasteiz-San Sebastian*. As I gave the driver our tickets, my upheld hands begged the question—*Is this the right bus?* The driver nodded.

Our bus traveled through the Basque Region's steep-sloped vineyards where elongated rows of shoots and canes sprung from hills. When a knoll veered, vines followed, twisting with the arc of the land, each geometric plot a tutorial in shades of green. During the ride, I studied maps and timetables and found San Sebastian the last terminal. I relaxed, taking in the rolled r's and lisping s's that bounced around the tall, bright seatbacks.

When the driver pulled into an open-air station and killed the ignition, we departed from air-conditioned coach to sizzling streets. A map rested under plastic in the outdoor terminal, but years of sun and wind washed out its coordinates. I glanced at the drawing, then the streets, and turned to orient myself. Wearing a flowy beach dress, I carried tourist's confusion next to my beach bag. Joel stood beside me in his American cargo shorts. The busman leaned against a pole and blew cigarette smoke, waiting to begin his return route. "La Concha?" he said. We nodded and he pointed.

"Gracias," I said. Every few blocks, I re-oriented with my map, but the driver's arm proved precise, and we found a crescent of sand that stretched for blocks, nestled against the city's perimeter. Out in the bay, tips of white foamed around Mount Ulia—no longer an observation point for now-extinct migratory whales. Closer to shore, waves curled and rolled, tossing floaters in the 23°C (73°F) water.

Shoes in hand, my feet suffered the blistering sand. When we found an open spot, I laid towels, slipped off the dress that covered my swimsuit, and read a magazine as Joel cleaned his snorkeling goggles. Soon, a mother and her adult daughters spread towels next to us. None wore more than a bikini bottom. My tankini looked prudish next to three sets of free-swaying breasts.

As the afternoon waned, we retraced our route to the terminal. I dozed most of the way home, and then Joel and I walked from the bus station to Gwen and Patrick's apartment, eager to talk about San Sebastian. "The weather was perfect...hot on the sand, cool in the water. But we'd like more time in the city. Any restaurants you'd recommend?"

Gwen said, "We've never been."

"How about Zurriola Beach?"

"Nope."

"Zarautz Beach?"

"Mom, we don't have time for travel. Every day is a training day."

With workouts seven days a week, Gwen and Patrick had not seen the most famous city beach in the world. I hoped they could find time to explore their new home. But Gwen worked six hours a day, swimming, biking, and running and between workouts, she answered emails, scheduled interviews, and posted to social media. Several times a week, she met with Beata and a physiotherapist, and when she had questions, she walked to Jamie's apartment next door.

"People don't realize how busy you are," I said.

"I'm lucky to have Patrick. Recovery—you know, rest, massage, and physio— is important, but athletes cheat themselves because they need to shop, and cook, and maintain bikes. Patrick takes care of that for me." I knew Gwen's primary reason in traveling with Patrick was emotional support, but his presence also served a practical advantage. "You don't even see everything. He edits my blogs and packs when we travel, and he has great ideas for what to say in interviews."

Most men wouldn't give up a cycling career to grocery shop, cook, and clean bikes. Patrick was a lot like Joel in his dedication to a woman and the satisfaction he found supporting her.

"Mom, can we stop by your hotel tomorrow? I have a phone interview and the Wi-Fi is stronger there." Several times, Gwen rode her bike to our hotel for social media posts or video conferences, and I realized her job required more than swim, bike, run.

ELIZABETH

It didn't surprise me Gwen wasn't seeing sights. There are so many elements to her job—and she has always prioritized training, more often than not denying recreation in favor of workouts and recovery. But if someone needs a favor, she obliges.

During my 2005 interview for an English teacher position at Arrowhead High School, the superintendent passed a list across the table. "Take a look and tell me which activities you could advise and which sports you could coach."

It wasn't a question, but a requirement, it seemed, of employment. "I'm willing to help wherever you need me."

"Great, we'll be in touch."

Later that day, the superintendent offered me sections of creative writing, journalism, and advanced composition. Seeing my high school track and cross-country experience—and knowing of my sister's athletic success—he referred me to the athletic director, who welcomed me as Arrowhead's assistant track and field, and cross-country coach.

For the next five years, between 2:45 and 5:30 p.m. every weekday, I brought up the rear pack of straggling runners, making sure we didn't lose any to the Mexican restaurant, friends' pools, or boys at the park.

In 2010, varsity runner Gabby Levac wanted to break the five-minute mile. With my talents better suited to end-of-the-pack round-ups, I couldn't maintain Gabby's practice or race pace. The boys' coach biked with his athletes to establish tempo, but I had a secret weapon: Gwen. I called her on the way home from practice. "I need a favor."

"Sure, what is it?"

"One of my runners wants to break five minutes in the mile, but she needs someone to race with her—set her pace and encourage her when she slows down."

"So, I would be her rabbit?"

Gwen used rabbits in meets, but I didn't know if she had been one herself. "Yeah. What do you think?"

"Sure. Just let me know when."

I was relieved. I didn't have a backup plan. "Okay, there's the WISCO Mile in a few weeks. It's an invitational where high school kids can run with adults, and it's a last chance to get a personal best. I'll sign you and Gabby up."

On a warm and drizzly day, typical for end-of-the-season meets, I layered on a poncho and carried an umbrella. Clipboard in hand, I compared Gabby's best time to the meet records when I saw Dad climb the bleachers. Dad had picked up Gwen from downtown Milwaukee, where she lived without a car. Mom stayed at school, rehearsing with her students for a performance.

The meet in progress, Gwen walked toward us. She needed no introduction because weeks earlier she had trained with my athletes. I counted on her to motivate and inspire—a division-one runner has a tendency to do that.

I ushered Gwen to Gabby. "Alright, ladies. Have fun. You can do this. Gabby, Gwen will pace you. Just stay with her."

Before the women's mile, the announcer said, "We have a very special person in the house today: Gwen Jorgensen! Gwen was an All-American runner at the University of Wisconsin." The crowd cheered and several parents pointed to her. "And now, the other athletes in the mile..." And then the gun sounded.

Gwen and Gabby led, matching stride for stride. Similar in soaring height and slight build, their ponytails bobbed in sync: one blonde and straight, one brown and curly. As they ran on the far end of the track, I saw Gwen converse with Gabby. For three laps, on pace, they flew. On the fourth and final lap, with 300 meters to go, when Gabby didn't stick to Gwen's heel, Gwen fell back into rhythm with her. With less than 200 meters, they approached the homestretch.

"GABBY! STAY RIGHT WITH HER!" I tried to focus Gabby on Gwen rather than her pain.

Gwen looked at her watch and then mouthed something. I imagined her saying, "Stay with me. Stay with my stride. You will break five minutes."

Gwen—maybe testing Gabby, maybe pushing her limits, or maybe unable to rein in her own competitiveness—strode ahead, leaving Gabby to stride the last 50 meters solo. I cheered for Gabby. "GOOOO GIRRRL! YOU. GOT. THIS!"

Each meet has a prize. The Masters: a green jacket. The Indy 500: a milk jug. Olympic Games: medals and wreaths. At the WISCO Mile, Gabby secured her prize: she broke the Arrowhead Union High School 1,600-meter record (4:57:77) and went on to run for the Duke Blue Devils. When Gwen won the race in 4:53.08, she set the WISCO Super Mile record and won an additional prize: the meet's traditional Sendik's Grocery pineapple.

After Gwen cooled down and packed her things, I said, "You were awesome today. Thanks so much. Gabby couldn't have done it without you."

"No problem. You're welcome. I have to get back home, working early at Ernst & Young tomorrow. I'm just glad Gabby got her time. And I won a pineapple! I can always use fruit."

NANCY

During our time in Spain, Gwen prepared for the July 20, 2013, sprint race in Hamburg. Three days before, we all departed for Germany. Once there, Gwen trained and familiarized herself with the course. Joel and I toured the city— bicycle tour of Town Hall, St. Michaelis, and the warehouse district; paddle boats on the Alster; beer and schnitzel at sidewalk cafes.

As one of the largest triathlons in the world, Hamburg 2013 hosted over 10,000 competitors and expected more than 250,000 spectators. Age-groupers raced first, the long weekend culminating in elite events. For days, streets shut down and we applauded the weekend warriors—men and women of varying skill and preparation. First, they swam the Alster's mucky water. Then some transitioned to worn, lace-up cycling shoes while others slid into elite gear. Some mounted expensive wheels, others hopped on beginner bikes.

"Hey, Nancy, look. That guy is using a city rental bike," Joel said. "There goes another one."

While we attended age-group events, Gwen holed up in her hotel, feet elevated. She ventured out only when necessary: subway ride to the pool, run in the streets, bike workout with Patrick.

When we stopped in their room, Patrick's rice cooker steamed as he decamped for the market.

"Patrick, can you get some chicken? And I really feel like tomatoes...and basil. And see if they have avocado. We need a salad too. Oh, I'm out of sparkling water. Can you carry all that?"

Ever agreeable, Patrick added items to his list. "Sure, sweetie." Pre-race, they prepared meals in their hotel room, postponing culinary adventures. I asked Patrick how he cooked on the road. "It's not so hard. I pack the rice cooker and a few utensils and once we check in, I look for a grocery."

"Gwen said she wanted chicken. How do you do that?"

"Oh, most places have pre-cooked meat. We buy it grilled and I cut it up for salads or a rice bowl." I knew Gwen raced with deliberate focus, and I realized Patrick performed his role as assistant/chef/mechanic/coach/emotional stabilizer with equal dedication.

Respectful of their rituals, we kept our visit short.

Hamburg featured two triathlons for elites. Gwen entered the individual sprint event on Saturday and, depending on her result, could be selected for Sunday's relay. We walked from our Barcelo Hotel toward City Hall—a towering neo-renaissance Rathaus of 647 rooms behind a pillars-and-bricks facade, topped by a sloping green copper roof and spire. In front of this 30,000 square-foot hall, a crowd packed the bleachers. As spectators squinted into the sun, volunteers delivered water in paper cups—free *wasser* for the tourists, courtesy of the Hamburg municipal water department.

Since the grueling uphill Kitzbühel race, Gwen refocused on swim technique. Jamie knew a strong performance in the 750-meters of calm water could put Gwen in the first bike pack. Gwen wore number three, behind Brit Jodie Stimpson and German Anne Haug, the hometown favorite. Although short, the Hamburg swim proved vicious. Gwen wrote later in her blog:

> *I got to the first buoy and was annihilated. I was held under water, swam on top of, literally grabbed and pulled backwards, and pushed into a kayak. This sounds brutal (and it was), but it's fairly typical.*

For most of the swim, a bright sun allowed athletes to eye the leaders and sight the buoys. But in the final meters, athletes swam through a tunnel. Overhead, cars and pedestrians traveled the bridge while below, swimmers stroked through the dark. When they emerged, a cheering crowd gathered within meters, 15-deep. Those in front dangled their feet in the water, while behind, on tiers of concrete stairs, fans shouted and cheered. Unlike most venues, where swimmers can't hear the crowd, in Hamburg, spectators made noise at water's edge.

Joel and I watched from the grandstand where we followed the leader board. Optimistic that Gwen's recent focus would show improved swim results, we scanned the scrolling names as women moved from water to transition. Gwen's name was absent. *Did she lose her timing chip? Where can she be?* We waited... and waited...to find her 43rd of 65 competitors, 45 seconds behind. It was more proof that Gwen's training for Kitzbühel's bike course sabotaged her swim progress.

Riding in a chase pack, Gwen lost ground on the flat course and 46 riders posted a better time. After the race, Jamie explained: "A poor swem affects boiking—when Gween is tired and strissed from swemming, she has no strength for coycling."

"Is that what happened?"

"Sure. And eef she iver geets better in both swem and boike, her run will geet strongah."

As Gwen attacked the 5K, two-lap run, I anticipated her disappointment. Barrie Shepley predicted she would run conservatively and save energy for the team relay, since she couldn't possibly finish better than 20th.

Three leaders (Haug, Stimpson and Britain's Non Stanford) dominated the race, soon joined by New Zealander Andrea Hewitt and Australian Ashleigh Gentle. The pack of five ran together up to the final kilometer.

Meanwhile, Gwen ran in the back. I had seen her recoup time lost in two disciplines with a dominant performance in one, but today, her deficit seemed insurmountable.

Up front, with 800 meters to go, Haug thrilled home fans as she burst into the lead. Germans rose from their seats, waving miniature flags of yellow, red, and black. They jangled cowbells and blew horns, underscoring fast-shouting announcers. We stood with the Germans, just to see the action, and I remembered the San Diego race when Gwen rode a swell of USA cheers. Home crowd advantage often propelled athletes. We witnessed it in action as Haug crossed the finish line first. The rest of the lead pack—four more—finished in the next 20 seconds.

As coverage focused on Haug's victory, we knew little of Gwen's position. I wondered how she progressed. Had she advanced? Could she make 20th? Or would she save energy for the relay? Then, within moments, I spied Gwen.

"Gooooo, Gweeeeen!" Joel stood on the bench and cheered like he would for gold.

But only five have finished...

Gwen sprinted and took sixth.

Although she did not take gold, her earnings proved valuable. The detrimental impact of Kitzbühel was clear—but she gained practical data on how bike workouts at the expense of swim training could affect her performance. She explored her run potential. And with prize money and points awarded on a sliding scale, she moved from 43rd—no dollars and zero points—to sixth—$4,000 and several hundred points.

ELIZABETH

When I watched the Hamburg race online, I wasn't surprised Gwen's final leg was her strongest, and I recalled her transition from mediocre swimmer to top-notch runner. For years, Gwen ignored her talent for running while she obsessed over freestyle strokes, diving blocks, and flip turns. Finally, as a college junior, she recognized her potential on land, quit the swim team, and joined the running program. Years later, she wrote me an email:

> *My biggest challenge was waking up in the morning and trying to walk on my sore, underused leg muscles. My body was not used to pounding on land. It took a while for my muscles to develop and during that time, I dreaded taking that first step out of bed in the morning.*

To ease her into running, Gwen's coach assigned 30 miles a week; her teammates ran more than 100. After several months, Gwen said,

> *Cross-country is going well—I'm loving it, which is great. I'm starting to actually run and not just jog.*

By the end of the season, Gwen qualified for the NCAA Cross-Country Championship meet—an accomplishment she never achieved on the swim team. So, in November 2008, we drove to the National Championship in Terre Haute, Indiana, where parking attendants, in parkas and stocking caps, directed us to a gravel spot. Arriving earlier than most spectators, we found white tents lining the finishing chute and volunteers assembling merchandise and concessions. A screen towered over hay bales. On this, the awards area, corn stalks decorated a wooden deck. In the surrounding park, bare spots dotted the sod where cleats had mangled grass. Athletes warmed up—sprinting, jogging, stretching—as coaches set up team tents. The speakers blared announcements. "Welcome to the NCAA Championships. There are four hours until race time."

Dad studied his course map, comparing his position to the diagram of trails. I wanted to visit the concession stand.

"Look, there's Sally Kipyego," Mom said. A future Olympian, Kipyego's talent drew attention—she had a stride to remember, powerful and elegant. A Kenyan studying at Texas Tech, Kipyego wore a winter headband and matching gray gloves she might have borrowed from the men's team—wide, too big for her hands, they threatened to fall off if she didn't curl her fingers.

We walked the course, matching the twists and turns on Dad's map, when we stumbled on the Badger tent. Inside, we spotted Gwen with a Bucky decal on her cheek, and we sneaked waves, Mom and Dad loath to distract her.

"Dad, what's the plan?"

"Every man for himself."

"What?" He couldn't be serious. We always watched events together. Was he suggesting we split up?

"I think we should go here." He pointed to the mile-mark on his map. "We'll see the start and this loop." He pointed again. "We'll head to the far end of the course and see her, and then sprint to the finish." Dad was determined to see the entire race, and it was up to Mom and me to stick with him.

Mom interrupted. "Is that enough time to see the finish?"

"You'll have to hurry."

"And you're serious about every man for himself?" I feared being lost or left behind, as I anticipated thousands of spectators clogging the course.

"Now you know the plan, so do your best. Worst case, we'll meet at the finish line."

Amid thousands of spectators, hundreds of athletes, and the swarm of media, we'll just find each other? Dad couldn't be serious.

We stayed together through the first miles, zigzagging and jogging as a trio. On our third stop, I turned after the last Badger passed and didn't see Mom or Dad.

Gwen referred to me in articles as the team's best fan: "I always have multiple people on the team asking me when she will be showing up because she's so good at cheering and motivating us." But, by staying to watch other Badgers, I missed Mom and Dad's sprint to the next location. Panicked, I realized I didn't have a map. Without Dad's pointing finger, I didn't know where I was headed, but I noticed a group bolting toward what I thought was the finish and followed. I ran along the roped-off chute, searching for Dad's hat. By chance, Mom and Dad spied me, called, and I squeezed between them, hanging over the fence in time to spot Gwen: tall, wearing a white singlet, thin black headband, and black gloves.

Gwen, pre-race, mentioned team goals. But she made no reference to personal ones. This was Gwen's first cross-country season since sixth grade. Mom and Dad and I, unconcerned with her time or position, were there to cheer and support, no matter the result. As the runners sprinted through the last meters, I screamed and jumped for the Badgers, but no one could catch Kipyego. Mom clapped as Gwen arrived much sooner than expected. When Gwen finished less than a minute after Kipyego, in 19th place for All-American honors, Dad cried. Mom hugged him, and he cried more.

I teased him. "You're for real crying?" In our family, I'm the one who cries— not Dad. No tears at funerals, or movies, or swim meets, Dad apparently saved his emotion for Gwen's running.

NANCY

Gwen's run talent was valuable in her triathlon career, as demonstrated in Hamburg. Based on her sixth-place result there, USA coaches chose her for the next day's relay.

Twenty countries lined up in teams of four. Each athlete (two women and two men per team) completed a 300-meter swim, 6-kilometer bike, and 1.6-kilometer run before tagging a teammate. Alternating woman-man-woman-man, the short distance required speed and strategy.

Joel and I joined spectators in the grandstand while other fans mobbed the exchange zone, eager to witness the fast-motion tag-offs.

As the first set of women began their 20-minute mini-triathlon, male competitors gathered at the water. At the top of a concrete ramp, men jogged in place, stroking imaginary water. After teammates tagged them, they rocketed down the ramp and launched themselves, soaring into the Alster. No graceful swan dives, these vaults created human missiles. Suspended momentarily in the air, athletes blasted into the waves and torpedoed through the water in search of the buoy. Most swim starts are sedate affairs, fans quiet as athletes pause in unison for the horn, but this relay exchange triggered shouts and cheers.

Once again, Anne Haug and the German team used hometown energy to take the lead. The favored Brits and tenth-ranked New Zealanders kept pace. No one expected Team USA with Sarah Groff, Ben Kanute, Gwen, and newcomer Cameron Dye to podium.

We caught glimpses of Gwen on the sidelines where she cheered and gestured to her teammates. I remembered Gwen's years with the Waukesha Express Swim Team. What she achieved in practice, she couldn't always replicate in individual races. But in relay events, Gwen surpassed her best times.

As predicted, the Brits dominated. Non Stanford, Britain's third athlete, led the race. The Germans and Kiwis were close behind, followed by USA—Gwen the third competitor. Suddenly, the Germans took over and the Brits disappeared.

Fans around me speculated. Was Stanford dropped? Was she serving a penalty? Did she have a puncture? I wondered how the best team went missing. Then, video showed Stanford laying on the concrete.

"What happened?" I said. "No one else was close enough to cause a crash."

"She must have lost focus."

With the favorites eliminated, I hoped Gwen could hold USA's position in third. Meanwhile, I listened for an update on Stanford, but information remained scanty and for the rest of the race I couldn't shake my mother's worry for someone else's daughter.

Germany, flying on fan energy, won. When New Zealand finished seven seconds later, Germany's celebration still blared. Thirty seconds after that, the 19th-ranked USA team won bronze to cheers from a few coaches and the Jorgensen parents at the top of the bleachers.

I knew if Stanford hadn't crashed, USA probably wouldn't have medaled. I celebrated Gwen's team winning bronze, but thoughts about Stanford remained.

Twelve athletes—three teams times four—crowded a podium built for individuals. After awards, each athlete clutched a two-foot tall pilsner glass full of beer—the traditional Hamburg trophy. Instead of spraying champagne, they deluged each other, and then drank what remained.

The victory was unexpected, and for Gwen, redeeming. She failed to execute her best in the individual race but contributed to a podium finish for Team USA.

> *Our team was super energetic, and ready to go on Sunday!...Ben...tagged me and I dove in the water fourth, right behind teams Australia and New Zealand...I exited the water in second (behind Great Britain's Non Stanford). This was a complete turnaround from the swim the day before. I was thankful for the decent swim, as I had three others and a country to represent. I rode the two-lap course and...unfortunately, Non had an accident on the bike. No one ever wants to see a competitor go down, especially when it's someone so kind, nice, and genuine. Thankfully we hear she is OK and on her way to a speedy recovery.*
>
> *I started running and could have sworn I felt others on my right shoulder, but I made the turn into the exchange zone in first. Cameron finished off our relay. He swam and rode like a rock star, and finished with a solid run in third. I couldn't be more proud of Team USA.*

After the race, Team USA invited us to a dinner for coaches and athletes. At a patio table, under summer umbrellas, we ordered house beer and studied a German menu. Gwen and Patrick shared entrees, salads, and a steak tartare appetizer. As a child of German grandparents, I nibbled raw beef and onions atop rye bread, but I abandoned the habit as an adult, concerned about bacteria and parasites. Post-race, Gwen and Patrick were apparently indifferent to *E. coli* or *Salmonella*. They dug into an eight-inch mound of ground raw steak, surrounded by capers and onions, crowned with a gleaming, raw egg yolk.

Bobby McGee, internationally renowned running coach, sat across from me. Gwen told me she worked a few track sessions with McGee, and I recognized him from online photos. Tall and athletic, he seemed about my age. He sported the same balding head and close-cropped fringe Joel wore, plus a neatly trimmed silvery mustache and goatee, handsome on his Afrikaans face.

"It was a great weekend," I said, hoping to start a conversation.

McGee smiled. "The USA relay came through. It was fun to see." A South African accent graced his words.

"Gwen tells me she's learned a lot from you."

"Gwen is just starting to explore her talent. She'll get better as she trains." I was surprised at his assessment. Gwen posted several race-best runs and articles praised her running. McGee obviously thought she could do better.

"Tell me more. I'm afraid I don't know much about athletic training."

"Triathlon has four disciplines...actually, five. Of course, there is swim, bike, run, and most people call transitions the fourth discipline. But the mental aspect is a fifth discipline, and Gwen hasn't begun to tap her mental powers." I expected McGee to tell me about stride or alignment, but he focused on Gwen's inner game.

"How often do you work with triathletes?" McGee coached South African runners for many years, but with Apartheid, his country was banned from international competition. When that policy ended and McGee's athletes proved successful on the world stage, his expertise was in global demand.

"They each have a personal coach, and I'm called in to specialize in run training. We have camps where athletes concentrate on one discipline." I realized USA Triathlon's hiring of top-level coaches like McGee supplemented Gwen's training and spurred her development.

The evening ended after dinner, athletes preparing for return flights the next morning.

The following day, still thinking about Stanford, I checked social media. Following an overnight hospital stay, she tweeted, "Tis but a scratch," and, "Out of hospital this morning relatively unscathed! Very lucky girl." She posted pictures of her red, raw back—proof she slid along the pavement. I was happy she sustained no major harm.

Gwen and Patrick returned to Vitoria-Gasteiz on a four-hour flight—convenient travel was one reason the Wollongong Wizards lived in Spain for the European race season. Joel and I endured a 15-hour journey home.

During the flight, I recalled Gwen's childhood dedication to—some might say obsession with—swimming. She maintained that discipline still, choosing workouts over vacations or socializing.

In high school, Gwen refused to miss swim practice. One year, I invited her to join my students and me on a New York City tour. She accepted only after confirming hotel pool hours—and then stroked through chlorine while the rest of us floated under Hilton sheets. She brought elastic bands for dry-land exercises, and while I herded 16-year-olds to airport check-in she jogged the terminal.

Her preoccupation with training continued in college and carried over to triathlon. But Jamie challenged her obsession. He recommended she vacation for a few days. Although reluctant, Gwen made reservations in Croatia.

> *...The day before we left I had a conversation with Jamie. I remember saying, "Jamie, I don't want to go on vacation anymore. I'm ready for some hard training!"*
>
> *Jamie looked at me with intent and responded calmly, explaining three days wasn't going to hurt my training (which I knew it wouldn't). I argued a bit until Jamie finally said, "Well, there is plenty of water in Croatia." I laughed and went on my vacation.*

I was glad Jamie could accomplish what I failed to do—he convinced Gwen to train hard, and then take time off.

> *Pat and I had an apartment/hotel in the heart of Split, Croatia. It was a cute town, with more tourists than I'd ever seen!...*
>
> *After an hour in Split, I looked at Pat and told him how nice it was to be on vacation. I had no idea how*

much I needed a break after eight months of training. The few days of no triathlon (no internet/emails about triathlon, no talk about triathlon, no swim/ bike/run...) were rejuvenating...

On our second day, we splurged. Pat and I love Anthony Bourdain. Our mouths salivate and our eyes bulge when watching "No Reservations". Naturally, the first thing I did when we booked our flight to Croatia was Google "Croatian Food"...a few clicks later I found perfection: The Secret Dalmatia Anthony Bourdain Experience: a 12-course wine pairing dinner at the Bibich Winery. It was amazing! Pat and I were driven about an hour away into the rural countryside of Croatia to the Bibich Winery. It was so incredible I'm not even going to try to describe it. [It was] a once-in-a-lifetime experience we will never forget.

Our third and final day in Croatia was spent at the beach. We took a boat to an island where we relaxed on the beach with good eats. This is what I was imagining Croatia to be like...

Two weeks later, Gwen raced WTS Stockholm. As we watched from home, Gwen scored her third WTS victory of 2013. After the race, I searched online articles for analysis. Triathlon.org recapped the event:

The USA's Gwen Jorgensen rediscovered her early season form in scintillating fashion in Stockholm on Saturday, making her third World Triathlon Series in 2013 win one of her best.

In yet another stellar run leg, where Jorgensen pulled back almost 40 seconds in about 3km to take

*the lead from Andrea Hewitt, she went on to win by
49 seconds...but that run wasn't even her favourite
part of the performance, that was given to her
impressive swim.*

*'I think I was just so shocked that I was in the front
of the group, besides those two that went up the road,
I was thrilled with my swim coming out of the water
there,' Jorgensen said when asked about her burst of
speed leaving T2. 'Jamie Turner (coach) and I have
been working hard on it and to see the hard work
starting to pay off just feels really good.'*

Uncharacteristically, during a video chat with Gwen after the race, she praised her own performance. "Yeah, it went really well today. Finally, my work with Jamie is paying off. I'm happy with my swim and my transitions." She talked from her hotel room, stretched out on the bed.

"Maybe vacation helped—gave your body some rest."

"That's what Jamie thinks." Gwen ate a banana, sipping from her water bottle.

"And you have three wins—you're tied with Paula!" Until the Stockholm race, Canadian Paula Findlay held the record for most wins in a season.

Gwen flipped around on the bed and propped her legs against the wall. "I try not to think about that. It's better for me if I just concentrate on each race. And today, it worked. I have to keep focusing on the processes." She targeted execution—high elbow in the swim, position on the bike, relaxed shoulders during the run—in favor of end result. Jamie taught her that success in the processes would lead to best outcomes.

Since childhood, Gwen rarely celebrated achievements, ruminating instead on elements that stymied her progress. When she was in high school, complaining about a 500-meter time, I said, "Gwen, are you ever happy with a swim?"

"One time in sixth grade, I had a good race."

Now, I was happy she acknowledged her Stockholm triumph. Jamie's input was influential—he trained her physically, and then cultivated a healthy mental game.

With a new coach, unfamiliar training partners, and life abroad, Gwen assumed the 2013 season would be a transition year. She didn't plan or expect top marks; her three wins were a bonus.

With the Stockholm victory, Gwen ranked first in the world, eight points ahead of Anne Haug, who was five points ahead of Non Stanford—the top three in a virtual tie. I never dreamed one of my daughters would be a world champion, but Gwen was poised to secure the title. The World Championship would be decided in London on September 14, at the Grand Final. Gwen had five weeks to prepare.

I longed to see the Grand Final live in London. But work commitments made travel impossible. Elizabeth and I were in the middle of a school year—teachers can't request vacation time—and Joel used his time off for our weeks in Austria, Spain, and Hamburg. For the biggest race of Gwen's life, we would stay home. I felt sorry, guilty, regretful. I lectured myself: we could never attend every international competition, and I would have to settle for online coverage.

On race day, we streamed computer to television. Elizabeth watched from her home.

I felt anxious about so much—weather, wet roads, Stanford and Haug—but excited about the possibility of a world championship title. Gwen described her preparation in a blog:

> We were prepared for the wet and the cold. We practiced what worked to keep me warm, as we refused to have a repeat of Auckland. I want to give a special thanks to USAT for helping me secure pool time at wicked hours to prepare me for the early race start.
>
> I walked on the pontoon nervous, excited, and ready. My fitness was ideal. Since Stockholm, I only felt stronger on the bike, swim, and of course, on the run. I dove in and was able to get on Emma Moffat's fast feet. I was pulled and yanked around the first buoy, but quickly turned it around and kept focused. I exited the first lap knowing I was in the front group, and I felt strong.

Gwen exited the water eighth. I felt confident—her strong swim portended a good race.

> *Wetsuit off. Helmet on. Bike mounted. Now, it was time for me to find some good wheels. Non was right there, along with Ashleigh Gentle. There were a lot of strong girls who quickly formed a group of about 20. I was riding in good position, and feeling comfortable on the bike. The rain started to fall and the temperatures began to drop.*

"She's doing good," Joel said. "Her swim put her with the top cyclists."

"The bike leg still makes me nervous."

Commentators mentioned misty conditions, but I was relieved it wasn't pouring. I tracked Stanford, who came out of the water in 18th, and Haug, who exited last, two minutes back. I relaxed a little more with Gwen ahead of her two toughest competitors.

Barrie Shepley recapped the previous day's age-group races when 35 riders crashed. He pointed out curves where riders went down in the 2012 Olympics. I wished he wouldn't mention crashes and moved to the kitchen where I could listen but scrub away anxiety.

At the end of the first lap, Gwen rode in eighth, part of the lead pack. Shepley surmised other athletes would be unhappy to see her, knowing she could outrun most of them by 60 seconds. I continued listening from the kitchen, and during the second lap heard alarm in Shepley's voice. He reacted to a crash—coming around a corner, a rider went down. I hoped this would be the day's only mishap. Although I didn't want to look, I walked to the television, just to make sure it wasn't Gwen.

An overhead camera spied the crash, and I thought the cyclist wore USA colors. My heart pounded. As the rider got up to check her bike, Shepley said he thought it might be Gwen. *No,* I thought, *that's not Gwen.* The camera zoomed in. "Oh, no! It is Gwen. What happened?"

Gwen stood as she checked her brakes and spun her wheels. I relaxed when I saw her moving.

"Looks like she's alright," Joel said. "Now, let's hope her bike isn't damaged."

Then it all went wrong. I wish I knew what happened, but all I remember is being on the ground. I don't remember a thing. Someone said I may have stood up, but I watched the replay and it didn't look that way to me. I don't remember grabbing my brakes. I had the best equipment. My tire pressure was low (70 psi). And everything we did prepared me for the best possible outcome; however, I ended up dazed, confused, and in a bit of shock. I remember getting back on my bike and thinking, Ouch, my hands hurt. I looked at the palms of my hands but they weren't even red. Strange. You must be fine. OK, you know a group is coming, along with the Anne Haug train. Just stay focused. You are still in this!

When Gwen remounted, she appeared uninjured. Commentators predicted she could latch onto a chase group, finish within 60 seconds of the leaders, and challenge them on the 10K run.

The first chase group approached. They whizzed past. A second chase group neared. Pedaling, Gwen's feet circled as fast as the rider's next to her, but she moved in slow motion. The second pack sped ahead, leaving Gwen solo.

Gwen went from race favorite to invisible as announcers focused on the front pack. I waited impatiently for an update. I remembered her solo ride after the flat tire in 2012, but this time, I wasn't sure if the cause was mechanical—or physical.

At the end of lap three, as the leaders came through, I fixated on the screen, searching for Gwen's helmet—no sign of her in the first minute after the leaders. I checked my computer for splits in case I had missed her. Two minutes after the leaders—nothing. Three minutes after the leaders, Shepley announced Gwen withdrew.

The next thing I knew two groups had come and gone. I remember some girls yelling words of encouragement, but nothing worked. I had to call it a day.

As I limped off the course, the crowd gave me a standing ovation. I was confused and overwhelmed

at the same time. I didn't feel like I deserved it—I
didn't even finish the race...

I had a feeling of loss, of expectation quashed. I anticipated a celebration at the end of this day, and now 60 athletes raced for a championship while my daughter walked off. Seeing her pedal fast and get nowhere, I assumed Gwen damaged her bike, but she explained later in her blog.

> *I got to the medical tent and was hysterical. All I*
> *wanted was to see Pat and Jamie. Thank you [coach]*
> *Jono Hall for quickly finding my support crew. The*
> *docs kept asking if I was alright, and I could barely*
> *manage to nod my head. I was nauseous, aching,*
> *sore, throbbing, and in a lot of pain. I had a deep*
> *wound on my hip (I bled through many bandages and*
> *I still can't walk without pain), and other abrasions*
> *on my elbows. I was hurting physically, but the worst*
> *hurt was how gutted I was.*

I felt powerless—unable to offer comfort from thousands of miles away—but grateful for Patrick, who I knew would care for Gwen emotionally and physically.

> *At the beginning of the season when Jamie and I*
> *talked about what I wanted to accomplish this year,*
> *it wasn't one, two, or three WTS wins, but it was to*
> *improve my swim and do well in the overall, and at*
> *San Diego, and London. Here I was in great shape,*
> *ready to race the best women in the world, and I still*
> *don't know what happened. It was either bad luck,*
> *or an error on my part that in the rain turned into a*
> *race-ender.*

When I realized her season was over, it felt like mourning. In only one year since her flat tire in the London Olympics, Gwen achieved extraordinary success. Each surprise victory accumulated until she ranked first in the world for much of the season. To lose the culmination of that work left me heartsick for my daughter and what she hoped to achieve.

2013 Race Results

2nd: OTU Sprint Triathlon Oceania Championships Devonport, Australia (23 February)
DNF: ITU WTS Auckland, New Zealand (6 April)
1st: ITU WTS San Diego, California, United States of America (20 April)
1st: ITU WTS Yokohama, Japan (11 May)
4th: ITU WTS Madrid, Spain (1 June)
18th: ITU WTS Kitzbühel, Austria (6 July)
6th: ITU WTS Hamburg, Germany (20 July)
1st: ITU WTS Stockholm, Sweden (24 August)
DNF: ITU WTS Grand Final London, United Kingdom (11 September)

CHAPTER 5

Chasing Victory

2014

NANCY

For much of 2013, Gwen ranked first in the world. She posted the fastest run in every WTS race but one. She scored the first USA gold in a WTS race. Reigning on the podium two more times, she shared the record for WTS wins in a season.

But a Grand Final crash took her out of the top rankings and while Non Stanford accepted the World Champion trophy, Gwen soaked through bandages in the medical tent.

Within a few days, she flew home. After nine months in Australia and Spain, Gwen spent only October, November, and December in the USA. Even when stateside, her schedule prevented frequent visits—she and Patrick lived in St. Paul, 325 miles away; they split holiday time between Patrick's family and ours; Gwen filled her schedule with sponsor obligations and media appearances; and triathlon training continued.

For years, Patrick rode Cable, Wisconsin's trails. Now, Gwen joined him for weekends there. Theory: if Gwen could master forest paths, contoured hills, and rock garden trails, she would surely improve her road skills. Back home, Patrick and Gwen competed in cyclocross and invited us to watch a November race. I never heard of cyclocross and was curious about biking in the winter. Joel and I drove to St. Paul. Atop a bridge in the park, mucous freezing in my nose, I stomped my boots and surveyed the layout. Stakes and fences marked muddy, snowy, sandy, and gravelly paths.

"This is cool. We can see almost the whole race," Joel said.

"How does this work?" I asked Patrick's dad Craig, who traveled from Fargo.

"It's sort of like a crit—they repeat the same loop. It starts in the open, then goes through the woods. After that, they pedal through the sand volleyball court, up and down the hills and stairs, and back to the beginning."

Gwen straddled her bike at the snow-packed start line. As I shivered, pulling the hood on my parka, Gwen adjusted her gloves and tugged her bike kit high on her neck. Even before the starting gun my feet felt numb, and I wondered how anyone could remain upright on the slippery, frozen turf.

Gwen took off with the pack. Once through the open area, she disappeared until, through the thicket, I glimpsed riders weaving a tight, tree-lined descent. I knew Gwen's bike handling skills needed work—was she ready to ward off branches and tree roots?

She materialized safely at the bottom, rode a few feet and sank into the sand pit. She seemed stuck in place but worked through.

"That looks like a steeplechase barrier," Joel said.

"Just watch. They'll dismount soon," Craig said. Gwen ran the short section, carrying her bike on her shoulder as she jumped the barricade. She remounted and, just when I thought there couldn't be more obstacles, approached wooden steps. "Now, they'll carry their bikes."

Gwen hoisted her bike on her shoulder as she ran up the steps, then hopped on the saddle and sailed down a twisted path. For an hour, she looped these sections—incline, descent, tight corner, dismount, run, remount. I thought it looked more like an obstacle course than a bike race.

After a middle-of-the-pack finish, Gwen warmed up in the car, changed clothes, and joined us on the bridge for Patrick's race. Craig watched up close while holding Patrick's spare bike.

"You doing okay, Gwen?" I knew she was cold, exhausted, and hungry.

"I'm fine, Mom. It's good for me to improve my cycling."

Skilled in cyclocross, Patrick rode at the front. He jigged around curves and trees, barreled down drop-offs, and stayed with the leaders. Then, after disappearing into the woods, Patrick emerged carrying his bike.

"He looks fine," Gwen said. "His bike must be damaged, but Craig will give him the spare." Patrick looped the course several more times and won silver.

When Patrick joined us at the car, Gwen congratulated—and then scolded—him. "Patrick, that bike is brand new. It's a lot of money to replace." They searched for cracks, but Patrick diagnosed minor wreckage with no financial loss—lovers' quarrel resolved.

****

Perhaps Gwen would have been a proficient cyclist if she enjoyed biking as a youngster. In elementary school, Joel often walked the girls home. One day, Elizabeth noticed her friends at the bike rack. "Dad, can we ride our bikes to school?"

"Mom drops you at the sitter's house in the morning. It just isn't possible."

"Please, Dad?"

Joel decided to engineer a solution. In shorts and jogging shoes, he carried the girls' bikes to the sidewalk. Resting one bike against a tree, he ran, his right hand guiding the other bike next to his hip. He tried again, this time with two bikes—one under each palm. Slow and awkward, Joel practiced until he could run several blocks. Eventually, he mastered his gimmick and frequently jogged two pink bikes to Heyer Elementary.

Elizabeth whirled her knees, blonde ponytail floating in the wind, as she spun over the bike path—"Dad, I'll wait for you at the highway"—while Gwen would rather have been swimming.

When Gwen was in middle school, Joel and I encouraged both girls to bike with us on the Glacial Drumlin, a rail-to-trail that starts in Waukesha and stretches 52 miles to Madison.

"Gwen, how far should we go?" I said.

"I'll stay here and do homework."

"Come on. Elizabeth is going. It'll be fun."

"No, it won't. I hate biking."

"We'll ride to Wales and get frozen custard at LeDuc's." She couldn't resist that, so we pedaled five miles and ordered the flavor of the day.

Years later, when Gwen trained for triathlon, in an upside-down rerun of our Glacial Drumlin trip, she invited Joel and me to join her. She needed practice with flying mounts, dismounts, and bunny hops.

"What's a bunny hop?" I asked.

"I'm supposed to launch my bike in the air and lift the front and rear wheels off the ground. Like over a curb or a rock." Her description sounded more like a BMX trick than a triathlon skill.

"Why do you need that?"

"It improves my bike handling. Plus, sometimes in a race, I might need to hop over a pothole, or a curb, or a rider who crashed." It sounded impossible.

Over and over, Gwen soared hundreds of feet ahead. While we caught up, she bunny hopped, dismounted, and remounted.

We're almost there, Gwen. Practice your flying mount a few more times.

Gwen went from a little girl who hated biking to a woman who competed with professional cyclists. To help her acquire skills, Gwen's sponsor, Specialized, supplied a professionally fitted bike, Patrick and other experts taught her technique, and Gwen worked to conquer her fear of speed. She developed a love of cycling.

****

In 2013, while Gwen trained in Minnesota, I prepared my high school choir students for the holiday season. While tenors and sopranos sang in the choir room, basses and altos gathered in the dance space. Soloists rehearsed at a piano in the hall, and section leaders finished attendance. From my office desk began a non-stop ringing.

"Mrs. J, your phone."—"Your cell phone. It's ringing again."—"Aren't teachers supposed to have phones on silent, too?"

When rehearsal ended, I found four missed calls and 15 texts, all from Gwen. "Call me right away."—"Call me when you can."—"I have to talk to you."

Heart beating in my throat, I willed my fingers steady on the screen. *What could be wrong? Bike accident? Car crash?*

Gwen picked up on the first ring. "Hi, Mom. Don't worry—nothing is wrong." I blew air silently past the phone. *Thank God.*

"We're engaged! Patrick asked me to marry him!" Usually like me in her restraint, Gwen unleashed a rare emotion that caught me up. I wasn't surprised at the engagement. Gwen and Patrick spent months together, living far from family and friends, relying on each other. Unlike most couples, who labor in separate careers, they partnered all day, every day. I knew Patrick would be a faithful caretaker for my daughter. Each time we visited, he showed affection for Gwen—a squeeze during walks, a kiss while cooking, a hug before his grocery run. He spoke love with, "Honey, what would you like for dinner?" or "Sweetie, can I get you anything?"

"Tell me about the proposal," I said.

With their upcoming departure for Australia, Gwen expected a proposal before they left. Weeks earlier, Patrick made plans for a December 1st bike ride on the Minnesota River Bottoms—his favorite trail. Gwen assumed his plan foreshadowed an engagement. But when Patrick's friends showed up, and Gwen was left to pedal solo, she lost faith.

Three days later, as a fluffy snow fell in St. Paul, Patrick suggested an impromptu ride. After a few miles, he stopped on the Ford Parkway Bridge to take winter pictures. "It's pretty, isn't it?" Patrick said.

Gwen dismounted, thinking it wasn't very pretty through the snow and fog.

Patrick grabbed her, kissed her, and said, "You know I'll love you forever? I'll love you a long time, 'til we're old and wrinkly."

Gwen's anger simmered as she wished for the absent proposal. "You can't say that unless you mean it!"

"What if I do this?" Patrick bent on one knee and offered a custom silver band inlaid with black diamonds. Gwen, astounded, took a step back and slipped. She got up and tackled Patrick, hugging him, refusing to let go.

Returning to their apartment above the bike shop, they called family.

"Have you set a date?" I asked.

"October 4, 2014. I hope you can help with planning. Patrick and I will do most of it, but mailings are difficult overseas. And I hope you'll make a wedding website?"

"Of course. Whatever you need. What about a dress?"

"I'll get that when we come back from abroad."

Twenty-seven days after their announcement, Gwen and Patrick departed for Australia. They would start a new life, traveling the world, committed to each other.

During their three months in Australia, Gwen emailed and texted, sometimes about training, other times about wedding plans. She, Elizabeth, and I collaborated on a save-the-date card and I set up an online RSVP.

Gwen's competitive season began on March 15, 2014, with a World Cup race in Mooloolaba, Australia. She won gold and once again posted the fastest run. Her next event was the more competitive WTS Auckland, New Zealand, race where, in 2013, frigid water forced her to withdraw.

We watched from home. With air at 27°C (80.6°F) and water at 20°C (68°F), wetsuits were not allowed. Gwen looked strong on the swim, exiting with the front pack. Her performance placed her with the lead cyclists.

After ending her 2013 season with a crash, I felt anxious as she leaned on turns and rode up to 40 miles per hour within inches of other wheels. But in pre-race interviews, Gwen emphasized bike-focused training—she intended to become a contender in every discipline.

"See, she'll be fine," Joel said. "She's been working on her biking."

"I know, but anything can happen, even to the best cyclists."

A few women surged, dropping Gwen to a chase pack, 34 seconds back. Commentators predicted Gwen a potential winner if the deficit did not increase. When she squeezed into the middle of the chasers, I wished she rode up front where there were fewer chances of a crash.

Patrick's dad texted.

> *Craig: She looked good on the swim.*

> *Nancy: Agreed.*

> *Craig: She worked on her biking this season. Let's hope it shows.*

> *Nancy: I hate this part.*

Craig knew the dangers and told me he watched with as much anxiety as I did.

Germany's Anne Haug pulled Gwen's tightly packed chase group. Before long, a competitor crashed and five or six riders, including Gwen, lay tangled on the pavement. With so many down, I strained to identify her. Gwen extracted herself, checked her brakes...and tires...and pedals...and finally remounted. The episode stole time, but I was relieved to see her moving.

Relegated to a second, slower pack, she entered the 10K run three and a half minutes behind. What is it that motivates a competitor? Why do some athletes succumb to defeat while others forge ahead? Although Gwen must have known she couldn't recoup three and a half minutes, she did run a minute faster than anyone else and claimed 12th. Announcers marveled at Gwen's race-best run. Articles praised her top-12 finish. Joel and I admired her fortitude.

But 12th had no place in Gwen's plan. Some triathletes spent years on the circuit, earning middling points and dollars. They considered top-20 a win, top-10 a victory; the podium a rare bonus. Gwen expected more. Only consistent podiums would justify her investments. Analyzing her performance, she diagnosed mental weakness. She questioned her swim strength. She debated her cycling potential. Perhaps, she thought, she should return to accounting.

On Jamie's recommendation, Gwen abandoned training for a week to reflect. She reviewed her progress, from 2010 rookie to 2013 world-ranked triathlete. She reread her journal—a personal record of her evolution. She discussed options with Patrick. And she concluded her best was yet to come.

One year later, in a blog post, Gwen recalled her decision.

> *Last year I debated quitting the sport after my race in Auckland. I thought I didn't belong. At the time, Jamie and Patrick told me to take a week and just think about it, and reflect on what I wanted out of the sport and if I wanted to continue. It was a rough time for me; but ultimately, I decided to continue... And, I am relieved I decided to stay in the sport. My advice for anyone struggling with something they love: surround yourself with those who will make you better.*

ELIZABETH

What is it that drives Gwen to compete? Is it a family trait? Do all Jorgensens have it? Perhaps Gwen's competitive drive is just more pronounced.

In the moments before the Friday bell in my journalism class, a 17-year-old boy with floppy hair, khaki shorts, and a designer t-shirt said, "Your mom, she's that teacher that won something, right?"

Puzzled, I said, "Yes." I wondered what triggered his memory. Mom won the *USA Today* prize for Best High School Musical in America. She also won the School Board's Arrowhead Award for "dedication and loyalty to Arrowhead... [and] passion for the profession and school."

But before I could respond, he added, "And your sister, she's always winning, too." The class nodded and smiled. I regularly showed recaps of Gwen's races. It was an opportunity to talk about resiliency, work ethic, effort. "*What* is with your family?" I heard his disbelief.

"We do like to win."

I was about to explain when the boy said, "But I never hear about *you* winning." He tried to bait me, clearly not aware of my obsession.

As I began framing my response, I said, "I do my fair share of winning too," but the bell rang and the boy waved.

"Yeah, okay, Ms. J," he said, rushing out the door. "Have a good weekend."

On Monday, I thought, *I should tell him about contesting.*

It started in high school. I entered scholarship contests, reducing my Marquette University tuition. In college, I was a regular winner at Saturday morning scholarship competitions. During my senior year, as the newly released Facebook scrolled graduation photos and senior parties, I noticed contest solicitations. I created videos and wrote essays. I enlisted friends, roommates, Mom and Dad, boyfriends—anyone—to help.

On one first date, I said, "If this is going to work, you need to help me with contests. You have to take videos, do funny things, and help me compete." We sat at a local bar, country music blaring, antlers decorating the walls.

He didn't get it. "Contests? What are you talking about?" He sipped his Miller Lite as I told him of my cousin Byron.

"Well, Carhartt asked customers to post a video to Facebook about their products. I recorded Byron pretending to fall off a six-foot ladder." I stopped to laugh. "After he fell, he popped up and screamed, 'Carhartt saved my life.' It was pretty funny, and Byron got really good at his pretend fall. And our video won!"

"Oh." He showed no interest, so there was no second date.

Months later, a radio station gave away a closet makeover. I videotaped mine, stuffed with laundry baskets, shoes, and drooping clothes and begged to be chosen. A $5,000 closet is now the focal point of my bedroom.

Another radio station offered an engagement ring for the best video. Directing Dad, I urged him to talk about his love for Mom. He mentioned their 30-year marriage, and how he never gave Mom an engagement ring. Dad's entry—the only from a senior citizen—was chosen.

I wrote a Father's Day essay, and Dad won a hedge trimmer, blower, and chainsaw. I wrote an essay about Mom, and she won a necklace and twelve months of flowers. I won a snowblower, four grills, and enough gift cards to pay for my trip to London. I won an iPad, three Amazon Fire tablets, a desktop computer, a 42" television, a Blu-ray player, a chandelier, and soda for a year. I won trips and airfare. In my creative writing classroom, I centered the curriculum on writers' markets. My students won national and local writing competitions. I also won things I didn't want—crafts, toys, stuffed animals, sports equipment, DVDs, coolers—so I dedicated basement storage The Prize Closet. Friends called me The Contest Queen. Patrick's mom, Jane, a radio deejay, preferred her industry's term: Contest Pig.

So, what makes the Jorgensens competitive? What drives us to compete? To win? My conjecture is something about the household Mom and Dad created combined with a string of DNA. For me, it's an addiction, fueled by adrenaline when a package arrives or an email announces, "Congratulations! You won!" Gwen said she feels the same high I describe, but she's motivated more by her hate of losing than her love of winning. And Gwen's wins are more complicated, her victories critiqued on the world stage. Her wins demand daily, hourly devotion—what she eats, how she sleeps, where she lives—her competitive Jorgensen drive gone viral.

NANCY

The International Triathlon Union revised their scoring system in 2014. In vying for the World Championship title, athletes would use points from five of seven World Triathlon Series races, plus the Grand Final. First place was worth 800 points, except at the Grand Final where it was 1,200. Points decreased with each place. At the end of the season, the athlete with the most points would be World Champion.

Points Table from Triathlon.org

Finish Position	ITU World Triathlon Series Grand Final	ITU World Triathlon Series events	ITU Triathlon World Cup events
1	1200	800	300
2	1110	740	278
3	1027	685	257
4	950	633	237
5	879	586	220
6	813	542	203
7	752	501	188
8	695	464	174
9	643	429	161
10	595	397	149
11	550	367	138
12	509	339	127
13	471	314	118
14	436	290	109
15	403	269	101
16	373	248	93
17	345	230	86
18	319	213	80
19	295	197	74
20	273	182	68

In addition to ITU points, a different system determined Olympic qualification. To complicate matters, athletes could qualify automatically for the Olympics at select races.

After the first race, in Auckland, Britain's Jodie Stimpson had 800 points while Gwen sat with 339. Twenty days later, on April 26, 2014, Gwen dove into Cape Town, South Africa, waters. Although air was 21.6°C (70.9°F), water registered 11.9°C (53.4°F). The chill could affect all, with Gwen especially susceptible. Recognizing perilous conditions, race officials shortened the swim from 1,500 meters to 750.

Gwen exited the wetsuit swim in 15th, 20 seconds behind. Nine women coalesced into a lead bike pack while Gwen joined the first chase group. Once again, we watched from home and it wasn't long before a crash left one rider face down on the road, USA clearly visible across the back of her suit. *Oh, no, not again. But maybe it isn't Gwen...does her body type look different?* Cameras refocused on the leaders while I paced.

"Could you tell who that was, Joel?"

"No, but definitely USA."

As coverage returned to the crash and I recognized Katie Hursey, I flickered between gratitude for Gwen's safety and regret about Katie.

In maneuvering around Katie, Gwen lost contact with the first chase pack. She finished the bike leg two minutes behind.

> *I struggled to put my shoes on in T2 as my feet were still numb from the cold water. Once I exited T2, I tried to execute a good run and didn't think about the time gap to the athletes in front of me. My legs felt heavy and slow, but I know feelings don't have to dictate outcomes.*

She told me recently about her mindset—confident her body could perform despite pain or discomfort. And I witnessed it. Facing insurmountable deficits, she rarely relinquished a race. When cold, or exhausted, or ill with flu, she still performed.

Chilled and two minutes down, Gwen gained on runners in front of her and attacked others up the road until, in the final lap, she passed all but three. She ran 1:07 behind Great Britain's Jodie Stimpson and Helen Jenkins, but only 33 seconds behind teammate Sarah Groff. Trevor Harris asked Barrie Shepley, "Can [Gwen] take Sarah Groff for bronze?"

Shepley answered decisively. "No." I also believed 30 seconds too much.

But with one kilometer remaining, as Groff faded and Gwen accelerated, Shepley backpedaled and suggested Gwen could win bronze.

Stimpson crossed the line first, followed within seconds by Jenkins. Destroying her two-minute deficit, Gwen nabbed third, 22 seconds behind the winner. I wondered what determined success. Was it talent—or mindset?

Stimpson now had a perfect score—1,600 points—while Gwen had 1,020. Athletes could use points from three more races to vie for the championship.

Joel and I listened to Gwen on speakerphone. "Yeah, that was tough. I had to work really hard for bronze." Hard work, yes, but perhaps validation for her decision to continue competing. "I just want you to know you may not be able to reach me for awhile. Patrick and I are staying in South Africa a few extra days."

"What's that about?" I asked.

"Patrick always wanted to do a safari, and we got some recommendations for a good one. Who knows when we might have this chance again?"

I was glad she learned from Jamie and her Croatian visit to take time off.

> Usually when I travel to a race we don't have much time to be a tourist; however, we had a few more days to enjoy the city this trip. Patrick and I enjoyed some local food recommendations (thanks, Liezel and Libby): bobotie, raw crocodile, braaivleis, ostrich, springbok, wines, chocolates, and more...We also went on a safari that Gavin and Siobhan [Specialized representatives] recommended. We saw the 'big five' (elephant, rhino, leopard, lion, and buffalo) and thoroughly enjoyed the drive to and throughout the safari. I learned a little about the lives of locals, saw many beautiful sights, and overall had a wonderful trip.

On Monday, after the Cape Town race, I showed a three-minute recap to my colleague, Wolfgang Calnin. A retired choir director about my age, he substituted for my regular partner that semester.

"Do you share these with the kids?" Wolfgang sported a bald head and forearm tattoos, a man's man who could reach students with a sports analogy.

"Not usually—I'm too pressed for time." I sometimes obsessed over notes and rhythms when I could be teaching life lessons.

"This is inspirational. The kids can see persistence." I trusted his perspective, set up the projector, and prepped students with a summary about Gwen, her career, and Cape Town.

Arrowhead High School in Hartland, Wisconsin, serves middle- to upper-income families. Most knew defeat through a failed test, a lost game, or an alienated friend. Using the example of Gwen's comeback from a two-minute disadvantage, I urged them to adopt her attitude: the race is never over until the end; no matter how bleak the circumstances, victory is possible; don't give up when faced with a challenge.

The 150 freshmen girls in Treble Choir listened attentively, watched the race, and asked a few questions. The 80 freshmen boys in Baritone Chorale, enthralled with the play-by-play, broke in with comments. "There she is! JORGENSEN!"— "How cool is that bike!"—"Look at her muscles!" They responded as if the race were live and applause erupted before Gwen crossed the finish line. Hands flew with questions. "What's her best time for a 10K?"—"Where's her next race?"—"Do you get to see any?"—"Was she in the London Olympics?"—"Will she go to Rio?"

Wolfgang was right. My students understood a sports handicap—and the urge to destroy it. I hoped they could take Gwen's lessons and apply them to their own lives.

****

Joel, Elizabeth, and I watched two May races from our respective homes. The first was in Yokohama, where the year before, Gwen took gold. She described Japan as a favorite venue—could she take back-to-back wins there?

On May 17, 2014, Gwen exited the harbor in 13th and gained time running to transition. After an uneventful bike leg, she and 45 competitors rode together into transition two. Gwen recorded the fastest run by 39 seconds and claimed victory by 36 seconds. She had one more reason to like the course.

With 800 points for the win, Gwen was second in world rankings behind Stimpson, who took ninth after a spill on the bike.

Following Yokohama, Gwen was registered for London. I grappled with superstition. A flat tire in the 2012 Olympics, and a DNF crash in the 2013 Grand Final—the course appeared to be Gwen's nemesis. I would have understood if she avoided London, but Gwen attacked it. For the May 31, 2014, sprint race, she said her goal was gold.

Gwen exited the water in fifth, one of three USA athletes in the top six, and joined the front group of cyclists. If she stayed with the leaders, I felt confident she could run to victory and lift London's curse.

Gwen held her position in a front pack that maintained a 20-second advantage.

After dismounting, Gwen ran with USA's Sarah Groff and Katie Hursey and others from the lead bike pack. She eventually surged and won the race by a 28-second margin. After two years of defeat in London, Gwen conquered the course. Once more, it appeared mindset secured victory, rendering previous disasters powerless against preparation and performance.

With three 2013 victories and two in 2014, Gwen tied the record for WTS career wins. Like chlorine infiltrating water, talk saturated the media. A current of promise coursed each article, creating suspense for fans—but encumbering Gwen with predictions. Adding pressure, her next race was in Chicago.

Only 100 miles from Waukesha, the Chicago event on June 28, 2014, offered friends, family, and fans a rare opportunity to see Gwen live. With only one 2014 WTS race in the USA (and some years none), national sponsors scheduled interviews, photo shoots, and appearances; Gwen's agent booked reservations; family members planned cross country travel.

For most races, Gwen remained relatively anonymous. She ran in cities thousands of miles from home where fans cheered their hometown favorite. But in Chicago, a grandstand crowd would overflow to city streets, all rooting for USA, with Gwen the presumed hero.

I knew Gwen assumed a responsibility—not only for herself, but for those who invested in her—to win. For aunts and uncles who flew from Tennessee and Colorado, for college roommates who traveled from Minneapolis, for hometown strangers who drove from Waukesha—she felt obliged to take gold.

Anticipating a win, Gwen's sponsors booked a post-race celebration. Even before the starting horn, they forecasted victory and invited guests to party.

Joel had family scattered around the country, and many followed Gwen's career. With nine children and no time to hover, his parents allowed each sibling to create a singular, sometimes eccentric, life. They were examples for Gwen and Elizabeth who grew up surrounded by risk-takers, path-forgers, a step-to-the-challenge clan. In deciding to abandon a corporate accounting career and train for professional sports, Gwen was not the first to follow a dream.

Gwen's Uncle Kenny, a professional paraglider, jumped off mountains, catching wind currents in Salt Lake City. Part performer, part teacher, he tutored US Armed Forces and traveled the world in search of mountains.

Aunt Charlene, 20 years ago, booked a ticket for the Virgin Islands and didn't come back. As a beach creature in shorts and sandals, she built a boutique business.

Uncle Randie, Gwen's godfather, consumed only what he hunted or grew, supplementing his diet with eggs from backyard chickens. He spent months in a remote cabin near Viola, Wisconsin.

Aunt Mary Beth raised her daughter in Hawaii and Japan, living a military wife's life.

Aunt Christine stepped in when the first five Jorgensen children lost their mother to cancer. At 12 years old, for a while, she raised Gary, Kenny, Randie, and three-year-old Joel.

Aunt Colleen supported herself for years as a dancer.

Uncle Greg traveled weeks every year chasing bird watching opportunities.

Uncle Gary, barely out of high school, fought in the Vietnam war.

Uncle Bill reunited with his birth family—the Jorgensens—to fulfill a dream of knowing his brothers and sisters.

In Chicago, seven Jorgensen aunts and uncles, their spouses and children, cheered for Gwen. They joined my brother and sister and their families, all with cameras and triathlon shirts, ready to celebrate.

Joel, Elizabeth, and I arrived in Chicago via Amtrak train—a 90-minute ride—a few days before the race. We would run errands for Gwen and snatch quick visits as she prepared.

In Gwen's Hilton room, bikes slanted three-deep against a wall, swimsuits and wetsuits dripped from the bathroom door, and suitcases perched in a tower behind the desk. As I edged around backpacks to get a kiss, I noticed computers on the bed, surrounded by charts and notes. Bags of laundry begged to be cleaned, and towels draped lampshades. Rice, vegetables, and oatmeal were heaped on the television while Patrick's rice cooker and knives decorated the dresser—a chef's itinerant kitchen. I saw the challenge of preparing for world-class racing in a hotel room. "What can we get for you?" I asked.

"Sparkling water? And a gallon of still and bananas?"

We returned with groceries to find Patrick's parents in the room and Gwen irritable. Reading her impatience, I prepared to leave. Not as familiar with Gwen's signals, Patrick's dad, Craig, lounged on a bed while his mother, Jane, studied brochures.

"Okay, I need some privacy," Gwen said. I twisted the doorknob before she finished. "I just need to be alone for a while." She walked her words over a tightrope, each syllable taut.

Craig eyed her from the bed. "Does that mean me, too?"

"Yes."

Joel, Elizabeth, and I were familiar with Gwen's pre-race moods and rituals. I hoped Craig and Jane would learn quickly and accommodate Gwen's needs too. This day, they trailed us out the door.

ELIZABETH

The next day, in the Hilton lobby, we piled in an elevator with a few others. One, a man in his thirties, with black hair, dark eyes, and a heavy Spanish accent, interrupted us. He struggled with his words. "Esscuze me. You...Gwen Jorgensen?"

Gwen nodded and smiled. "Yes." Gwen wore skinny jeans and a casual top, no athletic gear, no bike, no jersey to identify her.

"Sorry. English no good." The man smiled and gestured an apology.

"It sounds great to me." Gwen shook his hand. "Nice to meet you."

"You awesome. So good. Pleese...seelfie?"

We laughed at the universal term as I held my hand out. "I'll take it," I said, positioning myself at the front of the elevator.

Gwen put her arm around the man. They smiled and, after the camera's flash, her fan asked for another. "Maybe eye closeded?"

Maybe I should have let him take the selfie. Patrick, Mom and Dad, and the others stood to the side. I snapped—making sure both Gwen and her fan had their eyes open—as the elevator chimed our floor.

"Thanks you," he said, visibly giddy, as he checked the photos.

"You're welcome. Good luck this weekend." Gwen assumed he was an age-group athlete.

As we walked to Gwen and Patrick's room, I said, "How much does this happen?"

"At events like this? It's all the time." She seemed exhausted. "It's hard to get anywhere on time."

"Wow," I said. "I had no idea my sister was so famous."

"Elizabeth, I'm not. But at events like this, people recognize me."

Throughout the weekend, as we walked on Michigan Avenue, ate in restaurants, and watched age-group competitions, Gwen was stopped. Politely, each time, she posed for pictures and signed programs. I was proud of her. And I understood why she appreciated her anonymity in Spain and Australia.

> *Jamie was contacting my support crew to ask them for help in being my "body guards" around the media and event. I've been through this a million times, I can handle it, I reasoned; however, I couldn't have been more wrong. Without some sheltering from the media and a heavy dose of Silver Edition Red Bull, I'm not sure I would have made it through the week.*

NANCY

For weeks, Jamie warned Gwen about competing at home, but the pressure proved weightier than she imagined. On race day, thousands of fans in Chicago—and more streaming worldwide—focused on her performance. Professional sport was a public endeavor—blunders discussed on Twitter; gaffes analyzed in blogs; missteps simulcast for all to see. An audience of family and friends who traveled thousands of miles yanked the knot tighter.

Joel, Elizabeth, and I joined Gwen's fans in the grandstand, a six-row party complete with noisemakers and refreshments. Although Lake Michigan registered cold enough for wetsuits—19.2°C (66.6°F)—because of humidity and warm air—27°C (80.6°F)—officials chose a non-wetsuit swim. While a few from our group watched the start from Lake Michigan's shore, most spied Gwen on the jumbotron, where she dove for frigid water in two caps—thermal headwear underneath regulation silicone.

Gwen exited the chilly, choppy waters in 15th and joined a chase pack 30 seconds behind. On each lap, cyclists circled Grant Park's Clarence F. Buckingham Memorial Fountain, one of the world's largest, with 133 jets of water arching from a wedding cake design—an architectural magnificence that matched the athletes' prowess. Beyond its 280-foot diameter, racers disappeared eight times into the foothills of Chicago's skyline.

Gwen's chase pack lost time, and what began as a 30-second deficit ballooned to 66. My anxiety intensified—worried not only about the dangers of biking, but also about pressure on Gwen to win—and I wondered if the mental strain affected her performance. Or was she cold from Lake Michigan's water?

Patrick's dad, who sat a few rows over, walked to me several times. "She can do this. She can make up a minute."

Although Gwen typically bested competitors on the run, I knew a full minute would test her. "I really hope so." I wasn't in the mood for conversation, but I appreciated Craig's optimism and reminded myself of what I told my students about the Cape Town event: the race isn't over until the end.

As riders dismounted, the heat and humidity thickened. Two contenders asserted their dominance—Great Britain's Helen Jenkins and Japan's Juri Ide.

Family members, familiar with Gwen's typical victory-by-run, exuded optimism. "Okay, everybody! This is where Gwen pulls out the win!" said Aunt Mary Beth. Next to her, Uncle Greg palmed his video camera while Elizabeth shook a noisemaker, jump-dancing in place.

Uncle Randie conferred with Joel. "She can beat them, right?"

"I hope so. But maybe not 'til the second half of the run."

My brother Steve stood. "I want to see this up close. I'm going to street level."

At the end of the first lap, as women ran past the grandstand, I realized Gwen had made up time. The crowd cheered, shaking cowbells and waving flags. Aunt Christine slapped high fives. I tried to join the upbeat mood but remained anxious. To run 60 seconds faster than Jenkins or Ide would require pain and suffering—race components Gwen often referenced—in addition to strength and skill.

Craig appeared at my shoulder. "Well, what do you think?"

"I'm still really nervous. It's a lot of time to make up."

After the second lap, Gwen ate up 33 seconds and Craig said, "Okay, she's halfway through the run and she made up half the time. She can do it!" I could barely hear him, the crowd erupting as Gwen ran past. She was in fifth place, behind Jenkins, Ide, Mazzetti from Italy, and Sweetland from Canada.

Joel agreed with Craig. "You know she's going to negative split."

Around me, friends and family remained positive. "She looks strong. She's going to do it!" Aunt Colleen said.

"What a stride!" Uncle Greg put down his video camera for a second. "Doesn't even look like she's working."

"You'd never know she just swam a mile and biked 40K," Aunt Christine said, and then laughed when Elizabeth screamed, "GOOOO, GWEEENNNN!" while dancing on her bleacher bench, clanging a miniature cowbell.

I had to agree. Gwen looked strong.

As Gwen gained, Shepley said, "This is incredible...the predator coming in." He reminded spectators Gwen approached a two-time World Champion—Jenkins—and if Gwen could win, she would be the winningest woman in WTS history. I didn't care about stats. I just wanted her to take gold.

Air temperature soared. At every water station, women grabbed bottles—just a sip, then a dousing to cool core temperatures. On the jumbotron, the street crowd leaned over barricades, waving and shouting, as runners tossed empty bottles into the throng.

Shepley said, "This is brilliant running...something that happens so rare," and although competitors gained on Gwen in the swim and bike, "66 seconds is not enough [to keep her from winning]."

Completing the third of four laps Gwen trailed by five seconds, behind Jenkins and Ide. Elizabeth turned from where she sat in front of me and signaled a thumbs-up. "Mom, I think she's got it." It was hard to disagree, and as Gwen seemed poised to overtake the leaders, I felt twinges of relief, and anticipation—that Gwen might celebrate victory at home.

As she completed the final lap, Gwen passed Ide and pulled up next to Jenkins. It appeared they would run together to the finish. Shepley said this was "one of the three or four greatest runs we've ever seen in a triathlon." But he described Gwen's untested sprint, predicting the final meters could determine the winner.

The grandstand crowd remained riveted, eyes on the screen, when suddenly, without warning, and in a burst of energy, Gwen spurted ahead. Shepley said she "looked like somebody shot her out of a cannon...this race is over." The crowd's decibels exploded. Within seconds, Gwen ran 12 meters in front of Jenkins. Shepley later reported, "[Gwen said] the crowd was so loud...so USA, that she just found another gear."

"Oh, my, she's really going to do this!" I said.

Elizabeth reached back with a high five, and then jumped up. "GOOOOOO, GWEEEENNNNNN!"

As Gwen maintained her pace, not only did she destroy her 66-second disadvantage, she gained another 10. She ran solo toward the chute.

Each time I saw Gwen win, she donned a photogenic smile for the finish line photographers, followed by a stoic retreat—no theatrics, no dramatic collapse, no overblown celebration. But Gwen's victory in Chicago was historic—and her display of emotion a first too. Heading to the finish, when Gwen glanced back and saw no one, both hands came to her cheeks. I knew that expression. To me, it revealed her thoughts: *I actually did it! I won at home! I am ecstatic—and relieved!* Her smile was not just for the cameras. Gwen crossed the line first, buoyed by a cheering crowd—"USA! USA! USA!"

Joel and I spent long minutes hugging each other, then family and friends. We found brothers and sisters, nieces, nephews, and neighbors. Steve, a sports fanatic, said, "This was the most exciting sports moment of my life!"

Gwen's win thrilled me as a parent, and it was even better to share it. "Really? Of all the events you've seen?"

"Are you kidding me? To see my niece win like that...and hear the crowd cheering just for her? That was fantastic!"

While we waited for the medals ceremony, officials tabulated points and announced Gwen first in the world ranking (with 3,424), Jenkins second (2,666) and Stimpson third (2,396). But in the post-race interview, Gwen recalled a swim that left her behind, and a bike leg that further handicapped her. Shepley remarked that for someone who didn't know Gwen, "You would think [her humility] was just made up...but she keeps thinking this is a bubble that's going to burst...that she...should be working in an office and not someone who now, as we head toward Rio, has to be one of the favorites to win the Olympic Games." I knew Gwen's ultimate focus was winning gold in Rio. Lots of athletes aimed for the same. Hearing experts call Gwen a favorite made the quest possible. My daughter could be an Olympic champion.

Throughout the ceremony, the presence of family augmented every emotion. My pride was magnified when Gwen ascended the podium with family at the edge of the stage. My admiration was more teary as she accepted a medal while aunts and uncles snapped photos. My patriotism was more intense when the national anthem swelled. Then all around me I heard, "Gwen is my niece."—"Gwen is my cousin."—"Gwen is my godchild."

ELIZABETH

After Gwen's races, a mob often formed. Fans camped outside medical and mechanical tents, waiting for athletes. In Chicago, children and parents held Sharpies, photographs, t-shirts, bikes. Age-group racers wanted Gwen's autograph on swimsuits and helmets. Media stood by for photos and quotes.

Patrick exited first, walking with Gwen's gear. When Gwen appeared, we cheered and waved while dozens of fans, polite, but pushy, surrounded her. Gwen scratched her signature and posed for pictures. And as she finished with one person, another took his turn. With no professional security, the swarm heightened my nerves. I chatted with Mom and Dad but eyeballed Gwen. After a two-hour race, fatigued and drained, she remained calm and smiling.

Forty-five minutes later, the crowd dispersed, and Gwen strode to us. We congratulated her, and she hugged family and friends.

"Gwen! What a great race! Awesome job!" Aunt Mary Beth motioned to her husband, Marsh, who stood with camera at eye level, already zoomed in. "Can we get some photos too?"

"Of course! Thanks so much for coming," Gwen said. We laughed and smiled, still sweaty and exhilarated.

After family photos, Gwen mentioned the evening party and told everyone to check text messages for specifics.

Three hours later, we gathered at *Rockit* for drinks and appetizers courtesy of Red Bull. There, Gwen again shifted between coaches, sponsors, and family. Halfway through the night, she found me and apologized. "Elizabeth, sorry I haven't been able to chat. I just feel so..."

"Gwen, don't worry about it. I get to spend lots of time with you." I hadn't missed Gwen's presence. I was busy ordering lemon drop shots, sliders, and macaroni and cheese appetizers.

"Thanks. I just want to make sure I connect with each person." The evening reminded me of a wedding—of a bride's obligation to make sure everyone has fun, feels appreciated, is heard and seen. But unlike a one-time wedding, Gwen dealt with this pressure repeatedly. And on a wedding day, the bride didn't have to swim, bike, and run before the party.

I asked her to join my group for a lemon drop shot. I sat with Gwen's high school friend, Meg, and her dad. He said he never drank shots but, for the national champion, would make an exception. I was surprised Gwen agreed.

When the party ended after midnight, the Lemieuxs—Jane, Craig, Patrick, Paige—and Jorgensens walked two miles toward the Hilton when Gwen said, "I really want Ben & Jerry's. I feel like a core flavor."

"Core flavor? What's that? And what's going to be open?" I was tired, and drunk, and wanted to sleep.

"Cores have a different flavor in the center of the pint." She seemed surprised I hadn't heard of it. "You'll love it."

Jane spied a 24-hour drugstore. "I bet they have a freezer."

I teased Gwen that the world-number-one should get anything she wants.

The eight of us meandered through the nearly vacant store. When Gwen found what she wanted, Dad pulled out his credit card. We resumed our walk, sharing the containers. Most of us scooped a few spoonfuls; Gwen devoured the rest.

In the hotel lobby, hugs and final congratulations ended the evening. I was happy, and relieved, and ready for sleep, but even with media commitments the next day, Gwen seemed in no hurry. She told me sleep eludes her after a race. Competitive adrenaline haunts her system, and she dallies with books or movies late into the night until her body permits rest. I wondered if parties made it worse, staying up so others could celebrate.

The next day, at the men's race, Gwen joined Chicago's mayor, Rahm Emanuel, for photos. Typically the focal point, the mayor deferred to Gwen as they posed in front of Buckingham Fountain.

When she wasn't taking informal pictures, Gwen traipsed through parks and streets for a photo shoot with sportswear brand, ASICS. She spoke at press conferences and completed interviews. In her hotel room, she responded to race-related emails and posted to social media.

It was the first time I realized how taxing Gwen's schedule was, how demanding, how draining. I was exhausted, and I didn't compete—I couldn't imagine adding the stress of media, travel, and fatigue to the steady requests for selfies and signatures.

NANCY

Gwen would race one more time, in Hamburg, before the Grand Final in Edmonton. When Gwen discussed races or training, she created a theme of suffering. In tweets, she reminded competitors to suffer. In speeches, she expounded on its importance. In interviews, she recalled her race-induced suffering. In my own attempts to bike or walk, I quit when I was tired. If I felt pain, I surrendered. Curious about suffering, I group-texted Gwen and Elizabeth.

> *Nancy: Hey Gwen...I'm interested in the idea of suffering and why you don't just quit when it hurts.*

> *Gwen: I enjoy suffering. I see and use the word suffer in a positive light. That's what [people] don't get. Hmmm, how can I explain?*

> *Nancy: Is it because you are exploring possibilities? Because it means you are getting better?*

> *Gwen: It's a challenge, and when it's over, I feel like it's an accomplishment. I know that if I can get through the moment(s) of pain it will be worth it in the end.*

> *Nancy: Because it means you're working hard? Worth what? A better time?*

> *Gwen: Some people think sitting at a desk all day would be suffering. I can endure physical pain, but maybe not other pains, getting the most out of myself...This is all speculation. I don't think about it. I just do it. Not sure the why behind it.*

With so much emphasis on suffering, I was surprised she hadn't formalized her thinking.

> *Nancy: I know—it's just your personal experience. Hmmm interesting.*

> *Gwen: I think I'm horrible with some physical pain (like stubbing my toe, or something outside my control, or getting poked).*

> *Nancy: But when it's purposeful then you can take it?*

> *Gwen: It's a job, right? You just do it…? That's a theory I have :) [It's] true what you are asking me about suffering—I just don't know how to explain.*

> *Elizabeth: I think the pain you overcome is not the kind of pain I feel. You have the capability to push through because you consistently keep pushing—I think it's more about suffering a little more every day, and that builds up to wayyyyyyyy more than anyone else would do? Did that make any sense?*

> *Gwen: Ya I can see how the fitter you get the less pain at a lower level, but you just keep pushing that limit so always pushing more and more and it adds up.*

I analyzed our chat and concluded that for Gwen, suffering was a complicated concept about more than pain. I knew Gwen tended her body, noting twinges like I detected a piano string's buzz. When knees yipped, she reviewed her bike fit. When muscles squawked, she directed massage therapists to out-of-tune tissues. When she was too tired to recognize fatigue, she trusted Jamie's prescription for rest. Gwen endured suffering, while protecting herself from injury.

A few days later, Elizabeth sent me an interview in *W Magazine* where Gwen said, "Suffering is a strange word because it's often seen as a bad thing; however, in order to gain fitness in sport I need to push my physical limits which means I am suffering beyond what I thought was imaginable. My lungs burn, my legs scream for me to stop, and my entire body wants to shut down. It's a challenge to see how far I can push myself."

Gwen used mental discipline to push past physical pain. I wondered if it was an inherited trait. I regularly delayed gratification, working or saving toward a goal. And I taught for 30 years with fewer than five sick days—muscling through 12 hours of class and rehearsal with a cold or flu. But Gwen's suffering seemed magnified—beyond what I could demand of myself.

That's when Gwen sent me a screenshot of a memoir she read, hoping to explain her point. Fascinated with world titans, she studied successful people—athletes, chefs, business gurus. Alan Murchison, in *Food for Thought*, described the chef's pursuit of excellence:

> ...16-18 hour days...6 a.m. starts...pushing all day long...stressed...under pressure...50 covers booked for lunch...missing your wife and kids...forgetting birthdays...losing touch with friends...on and on...sore feet and the legendary chafing that is 'Chef's Arse'! The Glamourous life as a top chef!

> Why do we do it? If you have to ask that question then you don't understand the mentality of a chef in a fine dining restaurant...the satisfaction and obsession with gaining new skills while learning this incredible craft begins to define you as a person and becomes such an essential part of who you are, forever!

I did have to ask the question. Did that mean I would never understand the mentality? I tried to decipher Gwen's message: That complete immersion in an endeavor is grueling, that immense investments ingrain personal identity, and that the reward for suffering is transformation to a better athlete, chef, person.

****

A few days after the Chicago win, Joel and I flew to the Basque Region to once again spend time with Gwen and Patrick at their summer location. Although financially taxing, travel provided time together. Our interactions in Chicago were limited, and I looked forward to chats on the patio, nature walks in Salburua, and Spanish cuisine in local restaurants. Elizabeth stayed home, working her summer school job.

Arriving in Bilbao, we hopped from Lufthansa Air to lime green bus, choosing public transportation over a rental car. Before traveling to Gwen's location, we stayed in Bilbao for a few days. On a bike tour, our English-fluent guide spun us past the estuary and close to industrial buildings. "Look at the bridge coming up," I said. "It reminds me of the Calatrava addition at the Milwaukee Art Museum. It's that same bright white with the suspension cables and the lines pointing up to the sky."

Our guide overheard me and said, "I'm not surprised you see a resemblance. The Zubizuri [Basque for white bridge] is a Santiago Calatrava design too." The footbridge felt like home with its clean lines and soaring arch.

After our two-and-a-half-hour tour, we visited the Guggenheim. I lost myself in Richard Serra's 14-foot steel walls that serpentined a narrow walking path. I watched a boy navigate a glass maze. Beyond framed paintings, this museum filled its space with humor and interactive art. That evening, we enjoyed a public-square concert, yarn shops, and a sidewalk cafe. The next morning, we dragged our luggage to the bus station where diesel fumes floated in the terminal. A blue ALSA bus waited, gassed for its Vitoria-Gasteiz route.

After the 90-minute ride, we settled into our aparthotel in the complex Gwen and Patrick used.

"How was your time in Bilbao?" Gwen asked. Since our last visit, they had explored San Sebastian's culinary hotspots, but Bilbao remained just an airport hub to them.

"I'm not usually a museum fan, but I loved the Guggenheim." I still pondered how the Guggenheim transformed industrial Bilbao into an art lover's destination. I was glad we incorporated extra days into our trip and enjoyed sharing my impressions with Gwen. The Basques were proud of their art, industry, and language, and I knew she shared their pride.

For lunch, Patrick asked us to prep vegetables and chop meat, but Gwen encouraged us to cook an entire meal. "Don't tell Patrick, but I'm getting sick of the same dressing on every salad. Mom, could you do something different?"

I emulsified oil and vinegar into smashed garlic and salt, whisked in mustard, and discovered at dinner that Patrick hates raw garlic. He did like my baked potato soup.

"Mom, Dad, you should try a menu del dia tomorrow."

"What is that?"

"It means menu of the day and is served later than you're used to, from 1:00 to 4:00 p.m. But it's huge—appetizer, main dish, dessert, wine, bottled water—for a fixed price."

"And the menu changes?"

"Yup. Every day there are two or three choices in each course."

At a casual diner the following afternoon, where men in work boots crowded the tables, we started with bottled water and table wine. We said, "Sí," when the waitress offered diet white soda, and later learned we should have mixed it with wine, a Spanish custom. My paella appetizer—a steelworker's portion of rice with shrimp—preceded entrees, and when Joel's dense chocolate dessert arrived, I was glad I chose a light ice cream.

Later that evening, Patrick prepared Gwen's 7 p.m. dinner. "Are you guys ready for supper?"

"I can't even think about more food."

"Yeah, the Basques eat a late midday meal," Gwen said. "And their last meal is after 10 p.m. My bedtime is before that, so Patrick and I don't do menu del dia that often."

The next day, curious about a menu that emphasized quality over quantity, Joel and I walked to Casa Vieja in the old quarter. A waiter ushered us through an arched-brick vestibule—stucco walls and ancient wood beams—to a table with white cloths and crystal stemware. Antique clocks and rustic tables filled the space. He served us a bottle of wine, sparkling water, and a parchment menu.

Joel snapped a picture of the wine label and sent it to Gwen.

"Let's take our time. We should be more like the locals and not rush everything." This menu del dia arrived on elegant plates, brightened with an aioli swirl or carved vegetable. Chocolate mousse arrived in miniature jars with tiny spoons.

After our meal, we wandered the medieval quarter, starting on the hill dominated by the Cathedral of Santa Maria. We descended open-air stairs—flight after flight after flight—to the sunken city, where pre-1500 buildings housed modern-day businesses. We strolled streets where red geraniums trailed iron balconies and linen curtains wafted from casement windows.

Reuniting at the aparthotel, Gwen said, "We have to show you pintxo pote tomorrow. Every Thursday, bars offer an appetizer [pintxo] and a wine [pote] for one euro. It's like a fair with people walking the streets."

The next evening, we visited modern Victoria-Gasteiz where each restaurant and bar served appetizers on paper plates. "How do we know what they are?" I recognized mini burgers and cheese assortments but couldn't identify fancier creations.

"Let me know what looks good and we'll ask." Gwen, eager to practice Spanish, questioned bartenders and ordered cod fritters, sardines, potato tortillas, and anchovy skewers. We carried our choices, no more than a bite and a swallow, to outdoor benches or stand-up tables before meandering to the next bar.

As we stood around a sidewalk table, Gwen said, "Wanna go to the lake for our swim tomorrow?" She made a point to include us in her activities.

"You can ride in the van and watch the athletes in the lake," Patrick said, "and then while they run, you could swim at the public beach."

At the open water swim, the Wollongong Wizards practiced entries. When Jamie blew his whistle, 15 athletes charged, knees pumping above the waves. Then came dolphin dives, and finally freestyle to the buoy where they rested, treading water. Jamie whistled and the athletes swam back.

After swim practice, as the athletes ran lakeside paths, we lazed on a shady hill. I once again looked out of place, fully covered in my American tankini, next to bare breasted women.

After 10 days in the Basque Region, we flew to Hamburg for Gwen's next race. Bolstered by our success with Spain's buses, Joel and I relied on Germany's trains. At the Hamburg airport, we purchased subway tickets at an automated kiosk. As we learned in 2013, the U-Bahn operates on the honor system—no turnstile or scan. We kept our tickets handy, in case there was a passenger check.

Exhausted from a day of buses and planes, we collapsed for the 40-minute ride. After a few stops, a twenty-something man with close-cropped hair stomped into the train. Starting at the back, he checked tickets and high-stepped to the next row. He struck his military pose next to me. "Fahrkarten bitte!"

I offered our tickets.

He snatched them, scanned the information, and bellowed a string of German words. I cowered, focusing on the floor, baffled by his outburst. When I looked up, he narrowed his eyes and barked English: "Passports! Now!" and, "Sixty euros. Each."

I didn't understand—he had our tickets. As we fumbled for passports, a middle-aged woman next to me translated. "You purchased the wrong tickets and the penalty is €60." If we didn't pay, this man would escort us to the *polizei*.

The woman turned to the official and spoke in German. Her gestures and tone told me she argued on our behalf. A second woman joined, two aunties scolding the boy. I could only imagine what they said: "They're ignorant Americans. They tried to do the right thing and purchase tickets. Can't you let them off?"

The passenger load stared as the negotiation continued, the women apparently offering reasonable explanations countered by gruff retorts. I took shallow breaths and wondered why he needed our passports. Would he return them? We didn't have €120 in cash. What would happen at the *polizei*?

After several minutes, the official tempered his tone, but issued more threats, translated for us—"You must buy the correct ticket."—"Do not cheat the system." He sorted his packet of papers and with a menacing eye returned our passports. "This is your only warning!"

I was embarrassed but grateful two strangers interceded. I tried to vanish into my seat as we continued to Jungfernstieg station. When we arrived, I said, "I need to find an information booth."

"Don't worry about it, Nancy. We made it here."

"No. I have to figure out what went wrong." Speaking through an iron grill, I asked for help.

"First thing—find the English flag at the top of the screen."

I recognized my error immediately. Mired in travel fatigue, I missed the tiny English icon, and with only German instructions, botched our purchase. I vowed to be more conscientious.

****

Gwen entered the Hamburg sprint race owning the record for WTS career wins. A few years ago, I thrilled at top eight or a podium finish, but now the stakes changed, every race infused with assumptions and predictions.

While commentators anticipated another win, athletes from competing countries allied in one purpose: stop Gwen Jorgensen. Their theory: dropping her in the swim or bike would create an insurmountable deficit. Their plan: isolate Gwen in the swim lineup and place her far from the strongest swimmers.

Because she wore number one, Gwen chose her position first. Then, she watched as contenders ran past like playground bullies, leaving her friendless and alone. I wondered what she was thinking but knew she and Jamie planned for every scenario.

In the ideal weather—23°C (73.4°F) for both water and air—Gwen exited the water seventh; she advanced in transition, mounted her bike second, and joined the lead pack.

In the final stage of the race, she ran with a lead pack of six, and one minute into the last lap, surged, leaving Canada's Kirsten Sweetland and Australia's Emma Jackson to battle for silver. The victory bettered her record for total wins— seven—and consecutive wins—four.

The following day, Gwen raced the relay. Although not as dramatic as USA's podium in 2013, Gwen, Kaitlin Donner, Ben Kanute, and Alan Webb earned fifth.

Trolls persisted in social media, minimizing Gwen's victories by criticizing her swimming and cycling skills. Gwen, too, recognized her weaknesses and explored strategies for the Grand Final. With so much at stake—prize winnings, bonuses, sponsorship, the world title—she and Patrick considered using a domestique. In triathlon, teams routinely employ a strong cyclist to assist potential medalists. In the event of a poor swim, flat tire, or mechanical problem, a domestique could place the struggling cyclist on her wheel. When a domestique cuts the wind, the athlete behind conserves up to 20 percent energy. A domestique could also bridge a cyclist to the next pack.

Gwen and Patrick hired USA triathlete Sarah Haskins, a 2008 Olympian, as Gwen's domestique. USA Triathlon endorsed the plan, designating one of six spots to Haskins. If Gwen trailed, Haskins's cycling skills could pull her forward.

As Gwen solidified her game plan, Joel and I arranged our trip to Edmonton.

"Mom, Dad—Kassie would like to go too. Is that okay?" Elizabeth asked. Kassie Slotty was a piece of our family fabric since she and Elizabeth played violin together in middle school. Uninhibited, Kassie lived with abandon and spoke with humor and honesty.

"She'd be fun to have around. Would we all stay in the same room?"

"Well, Kas is nervous about passing gas in her sleep, but it would save us money."

I laughed. "Tell her not to worry. We'll get a room for four."

****

In high school, Kassie, Elizabeth, and Gwen carpooled to the Milwaukee Youth Symphony Orchestra where Gwen pouted about missing swim practice and Kassie and Elizabeth dispelled myths of the quiet, serious musician.

Although Gwen whined about violin, her talent drew attention. At high school parent teacher conferences, orchestra director, Lygia Topolovec, tilted her silver bob and said, "I want Gwen to be our concertmaster this year."

I was nervous for Gwen. "I'm not sure she has the personality for that." A concertmaster tunes the onstage orchestra and guides the string section through subtle body movement. Gwen played violin like she swam—eschewing public attention, her pursuit of excellence a private one.

"Gwen is our best violinist. I need her to lead the orchestra."

That night, I mentioned Topolovec's suggestion.

"I don't want to be concertmaster."

"I know, honey, but the orchestra needs you. You wouldn't turn down a relay spot for your swim coach."

"I don't want to talk about it."

When I broached the subject a few days later, Gwen clipped her words. "Yes, Mom. I'll do it. Don't ask me again."

At the October concert, Gwen stood center stage in her long black dress, hair damp from the pool, tuning woodwinds, brass, and strings. As the orchestra performed, Gwen should have nodded and swayed to indicate phrasing, but self-consciousness prevented that. She did accept Topolovec's handshake during the applause.

Ten years later, Gwen entered Edmonton the leader of Team USA, and I believed her backbone was strengthened by at least a few musical vertebrae. Kassie's presence reminded me of Gwen's orchestra days, and I was happy she remained an extension of our clan.

London 2011. *Gwen's bike racked before the Olympic qualifying event.*

London 2011. *Gwen qualified for the London 2012 Olympics.*

London 2012. *Gwen with Lolo Jones at the Opening Ceremony.*

London 2012. *Patrick and Gwen on the streets of London.*

London 2012. Gwen with college friends Sarah Hurley and Sara McKinley.

London 2012. Gwen with high school friends Maggie Lach, Kate Fahje, and Hannah McDougall.

Milwaukee 2010. Gwen and Gabby Levac at The WISCO Mile.

Photo courtesy of Amy Horst.

Terre Haute 2008. Family at the national cross-country championship.

Hamburg 2013. *Joel with the pilsner trophy. Gwen's numbers indicate relay team #19, athlete #3.*

London 2013. *Gwen bandaged after the World Championship crash.*

St. Paul 2013. *Gwen and Patrick on their engagement bike ride.*

Chicago 2014. *Gwen and Elizabeth with fans.*

Edmonton 2014. *Joel, Kassie, Gwen, Elizabeth, and Nancy with the World Championship trophy.*

Cable 2014. *Wedding photo with Craig, Jane, Paige, Patrick, Gwen, Elizabeth, Nancy, and Joel.*

Photo courtesy of Jonathan Pavlica.

Cable 2014. *Breakfast the morning after the wedding.*

Waukesha 2015. *A wall in Gwen's childhood bedroom.*

2015. Gwen's custom bike.

Rio de Janeiro 2015. Family lunch at an outdoor cafe.

Rio de Janeiro 2015. Nancy, Joel, Gwen, Patrick, and Elizabeth after the Olympic qualifying race.

Rio de Janeiro 2015. Men's Olympic qualifying race.

Rio de Janeiro 2015. Elizabeth walking along street art.

Rio de Janeiro 2015. *Gwen and Elizabeth sharing a Brazilian grilled lunch.*

Chicago 2015. *Nancy, Elizabeth, and Joel at the Specialized booth in Chicago.*

Chicago 2015. *Elizabeth and Patrick navigating the stormy Chicago streets.*

Chicago 2015. *NBC filming our family lunch after the Olympic qualifying race.*

Waukesha 2015. *Camera crew set up in Nancy and Joel's kitchen; Elizabeth at the table.*

Maple Grove 2015. *Gwen, Paige, and Elizabeth at the Christmas Day Joyful 5K.*

Rio de Janeiro 2016. *Kristi Castlin, Olympic medalist, and Elizabeth.*

Rio de Janeiro 2016. *Futebol stadium.*
Photo courtesy of Josh Olson.

Rio de Janeiro 2016. *Elizabeth and the Brazilian who befriended us on the subway.*

Rio de Janeiro 2016. *Family portrait at the Oakley House.*

Rio de Janeiro 2016. *Gwen's friends and family about to leave for the Olympic race.*

Rio de Janeiro 2016. *Post-Olympic victory. Elizabeth with Hannah McDougall, Meg Gross, Natasha Hanson, and Maggie Lach.*

Waukesha 2016. *Family friend Emily Reddy watching Olympic coverage from Wisconsin.* Photo courtesy of Emily Reddy.

ELIZABETH

Edmonton bombarded us with its slogan—"This is going to be EPIC!" Banners plastered subway cars, billboards, and elevators, and we teased each other that if Gwen won, this would indeed be epic.

Race day was clear, sunny, and cool. After breakfast in a French brasserie—thick bread in a pudding of cream, eggs, and cheese, served at cafe tables below street level—we walked toward the shuttle buses. Confused by our map, we called to a woman hurrying by. "Ma'am, do you know how to get to the triathlon?"

She smiled. "Follow me. My volunteer shift starts soon, and I'm trying to catch the shuttle." We hustled, skipping steps.

We arrived in the age-group area where thousands of bikes hung in racks and continued across a sunny open field toward the grandstand. "I bet we can find some free stuff at the vendor tents," I said.

Mom, Dad, Kassie, and I looped through the offerings. It was a place to score deals on gear. Booths lured me with games, raffles, and the promise of a prize. I picked up free lip balm when I spotted Uncle Greg and his wife, Chinchi. They made a road trip of the event, driving from Wisconsin to Canada, stopping to bird watch and camp. "I'm so glad you guys made it," I said.

"It was a long trip, but I'm so glad we're here. Have you seen Gwen?"

"No, and I don't think she'll chat before the race." As Chinchi mentioned her name, I spotted a life-size poster of Gwen. "Look! I see Gwen! Let's take a photo." I asked a volunteer to take our bizarre family portrait, the centerpiece a screen-printed Gwen. Gwen hated silly antics like this, but I tagged her on Facebook anyway—twice—once on her poster face and again on my t-shirt.

At the next booth, rowing machines teased guests to test power and speed. "Kassie, wanna take me on?" Kassie, a division-one, collegiate decathlon recruit, swam with Gwen in high school. She and Gwen were on the 4x100m relay team that broke a 20-year record. Tall and lanky, she used headbands and state fair jewelry to accent her bohemian look.

"For sure! Let's do it." Kassie reclined in her machine, hands on a mechanical oar, feet ready to row.

The worker buckled us in and started his timer. "Ready? Set?"

Why do I need a buckle?

"BEGIN!"

As we pulled and pushed, Mom, Dad, Uncle Greg, and Aunt Chinchi cheered. We drew onlookers, none realizing they were watching the potential World Champion's sister and her former teammate. Using her collegiate athleticism, Kassie doubled my power in the three-minute contest.

With hours until race time, I searched for activities. "Look—a photo booth. Everyone grab something." Mom gave me a sidelong look, but I convinced even her to try on a pirate hat, wacky glasses, and a fake mustache. After several attempts, we scored a picture with everyone jumping mid-air.

On our way to the grandstand, Patrick's parents found us.

"Craig, where is the best place to sit?" Uncle Greg wanted to get video.

"I think up higher we'll see more of the bike course." I knew he shared Mom's anxiety about biking but wanted to see every minute.

"Let's be close to the finish," Dad said.

We settled in front of the screen and wiped the moist bleachers with our coats. Under the jumbotron, in the transition zone, athletes checked bikes, ignoring cameras that lurked inches away.

Accustomed to watching races online, Kassie seemed awed by the event's scale and grandeur. Music boomed. In the warm-up area, competitors pumped their knees in pre-race strides. Helicopters hovered, ready to relay footage. Kassie slipped into home-watching mode, firing questions. "So, are you sure the domestique is legal?"

I looked around. Gwen told me not to tell anyone about her plan. "Kas, you know Gwen would never do anything that wasn't. Gwen and Pat told me the British team does it all the time. They even had a domestique in the last Olympics. It's just part of the sport."

"Right, but explain it to me. Is it a secret?" Kassie whispered.

"I don't think she's posting it all over social media. She doesn't want competitors to know her race plans."

The jumbotron zoomed in on wetsuit-clad athletes at the manmade lake.

"Oh. I see." Kassie seemed unconvinced.

I drew a comparison to a rabbit in track. "Plus, Patrick explained it as a common part of cycling. I guess they use drafting to save energy and let the domestique do the work. I just hope everything goes well and she doesn't need her."

NANCY

For the second consecutive year, Gwen entered the Grand Final as the series leader. In 2013, she crashed and withdrew. This year, ahead by 848 points, she needed 16th or better to win the World Championship title. But I knew Gwen wanted more. Her goal: win both race and title.

During the swim, commentators Barrie Shepley and Trevor Harris reviewed the bike course. Harris said, "[There are]...a couple of hills. We should see some drama. It's made for a breakaway." Already he alluded to competitors' attempts to drop Gwen on the bike.

Shepley said, "I think to have...any chance to knock Gwen Jorgensen off, they're going to have to get a group of five or six away and have at least 90 seconds at the end of the bike." He noticed Haskins—an Ironman triathlete—on the start list. "I think the United States has a few tricks up their sleeve that might make it more difficult." Triathlon fans would understand the implication that Haskins served as Gwen's domestique.

Gwen completed the swim—air and water at 18°C (64.4°F)—in 13th. I felt confident, knowing Haskins could help on the bike leg.

"Let's see if Gwen can stay with that front group," Joel said.

Twenty cyclists formed a pack, but Gwen couldn't latch on. The leaders got away and the jumbotron featured Gwen riding solo.

"Can you tell what's wrong?" I asked.

While other women rode in the saddle, Gwen stood to pedal.

"Is she cold?" Elizabeth asked.

Shepley noticed Haskins riding next to Gwen. "Haskins, if any person is able to get you to the front end of a race course...[it] is Sarah Haskins. She would be one of the greatest swim/bikers in the world, hands down, at any point in...history. If Gwen Jorgensen is having any kind of a day, she's going to get herself ridden up."

Haskins moved Gwen into the chase pack, and Shepley said, "That was a very worthy airline ticket the United States spent on Sarah Haskins." He apparently didn't know Gwen and Patrick hired and paid her.

I felt hopeful with Gwen in the chase pack. But when Haskins pushed the pace, Gwen dropped to last in the group.

Craig tapped me on the shoulder. "That's a terrible place to be—too easy to get caught up in a crash. And every time she gets shot off the back, she's wasting energy to catch up."

ELIZABETH

During the bike, the sun faded the jumbotron's images. I relied on announcers. Then, race commentary was muted as drummers assembled in front of the grandstand. In costume, they executed complex rhythms on leather drumheads. For several minutes, I heard only their beat. The fortissimo heightened my panic, and I was frustrated, wishing for race updates.

Kassie leaned over. "Why are they playing those drums?"

"I don't know, but I wish they would stop."

NANCY

At the end of lap one, Gwen's pack rode 45 seconds back. The lead group of 18 included top runners like USA's Sarah Groff and New Zealand's Andrea Hewitt.

"Oh my, they gained that much time in one lap?" Elizabeth, like all of us, knew continued gains could add up to three or four minutes. What if 18 were ahead by three minutes at the end of the bike? Could Gwen make top 16?

As Haskins led Gwen's chase group, Shepley said, "A lot of those women are all looking for one person, that's Sarah Haskins, to keep the pace going as rich as possible so they can get a chance [at the podium]."

While I hoped Haskins would maintain a competitive pace, I worried Gwen, who rode at the back, couldn't stay with her. "Should Haskins slow down?"

"They'd lose too much time," Joel said. "Gwen's only chance is for Sarah to keep pushing."

At the end of lap two, riders approached the grandstand. The screen featured Italy's Mazzetti speeding toward transition, crouched low over her handlebars. But as she leaned into the turn, her body tipped, her wheels lost grip, and she tumbled. "I hate watching that." I suffered a familiar panic that comes with every crash. But Mazzetti got up, checked her chain, spun her tires, and remounted. When my attention returned to Gwen, I realized her pack lost more time, down now by 65 seconds.

ELIZABETH

Patrick's mom, Jane, sat behind Kassie and me. She worked as a radio deejay, her giggle and banter part of her daily conversation. Midway through the bike leg, Jane left to find a hamburger. *I can't believe she came all this way to leave mid-race.*

When Jane returned, she collected cowbells race organizers provided. "I think these would be fun to put out at the wedding. I can spray paint them and tell people to ring the bell instead of banging on glasses to get Gwen and Patrick to kiss." Jane had three cowbells in one hand and more in her bag. "Elizabeth, help me find more."

"Can we do this after the race?" Mom cleans while Gwen races, so maybe this was Jane's nervous habit? I grabbed my cowbell and hoisted it as Gwen came through.

NANCY

Shielding my eyes from the sun, I searched for Gwen's red bike and blue helmet as her pack pedaled past.

"Oh, wow! She's second in the chase pack," Elizabeth said. "She must be feeling stronger."

Shepley said, "She doesn't want to win the title today by coming in 16th... Anytime you're a superstar, you want to finish off the title with a win."

Even after Gwen's string of golds, the word superstar surprised me. I knew Gwen didn't consider herself a superstar either.

Shepley calculated that if Gwen's pack continued to lose time, they could face a 90-second deficit. "They're setting this up for Gwen to either implode or have the greatest run in the history of women's triathlon."

"If she can stay with Haskins, it shouldn't get to 90," Joel said.

Cameras ignored Gwen's chase pack and focused on the 18 up front. To confirm Gwen's position, we waited until she rode past. At the end of lap four, her pack trailed by 81 seconds.

The gap aggravated my anxiety, but seemed to titillate commentators—a cliff-hanger, live from the pages of triathlon history. Shepley said, "...can [Gwen] have maybe the greatest run in a triathlon ever? And it's gonna take that...I have not written this woman off yet. She's done spectacular things...and...she's not panicking." I hadn't written her off either, but with the mounting deficit, it was hard to imagine a gold medal.

Gwen rode on Haskins's wheel, the chase pack single file behind them. Haskins, a world silver medalist, left her one-year-old baby for the first time and presumably worked at capacity.

Shepley said, "If it's 75 seconds, Gwen Jorgensen has a legitimate chance [to win this race]."

Gwen dismounted with a 78-second deficit and Haskins walked off the course, confirming her role as domestique.

"So, Gwen had a domestique, but she's still behind," Kassie said.

"It would have been a lot worse if Haskins didn't help. Right, Dad?"

"Good thing they hired her."

Three women led the run—Hewitt, Japan's Juri Ide, and Groff.

"So how tired is Gwen?" I knew strenuous cycling could affect run strength.

"She'll be fine," Joel said.

Gwen advanced to the front of the chasers, and Harris noted her atypical burst of speed. "That long, rangy stride."

Shepley agreed. "Usually it's about 3K in before she starts to unwind that bad boy."

After 1.25K, Gwen decreased her deficit to 60 seconds, and Shepley said, "Can she do the...almost impossible?"

"How much time did she make up in Chicago, Mom?"

"That was 60 seconds. Today, it's 78."

Kassie leaned in. "Liz, this is getting exciting!"

> *I started running, and my legs felt like they were made of bricks. I thought my muscles were going to give out and I was going to collapse to the ground...After lap one of the run (out of four), I felt like I hadn't gained time on the leaders. I had no idea how many women were in the first pack, but it looked like more than 16. I stopped thinking about what place I was in; instead, I ran as hard as I could, remembering my original game plan: to cross the finish line in first.*

By the end of lap one, Gwen decreased her deficit to 49 seconds. "She wins if she keeps that up," Harris said, and I prayed he was right. "The lioness has given the gazelles a big head start, and she's still going to snare them." I longed for his surety.

During lap two, Gwen infiltrated the top 18. Feet striking the ground 180 times per minute, she passed competitors, one by one, her pace painting them a still life.

"GOOOOOOO GWEEEEEENNN!" Elizabeth was on her feet. "YOU CAN DO THIS!"

Kassie joined Elizabeth, standing to ring her cowbell. "You go, Gwen!"

The couple in front of us turned around. "Are you Gwen's family?" I acknowledged my pride but didn't reveal my anxiety. "You must be so excited."

Gwen positioned herself in 16th.

Shepley said, "[She] will be World Champion, [but] will she be the race champion? If [Hewett, Ide, or Groff] want to win, they have to go faster."

Gwen put more runners behind her and penetrated the top 10.

With two laps to go, Gwen rounded the corner in front of the grandstand—17 seconds behind—and Shepley said, "Gwen Jorgensen has that special gift right now. We've seen it a few times, where somebody is in a moment in their career where they're just different than everyone else."

While I focused on Gwen's race, Gwen's ranking, Gwen's opportunity for a title, other battles raged. Groff needed sixth to earn second on the World Championship podium; Hewitt needed silver to earn third. Knowledgeable fans understood the stakes and cheered for various campaigns.

On lap three, the jumbotron showed street spectators leaning over blue fences, shaking cowbells, and shouting encouragement. When Gwen's natural stride carried her past teammate Groff, Gwen tapped her on the backside, a nonverbal vote of confidence.

Beginning the final lap, three leaders ran together—Hewitt, New Zealand's Nicky Samuels, and Gwen. They formed a trio, each tapping her own tempo. Was it easier to run with companionship? Or was Gwen too fatigued to accelerate?

Midway through the last lap, Gwen laid down a cadence the others apparently couldn't match. On the jumbotron, street fans shouted, "Good job, Gwen."—"Go, Gwen." They passed their cheers along, like a relay baton, as Gwen surged to lead. The grandstand erupted, "Go, go, go, go, go, go!"—"Woo-hoo!"

Shepley said, "I hope they understand that this is one of the greatest runs that we have ever seen."

We started our early celebration. Kassie and Elizabeth high-fived me. Chinchi hugged me and said, "I'm as nervous as you." Joel shouted, "You got this, Gwenevere." For five minutes, we enjoyed the anticipation, standing on the bleachers reveling.

Down the road, Gwen approached the grandstand, and I followed every step until she touched her toes to the blue carpet. She ran with a confident stride but checked over her shoulder. She put up her sunglasses, smiled, and raised the finish tape. She paused for photographers, and then lowered the tape with a shake of her head, as though admonishing herself.

Gwen waited 16 seconds for Hewitt to finish, and another ten for Samuels. She gathered them in, an arm around each, and posed for a photo. One minute and fifteen seconds later, Groff finished in fourth.

> *As I was running down the blue carpet towards the finish tape, I didn't relish the moment. I didn't think about what I was accomplishing. I was just running. It felt like any other race. I never thought, "This is it! You are the World Champion!" It's a strange thing, racing.*

> *I crossed the finish line and wanted to give Patrick and Jamie a hug. I wanted them to know this was for them. There are only a few people who know how hard Patrick and Jamie work for me. I didn't want to celebrate. I wanted them to celebrate.*

As competitors crossed the line, several collapsing, cameras stalked Gwen. "I made that difficult for myself, hey?" she said to someone off-screen. She adjusted her sunglasses, yanked the brim of her Red Bull hat, and mopped her face. As she wove a side braid, using sweat like gel, she checked her appearance for post-race interviews. "Pat...Patrick! How does that look?"

Across a security fence, Haskins leaned toward Gwen.

"Sarah, thank you. I'm sorry. I was just...oh, that first lap." Gwen turned to someone off camera and, shaking her head again, said, "I made that difficult for myself."

I read her frustration and wondered what handicapped her performance.

On the jumbotron, Shepley interviewed Gwen as she thanked Patrick and Jamie and then said, "I couldn't have done it today without Haskins, and I owe her a lot and I'm really grateful that she was here." I was glad she acknowledged Haskins's role.

Shepley asked what Gwen thought about the bike leg. "I didn't really execute too well on the swim and the first lap of the bike and...um...I think I got a little nervous and let that get to me. But towards the end, I was able to reel it back in so I'm really happy." Shepley inquired about Gwen's 2013 Grand Final crash and the motivation it spurred. Adept at ignoring tough queries, she answered a different question: "Hopefully, I can execute a little better in the upcoming years."

ELIZABETH

We watched Gwen's podium preparations but didn't capture photos—we could find better ones online.

"Look at Gwen! I'm so happy for her." Kassie shared our family's joy and relief.

Growing up, I hadn't envisioned my sister a World Champion. Always a successful athlete, she now was a dominant one. I wondered how important this win would be. Would it change Gwen's life? How long would her reign last? And as I watched my little sister, I noticed her body—muscular, defined, a World Champion's physique. So much changed: she was engaged, living abroad, dominating the world of triathlon.

Kassie put her arm around me and we looked at each other. It wasn't the first time we'd celebrated a family success, but this one was grander. "I'm so happy she did it," Kassie said.

"Me too."

We shifted to see the podium. Gwen took the top step twice—once as race champion, and again as 2014 World Champion. The first time, Gwen waved to us as she recognized shouts, "YAY, GWEN!" and "GW! GW!" and "Good job, Gwennie." During the *Star Spangled Banner*, I gazed from waving flag to Gwen. She looked regal, satisfied, happy. During the second podium, Gwen held the Series Leader trophy—the World Champion's prize. Gwen, Groff, and Hewitt held their arms up, struggling with trophies heavy above their heads.

NANCY

After the ceremony, a camera captured Gwen's reunion with Jamie. For the third time, Gwen chastised herself. "Oh, I made that difficult for myself." Jamie, a few inches shorter than Gwen, lifted her as she squeezed him and Gwen said, "Thank you, thank you, thank you." He raised her once more, and she reprised her hug with, "Sorry...I know." I assumed she apologized for allowing nervousness to affect her performance. Jamie taught her that feelings shouldn't determine outcome.

To spectators, Gwen's run of victories seemed easy, a given, assured. She had an historic five consecutive WTS wins and eight total. I knew the victories were hard fought, especially under the pressure of expectation.

We gathered at the finish, but security held the winners for drug testing. Barry Siff, President of USA Triathlon, spied us and waved.

"What a race!" I said.

"It was a great day for USA," Siff said. "Sarah and Gwen both on the world podium! Can't get much better. Our women and the recruiting program are strong right now. It's an exciting time."

While we waited for Gwen and Patrick, I spotted Groff's parents and approached. "Congratulations!" I said.

"You too," Sarah's mom said. "So fun to see both girls do well today." If there was competitive tension between USA's two top performers, she and I refused to succumb to it.

Finally, after autographs and selfies, Gwen joined us. "I'm so proud of you." I referred to more than the win. She made me proud with her perseverance, hard work, intelligent interview, and sportsmanship.

Back at the hotel, a small group met in Gwen's room.

"Can I hold the trophy?" Elizabeth asked.

"Of course, but it's heavy. Don't drop it."

"How does it feel to be World Champion?"

"The way that race went, it's amazing I am."

"You were great—you pulled it off in the end. Can we get a picture?"

Gwen agreed and then mugged a funny face.

Although the triathlon world predicted this championship, it took Gwen days of living with the trophy, seeing it every morning, to comprehend her accomplishment.

> *World Champion. It all just doesn't seem real. I feel*
> *like I am living in my own fantasy world and it's*

awesome! I don't know where to start to explain my journey and thoughts on winning the 2014 ITU Championship.

Winning didn't fully sink in until a day later on the flight home with Patrick. I was relieved, happy, and gratified. I have woken up every day since feeling amazing. I had no idea how much pressure and stress I was putting on myself (and for how long I had been putting stress on myself...). It was silly.

That evening, friends and sponsors gathered at a local restaurant. I found Haskins and said, "You were great today. I know Gwen appreciates everything." In my mind, Haskins was an imposing figure, controlling the race, dominating the bike. Here, in front of me, pretty and blonde in a summer dress, she seemed slight, in perfect form. "You must miss your baby."

"It's hard to be away, but my parents have her for the weekend, which took some arranging, but it's all fine." She shared her struggle to simultaneously train and breastfeed as the two forces drained nutrients from her body. Knowing Gwen's plan to give us grandchildren, I wanted to hear more, but Haskins pulled away to chat with others.

Jodie Stimpson, top British athlete who finished 13th, appeared at the door. She celebrated in a different room but brought Gwen a drink. Fiercely competitive in races, women established friendships off the course, their finish line hugs revealing genuine affection for compatriots, squad partners, and friends.

ELIZABETH

I saw Stimpson and Gwen and rushed to them. The second-floor dining loft was dark. Men in suits and ties stood at the entrance. I wore a cotton shirt and skirt and TOMS. "Jodie, I'm your biggest fan. Seriously."

Gwen shook her head and said, "Jodie, this is my sister, Elizabeth."

"You're such fun to watch, and I really like your post-race interviews." I found Stimpson animated and honest, endearing, and complimentary. Even on the worst days, she was optimistic and upbeat.

"It's nice to meet you." Stimpson gave me some other compliment, but I was too star-struck to remember.

"Can we take a selfie?"

Gwen offered to take it, and Stimpson said she was surprised I didn't want one of the three of us.

After the photo, I joined the Lemieuxs and Jorgensens at a rectangular banquet-type table. Gwen joined too.

Patrick's mom sat across from me. Curious about Jane's background, I asked questions. I learned about her complicated family of birth and adoptive parents. Jane told stories, laughing at her own jokes. I imagined her accustomed to entertaining, chattering to fill airtime. Patrick's sister, Paige, discussed social work and her master's degree. We talked about religion and contesting. We drank beer and asked Gwen about the people in suits.

Before the night ended, I bought a souvenir: a pint glass packaged in cardboard. Little star-filled flags, perched in cups, decorated the tables; I stuck a few into my purse. I couldn't think of better World Championship mementos.

We moved the party to our hotel lobby. At a table, Patrick and Gwen sat flanked by Mom and Dad, family, friends, Jamie, Kassie, and me.

Jamie made fun of my headband and American accent, and how often my family praised each other. "Ya Ameericins. Always soying good job thees and good job that! Iverything isn't always good."

"But I like praise," I said. "It's positive."

"It's meaningless when ya repeat it oyver and oyver."

"So what do you say?"

"I teel the truth. Eef Gween does a bad job, I teel her that."

Gwen rolled her eyes and said to our waiter, "Can I have a milkshake?" She hadn't found one on the menu, but probably thought any chef could blend chocolate and ice cream.

"Let me check if we can make that for you."

"Yes, that would be great. And a water, please. No ice."

I remembered Gwen's similar order at my bachelorette party as we watched wannabe Chippendales. Tonight's waiter, like the strip club server, topped Gwen's order with whipped cream. The rest of the group drank a few more rounds, the evening ending hours past bedtime.

NANCY

At the end of the night, Gwen said, "So I've got sponsor stuff tomorrow, but you could come along for the magazine interview and photo shoot."

"For sure!" Elizabeth said.

"EJ, you and Kassie could help with hair and makeup."

The next morning, we walked from our hotel to the studio. "What is all that stuff in your bag?" Elizabeth asked Gwen.

"Just different outfits. The photographer may want to try different colors."

I peeked in. "Why so much Red Bull gear?"

"I agreed to an unpaid interview if I'm on the cover with a Red Bull logo. That's how I'll get paid—a bonus from Red Bull."

We entered an office building, deserted that Sunday morning. The editor in charge of the interview led us through a maze of hallways. "You can do makeup here, and down the hall is a restroom."

"We'll let the girls do that," I said as Joel and I settled in a space no bigger than our living room. There were two chairs. "I'll sit on the floor."

White seamless paper, suspended from the ceiling, rolled six feet along the ground toward a tripod. The jean-clad photographer, his back to the windows, adjusted settings while his intern aligned a reflector. I squeezed against the wall and tucked my feet under me.

Gwen, Elizabeth, and Kassie returned from applying makeup, and even after yesterday's exertion and late celebration, Gwen looked ready to work. She carried her Red Bull water bottle, Red Bull visor, and Red Bull hat in addition to a bag of shirts, tri suits, and shoes. Leaving her bag with Elizabeth, she stood by the white paper.

"Do you want to wear the earrings?" the photographer asked.

"Well, I think they make me look more feminine..."

The editor agreed. "Let's keep them."

Over and over, Gwen ran diagonally across the white background. Each time, she pre-set her arms and appeared to mentally calculate her stride. With room for only two or three steps, the photographer click-click-clicked, and Gwen returned to start again. "Am I doing okay? Did we get a good one with the Red Bull gear?"

"Yes, come look."

Gwen checked the camera, and then repeated her truncated runs.

ELIZABETH

After 90 minutes, as the photo shoot concluded, the photographer asked,."Do you want one as a family? I can send you the file later." Mom and Dad said yes. I was less inclined. I hadn't showered or brushed my hair.

"Come on in, family." The photographer said we all looked natural except Dad.

"Dad, you have to smile!" Gwen said.

That got him to laugh and the photographer captured a shot.

Transitioning to an interview, Gwen and the writer perched by the window, knees almost touching. Gwen wore a casual top, fashioning her Oakley sunglasses into a headband.

"Tell me how you got into running." The writer propped up a mic and jotted notes on a pad.

When the photographer snapped candids, Mom, Dad, Kassie, and I shifted to avoid the frame. Kassie whispered, "I'm star-struck."

Gwen had a few stock answers. "My high school coach, Eric Lehmann..." And when she said, "Elizabeth was on the track team in high school," I wanted to butt in with the big sister's version but quieted myself in favor of professionalism and decorum.

"Tell me about hiring Jamie Turner."—"What makes you successful?"—"How will you improve your cycling?"

Gwen didn't stumble over words, she didn't stutter, she didn't get a saying wrong. Her speaking, like her triathlon, was world class.

NANCY

The next day, Patrick and Gwen would return to St. Paul. Of 90 days in the United States, they would spend 35 in Minnesota. The rest, Gwen would travel for sponsor obligations—more interviews, photo shoots, and appearances.

Before we left, Elizabeth and Gwen planned next week's visit to St. Paul. "Elizabeth, can you still make wedding dress appointments?"

"Sure. How many places do you want to try?"

"I trust your judgment. And the bachelorette party?"

"Yes, I have ideas for that too. I'll send you some choices."

"Thank you so much. I just don't have much time right now."

"No problem. That's what sisters are for."

Elizabeth, Kassie, Joel, and I left for Waukesha. Several times on the plane, I said to Joel, "Can you believe our daughter is a World Champion?"

He nodded each time and said, "I know. It's crazy."

"I see parents at these races and sometimes they're alone or with step-children. This wouldn't be as much fun if we couldn't do it together." I leaned over to kiss him.

A few weeks later, Gwen called to say the magazine featuring her interview was in stores. "I'm really mad, though."

"Why? What happened?"

"They broke their promise. I'm on the cover, but not with any Red Bull gear. So now I won't get paid—and they got their interview for free."

For legal advice, Gwen trusted her agent, who decided the loss not worth pursuing. Breaking the contract was unfair and dishonest, and I wondered if the magazine ever intended to use the Red Bull images.

Gwen's 2014 season was complete.

2014 Race Results

1st: ITU World Cup Mooloolaba, Australia (15 March)
12th: ITU WTS Auckland, New Zealand (6 April)
3rd: ITU WTS Cape Town, South Africa (26 April)
1st: ITU WTS Yokohama, Japan (17 May)
1st: ITU WTS London, United Kingdom (31 May)
1st: ITU WTS Chicago, United States of America (28 June)
1st: ITU WTS Hamburg, Germany (12 July)
1st: British Sprint Champs Liverpool, United Kingdom (10 August)
1st: ITU WTS Grand Final, Edmonton, Canada (1 September)

CHAPTER 6

The Love Bug and Other Syndromes

2014 OFF-SEASON

ELIZABETH

On September 1, the Grand Final race in Edmonton made Gwen the 2014 World Champion. One month later, on October 4, a ceremony in Cable, Wisconsin, would make her Mrs. Patrick Lemieux, and I was in charge of finding a dress. Where to begin? What kind of dress? How many did she want to try? New ones? Used ones? Price?

After research, I called her. "Gwen, there are so many options."

"We have to get all the shopping done in one day. So, find shops that are close. And I'm not sure what kind of dress. I think something casual, but maybe traditional? I know I don't want it poofy."

I relied on Google and online reviews, scheduling five appointments on September 6. That would give us four weeks until the wedding. We started at a boutique in a converted two-story home. In a bustling basement check-in, we met two of Gwen's college roommates. Dad stood to the side, looking bored and out of place. Jane drove from Fargo to join us for the day too.

The receptionist scanned her list, made a call, and said, "We have no record for a Gwen. Could it be under a different name?"

I panicked, scolding myself for not double-checking my reservation. "Maybe Elizabeth? Or Jorgensen?"

"No, none under that, but we did just have a cancellation, so you can have that appointment."

As Gwen met her consultant in a dressing room, I confirmed our later appointments and returned to watch Gwen try knee-length dresses, sticking to a casual theme. None impressed our entourage—Dad included. On the way out, I said, "Well, the other places have us scheduled. Hopefully, it will get better." Gwen and Mom said it was probably the store's mix-up. "Seriously, I made the appointments."

"We believe you. And this is why we have lots of appointments: to find the perfect dress." Gwen seemed relaxed and confident.

But at the next store, in a run-down strip mall, through the cracked glass door, I saw peeling carpet and yellowing walls. "Do we bother going in?"

"We never know what we'll find. Maybe a good bargain?" Gwen opened the door.

She found one dress she liked—it sparkled, long and heavy with beads. I wondered why Gwen liked this dress, and why reviewers gave this shop top recommendations. As we left, I apologized. Again.

Gwen squeezed between Mom and me in the back seat and said, "Elizabeth, this is fine. We'll find something. Don't stress. Let's get lunch, and you'll feel better." Jane rode shotgun, snacking and chatting while Dad navigated.

Outside the wedding resale shop, we spotted a Latin small-plate restaurant. We went in, ordered more food than fit our table, and I added a margarita, giving me enough optimism to believe we might find something before our end-of-the-weekend deadline.

After lunch, Gwen tried headpieces, sparkly belts, and traditional lace dresses. Nothing was right, and I sensed Mom and Dad waning. "What if you don't find one?"

"I will find one. I have to. There's no other time."

Her body made every dress beautiful, but Gwen continued to say, "I'm not sure Patrick will like any of these."

I was tired and wanted her to decide. I also wanted the day to be a success—my duty fulfilled, my sister happy. "I think Patrick will like anything you wear, Gwen. You should pick the dress you feel best in."

"Yeah, but I really want him to *love* it."

Her devotion to pleasing Patrick surprised me. Patrick loved Gwen in athletic shorts with sweaty hair snarled under her bike helmet.

When Gwen's friends left, we began the final appointment. This was Gwen's last chance. A second-floor showroom featured model-worthy saleswomen and vaulted ceilings. Dresses hung by designer, one from last season's Project Runway. Long plank floors, caramel-colored in the natural light, led to a private room. A saleswoman selected dresses for Gwen's body type. We sipped complimentary champagne as she tried short dresses, casual dresses, long dresses, formal dresses, expensive dresses, and sale dresses. An hour and a half later, she narrowed her choices to two. One, short and ethereal, looked like it belonged at a royal tea party. Petals covered the dress in an ombré effect, mutating from pink to white—elegant, formal, but not showy. The other, a traditional floor-length lace dress, featured a sweetheart neckline, cinched waist, and A-line skirt.

"I have to go home and show Patrick these pictures. I can't decide."

"What? Why?" I was tired and frustrated after eight hours of shopping. "Why didn't Patrick come if you wanted his opinion?" I wondered why I stumbled through racks and squeezed into changing stalls so Patrick could swipe through pictures.

"I don't know, Elizabeth. I thought I could decide but I really want Patrick's input. So much of my life is public, but this is our day. I want to make it perfect for both of us."

"Well, he better like one of these because there is no time for more shopping."

Mom must have sensed my frustration and fatigue. "Gwen just wants to be a stunning bride. And Patrick wants a memory of how beautiful she looked on their wedding day." I knew she was right.

The next day, before her flight, Gwen and Patrick revisited the shop. She called as we drove to Wisconsin. "I tried on both dresses for Patrick."

"And which one did he love?"

"Both."

"So now what?" I couldn't believe even with Patrick, she couldn't make a decision.

"I'm going to wear one for the ceremony and one for the reception."

I teased my typically economical and practical sister. "Aren't you fancy! Two dresses?"

"I think the long one looks like a wedding dress. And I like that. I really like the other one, but I just don't know if it's enough for the ceremony."

"It's your wedding. You should do what you want."

"I think I like them and I'm happy."

"You think?! Gwen, they're both great. You should feel good about your decision." I wanted her to be satisfied and not the least regretful.

Gwen said she scheduled alterations. "You should come and help with that too."

"Of course, I'll be there. And for the bachelorette party."

During the next weeks, Mom, Dad, and I traveled from Wisconsin to Minnesota several times for pre-wedding events.

NANCY

We arrived in Cable, Wisconsin—population 825, starting point of the American Birkebeiner and Gwen and Patrick's favorite biking getaway—just in time for the pre-wedding bike ride. On this rainy Friday, family and friends met at a cafe next to the trailhead. Fifteen riders wore waterproof gear, adding winter hats and lobster gloves for the 37°F chill. After the group pedaled off, Joel, Elizabeth, and I lingered in the cafe watching drizzle morph into giant, fluffy snowflakes. Anticipating the riders' return, we retrieved apples from our car— Honeycrisps in a wicker bushel basket—and met them at the trail.

"Whoa, it's cold out there." Gwen's nose dripped and her cheeks flushed. "And wet...but fun." The group dispersed quickly, hurrying to get in dry clothes. "See you tomorrow at the wedding!"

ELIZABETH

For the wedding weekend, the Lemieuxs and Jorgensens reserved all eight rooms in a woodsy, rustic lodge. The owner's dog greeted us, sloppy, wet, drooling on our bags. Wooden staircases took us to a second story entrance. In a gathering area, next to the fireplace, Dad perched on a cooler of beer, waiting for room assignments. Craig had a plan: Lemieuxs on the right, Jorgensens on the left.

"Let's shower and then meet downstairs for dinner at six," Gwen said.

That evening, waiting for Jane, we sipped wine and reviewed tomorrow's schedule. When she arrived, she carried boxes. "Gwen, I found this great sale on shoes. I thought you might like them for tomorrow. You still don't have flats, right?"

Gwen opened the box and held up a shoe. "They're perfect! Jane, thank you." We all agreed they were cute and well-suited to her petal dress.

"It was such a good deal, I got the same shoes for Paige and a pair for myself."

We chuckled at the thought of the mother of the groom, the groom's sister, and the bride in identical shoes.

The next morning, Jane, Mom, Paige, Gwen, and I mixed mimosas while Gwen debated hairstyles. We sat in a salon, opened just for us, where a stylist prepared her station. Every 30 minutes, one of us rotated to the chair.

"I want my hair like it normally is," Mom said. She typically lamented salon-done hair as not quite right.

"I need my hair done," I said, "and I want something casual: down with loose curls and a braid on top, kind of like a headband."

Gwen looked up wedding hairstyles on the internet while eating our to-go breakfast. Bagels and juice, fruit and cheese lined a bar-height table usually used for lipstick samples and mirrors. "Do you think I should have my hair down? Or half up?"

Gwen is notorious for bad hair days, frizziness, and panicky childhood moments about imperfect bangs. "Patrick says he wants to be wowed."

"Maybe have an idea and let the hairdresser decide?" I was amazed Gwen deferred to Patrick. In triathlon, she was opinionated and decisive, and now I saw a new side of my sister's personality. So much of their life centered on Gwen's training, Gwen's races, Gwen's nutrition. This weekend was about Gwen and Patrick, and she wanted them both to be happy.

As Gwen settled into the chair for a side-swept curly look, Jane and I shopped the downtown stores. I purchased earrings while Jane perused tchotchkes.

"Elizabeth, I have the cowbells. When we get there, we need to find a place for those."

"Yes, and put out the water bottles." Gwen and Patrick's gift to guests, a white athletic water bottle, featured a picture of them and their wedding date.

NANCY

Gwen's wedding day brought fairy tales to mind. It was autumn in Wisconsin—crimson and copper leaves, a breeze, a woody smoke in the air—and before the ceremony, nature added her white lace to the landscape. The soaring pine trees, the scent of decaying needles, the rustle of wildlife—no wonder Gwen and Patrick chose this place in the middle of the Chequamegon National Forest to escape and relax and now to get married.

The October afternoon felt like winter as we posed for outdoor pictures, toes numb in the frozen turf. Before each shot, we shed our winter coats and ran to assigned spots. Then we huddled to get warm before the next round of pictures.

At 4 p.m., we arrived in Cable's quaint downtown area, just a few blocks long, to find The Rivers Eatery where athletic paraphernalia decorated the walls—memorabilia from those who cycled or skied. To accommodate 150 guests, owners attached a white tent to the side entrance and installed portable heaters.

Waiters readied an S-shaped 14-tap bar while cooks stoked a 10-foot stone oven. After we set up decorations—cowbells, pictures, flowers—the owner/chef toured the grounds with us, ending in a back-of-property cabin where Gwen and Patrick waited.

"I opened this up for Gwen and Patrick to have privacy," he said.

"Is this where you'll say your vows?" I asked. Gwen told me they would exchange them before the ceremony. I guessed they would confirm a unique commitment—something no standard-issue script could say.

"Yes. And we don't have much time." Gwen held handwritten pages, and I sensed she wanted to be alone with Patrick.

"We'll see you in a few minutes," Patrick said. He stood with his arm around Gwen's shoulder, a calming influence as wedding day nerves seemed to make her irritable.

"Elizabeth, wait, I need you to help with this dress. It keeps falling down. Mom and Dad, we'll see you in a little bit."

ELIZABETH

I adjusted as Gwen tugged. "Stop doing that," I said. "It's not going to fall down. I barely got the thing to zip."

We stood between a bar and couches from the early nineties. "I just don't know if this looks okay."

The wedding officiant, Dennis, leaned on the bar, reviewing his notes. "It's perfect. You look amazing." She did—her hair swept to the side, curls resting on her shoulder, pearls gracing her neckline.

"I just never wear anything that's strapless. I feel like it's going to fall down."

Patrick walked over and kissed Gwen in a romantic, sweeping gesture. They embraced, and he said, "Gwennie, you are stunning."

"Okay, Elizabeth, go tell the band we're ready. They can play one more song and then we'll come in."

NANCY

While Gwen and Patrick said their vows, the crowd gathered. A bluegrass ensemble—violin, percussion, singer/guitarist tapping tambourine with her foot—jammed, and then switched to a processional as Gwen and Patrick entered.

Tall and erect, Gwen inhabited her strapless dress with an athletic, feminine grace. Creamy cotton lace hugged her slender hips before A-lining to the floor where it barely grazed Patrick's suit. Friends and family stood around white-clothed tables as Patrick escorted her down the makeshift aisle.

Immediate family waited at the front with Patrick's friend and octogenarian, Dennis. There, in a corner decorated with hay bales and corn stalks, he conducted the ceremony. Dressed in formal lederhosen, he said a prayer, explained the private vows, and prompted Gwen and Patrick to exchange rings. The gathering applauded, and Gwen and Patrick retraced their entrance. The ceremony lasted only minutes—and then the pizza party began.

Guests from around the world mingled. Family from Wisconsin. Family from North Dakota. Coach Jamie from New Zealand. Triathletes from Florida. Triathletes from Canada. College teammates from swimming and track. Ski buddies. Bike buddies.

I found Gwen's high school teammates and felt small, dwarfed by six-foot tall blonde swimmers. I talked with Jamie and a triathlete from Florida who thrilled at seeing their first big-flake snow. Jane interrupted conversations for cowbell ringing and newlywed kisses. Gourmet pizzas—cranberry barbecue, Thai peanut and pepper, basil and pine nut—appeared on the bar top and vanished.

174

My brother Steve found me. "So, will Gwen use Lemieux for her name?"

"Legally, yes. But she'll use Jorgensen professionally."

After an hour, Gwen disappeared and returned in her short ombré petal dress. I decided my daughter was a stunning bride as she moved table to table, comfortable and at ease. But I was surprised she wasn't cold. The white tent sat abandoned, frigid despite space heaters. I wore my coat, chilled from the draft. Others kept warm dancing in front of the band, modern steps to country blues. I walked to the dessert bar where a soda jerk scooped ice cream from a glass case. While there, I overheard Gwen's conversation with a friend.

"So, where is the honeymoon?"

"We don't have time now, but I told Patrick he could pick a location. On our next break, we'll go wherever he wants."

I admired Gwen's flexibility as she scheduled major life events around her demanding professional calendar.

ELIZABETH

Gwen had no official bridesmaids, but she wanted to thank the girls who attended her bachelorette party. "Elizabeth, is now a good time?"

"Perfect. I'll get the gifts. You get your friends." I wove through groups at the bar. From under the gift table, I pulled a cardboard box and toted it, excusing myself, drawing stares.

Gwen grabbed the box. "You girls are such an important part of my life. Thank you so much for coming to the bachelorette party and wedding. I want to thank you with these." When she pulled out the gifts, the half dozen girls gasped and giggled. UW running alums, they appreciated the practical, Gwen-themed gift: hot pink ASICS running flats. We put them on and stood in a circle for a photo of our matching shoes.

With no assigned tables, guests milled near their coats, purses, and water bottles, and a few people danced. I saw Gwen's godfather, Uncle Randie, at the bar. "Wanna get this party started?"

He grabbed my hand and twirled me toward the band. He spun me, dipped me, and others joined. Soon, there was a group of us—including a handful in hot pink ASICS—swinging and clapping, laughing, and two-stepping. Gwen cut in, and I stood near the tambourine, pumping my arm.

NANCY

The evening ended after midnight when the band packed up and Patrick's dad gave a long story-speech-toast in the tent, his words fogging the air. We said goodbye to people we wouldn't see for months and others we may never see again.

The next morning, at a cabin in the woods, we joined Dennis and his well-mannered but large, shaggy hound. A wood-fire stove warmed the kitchen and gathering space. Gwen seemed happy and content, helping Dennis with batter. We ate pancakes and bacon, Gwen smiling, kissing Patrick, holding his hand. Then, Gwen and Patrick signed the marriage license and we left for home.

A few days after the wedding, Gwen and Patrick invited both families for Christmas in Minnesota. I wondered how they could serve dinner for eight in their apartment above the bike shop. With bicycles hanging from the wall, a kitchen too small for a table, and seating for three in the living area, it seemed impossible. But we said yes.

****

Before Christmas, I would conduct holiday concerts with my high school singers. Our first performance was on December 9 with the Wisconsin Philharmonic Orchestra.

"Bizzie, would you please get the sopranos?" I asked. "And David, call the basses back." One hundred and twenty singers moved to the risers. "Did everyone get the email on tickets? If your parents pre-order, they'll get a discount on the $25 price."

"Mrs. J, can you review the schedule for next week?"

On Monday, we would practice with the orchestra, and on Tuesday we would present our concert at Carroll University, the choir singing the entire second half.

Over thirty years of teaching, I bragged about my good health, rarely using a sick day. But after school that Friday, chills and a fever grabbed me. On Sunday, I visited Urgent Care.

"Your swab tested positive for Influenza A," the doctor said. "I'll prescribe Tamiflu, but don't return to work until you are fever-free for 24 hours."

That evening, I texted my teaching partner.

> *Grace, I'm running a fever. Can you handle the Monday rehearsal? I'll be there for the Tuesday concert.*

When the fever continued, I considered my choices. Muscle through the performance, but risk infecting the choir? What if they all got sick before our home concert the next week? With unrelenting nausea, I couldn't imagine an hour under stage lights or a 45-minute bus ride. Feeling guilty and regretful, I stayed home—the only performance I missed in more than 30 years.

Confident I could recover, I returned to rehearsals, ignoring my queasy stomach and abdominal ache. But the next Sunday, an explosion of pain engulfed my abdomen and chest. Collapsed on the couch, the slightest movement mushroomed into pain. Was this influenza? Or something else?

Joel said, "Should we go to the emergency room?"

I wondered if I could walk to the car and wished he would tell me what to do. "Yes."

At 9 p.m., hunched in pain, I saw Elizabeth's friend Kassie working at admissions. As she whisked me to an exam room, I was grateful for the special treatment.

Nurses attached patches to my chest, drew blood, and checked vitals. A doctor ordered a CT scan. I returned from radiology, my abdomen swollen and rigid. I complained of pain, and the nurse nodded. "We're starting morphine."

Most emergency room visits end with a prescription—a remedy—but this doctor said, "Your CT scan shows irregularity. I contacted our surgeon." I never had surgery and the proposition should have frightened me, but I welcomed any solution for my pain.

At midnight, Dr. John Touzios—tall, youngish, balding—introduced himself. "I looked at your images, and your abdomen is a mess. You're full of air and abscess, but the CT doesn't show where the infection is coming from." He seemed frustrated—even a little angry—at the uncertainty, his forehead tinting red.

"What are my choices?"

"There aren't any. We have to surgically clean your abdomen. And we need to find the source of infection, but I have no idea where to look."

A morphine haze rendered me compliant as Dr. Touzios answered Joel's questions.

"How long will this take?"

"By the time my team gets here, it will be 1:30 a.m. We should finish up by 5:00."

A nurse leaned in. "The doctor wants you to use the bathroom. I don't think you can walk that far so I'll bring a commode."

I used it, dropped back on the gurney and yielded to the pre-op sedative.

ELIZABETH

Every morning at 5:15 a.m., when my phone sings, I hit snooze and check messages. This morning, uncharacteristically—alarmingly—I saw six missed messages from Dad.

Mom not so good.

Going to hospital

Call me.

She needs emeg surgery.

Going home.

Call when up.

Jittery and scared, tears formed, but I pulled them back to dial. I wiped my eyes. "Dad. Oh. What is going on?"

"She's going to be okay. But, bud, she's sick." I wondered if I woke him. He sounded tired and long pauses interrupted his words. "She had an abdominal infection and needed emergency surgery. They said it was good we came in when we did. We should call Gwen."

Dad's details typically are kind of close, almost right, but also utterly mixed up, and I still didn't understand. I never heard of surgery for an infection. "Dad, what about work?"

"You should tell them she won't be in for a while." Since Mom and I taught at the same high school, he assumed I would contact administration.

I gasped. "Sure, yes." *A while? What would I say? And who else should I call?* "I'm coming to the hospital."

"She's not awake and I'm not there now. Let's have pizza for lunch and then go."

Lunch? My stomach left me too heavy to sit up, much less plan meals. But Dad said Mom had hours before the sedative ebbed. "Okay, I'll call Gwen and tell her what's going on."

I tried to hack Mom's account on our school's web-based substitute program. But after several failed attempts, I doubted Mom set up her program, since she didn't use sick days. Still pushing back tears, I called Mom's teaching partner. "I don't know, Grace. It just sounds scary. Dad said it's good they went up there when they did. Emergency surgery for an infection? I don't really know. I thought she just had the flu. I'm going up to see her, and I will keep you posted."

"Liz, tell your mom not to worry about the concert." Grace promised to send prayers.

The secretary—unalarmed at my early morning quiver—told me, "Your mom needs to use the web-based system to request a sub."

I started crying. "You know, I'm just trying to do you a favor. She's not going to be in today or the rest of the week. She's not conscious, so she's not using the computer."

The secretary heard my panic and took a moment before saying, "Liz, I'm so sorry. Please let me know if there's anything we can do."

I called Gwen. "I don't know what's going on really. Dad just said that she is bad."

"Do you think we should come?"

"I think you should. You don't want to regret it if you don't."

It was good we came in when we did.

NANCY

I woke the next morning, December 15, with a 10-inch incision and anesthetic-induced nausea. Diagnosis: peritonitis. Source: unknown. Something more than flu invaded my body. The surgical team had flushed my abdominal space to eliminate bacteria and toxins. The doctor suspected diverticulitis but found no perforation.

"Did you get all the infection?" I asked.

"That would be impossible. We got as much as we could." Estimated hospital stay: seven days. Estimated recovery: eight weeks. I would not be conducting my choir concert on December 17 and would not return to the classroom until March.

Later that day, Elizabeth sat in my hospital room. "Mom, I cancelled your dentist appointment and called off your renaissance music rehearsal. Anything else?" She concealed her lifelong aversion to hospitals. I had a catheter, oxygen line, abdominal drains, and a tube down my nose and knew my condition must have unsettled her.

By the next day, Gwen appeared in my room, straight from a Minneapolis to Milwaukee flight. She stayed two days, and I felt guilty about interrupting her off-season training.

ELIZABETH

I didn't know what to say as Mom lay listless, gray, and weak, her hair unwashed since her surgery. This was so much more than sick. Mom could barely walk. She looked pregnant from the swelling and couldn't eat; she wasn't wearing her own clothes; she wasn't asking me lots of questions. I fought back tears and said, "It's bad," when people at work asked. I relayed Mom's morphine-filled messages to her teaching partner; I brought gifts from students and teachers; I reassured Mom with a video of the Christmas concert; I took notes when the nurses explained doctor-speak, and then sent mass texts to family and friends. I hoped the doctors could contain the infection. I just wanted to be able to say, "She's better," when people asked.

I refused to see Mom's scar—close to a foot, squiggling from her breasts to her pelvis. Dad described it as open, red, lumpy, and oozing green sludge. I felt like fainting.

On December 24, a week and a half after surgery, Mom was still hospitalized, and I called Gwen to discuss holiday plans.

"Well, what do you think? Should I come there again?" Gwen asked.

"If you ask Mom, she'll tell you to stay in Minneapolis and just relax before you leave for Australia."

"Patrick thinks we should come." Patrick and Gwen answer calls on speakerphone, and I imagined him signaling boarding a plane and eating Christmas dinner in the hospital cafeteria. "Can you pick us up at the airport and have dinner?"

"Dinner? Are you out of your mind? What's going to be open on Christmas Day?" I pictured my pantry: a few cans of tuna, half a bag of bagel chips, and some week-old fruit.

NANCY

On December 25, Joel, Elizabeth, Gwen, and Patrick crowded my room. I had worried about Gwen's tiny apartment, but here we were—five of us eating leftovers in hospital quarters. Elizabeth and Gwen simulated a holiday gathering, complete with organized games. Weary from infection, I clutched my Cards Against Humanity hand and argued with sagging eyelids.

At the end of the afternoon, Gwen and Patrick said goodbye with an awkward hug, encumbered by machines and an IV stand. "Gwen, I feel bad you flew here twice when you should be getting ready for Australia."

"We wanted to see you, Mom."

Our next visit would be in August at the Rio de Janeiro Olympic test event. I regretted losing holiday time and couldn't envision myself well enough to travel to Brazil.

On December 29, two weeks after surgery, I arrived home attached to a portable wound vac. Between naps, I forced myself to walk 10-minute intervals around the house. Joel cooked meals I only nibbled, and my students posted Facebook videos of rehearsals without me.

Six months earlier, Joel had retired. We lived on one income while I considered my own retirement. Being homebound gave me time to think.

Retirement would mean I no longer shared a career, in the same school, with Elizabeth. Retirement would mean I no longer heard the guitarist singing a story to his accompaniment, or the soprano silencing a room with one perfect note. I would no longer brave 90 freshmen boys singing out of tune. Or one freshman boy singing perfectly in tune. No more early American hymns. Barbershop quartets. Madrigals. Show tunes. Dance tunes. Dance captains. Vocal captains. Attendance captains. Field trips to New York. Field trips to nursing homes. Candlelight Christmas concerts. Tickets. Programs. Final rehearsals. Repetitive rehearsals. Endless rehearsals. Applause. Standing ovations. Parents who send thank you notes. Parents who send angry emails. Auditions. Summer camp. Summer workshops. Lunch with students. Dinner with students. Grades. Progress reports. Homecoming week. Shy freshmen. Exuberant sophomores. Know-it-all seniors. A paycheck. Checking on a sick student. Inservice. Curriculum. Meetings. Directing the pit orchestra. Phrases, intonation, expression, style, song.

I knew teachers who retired late and died before enjoying their freedom. Teaching was a pleasure, but I wanted time for other pleasures. If I returned to school the following year, I would face an overhauled administration. Due to political turmoil in the state of Wisconsin, Arrowhead High School would welcome a new superintendent, school psychologist, vice-principal, director of learning, and special education director. I decided it was time for a new choral director too. "Joel, I think I should retire at the end of the year. We'll have more time to travel and see Gwen, and we should have enough money." He agreed.

When I returned to school in March, I found my office decorated with balloons and streamers. I left them up the rest of the year. I composed a letter for the school board and told my students I would be retiring. There were some tears from next year's seniors, and I was reminded I would miss their raw emotion, their commitment to music, their respect and collaboration.

****

In the midst of 2014 sponsor obligations and a wedding, but before I got sick, Gwen and Patrick pursued one more dream.

Throughout Gwen's triathlon career, individuals and organizations invested in her. Gwen was grateful for USA Triathlon's Barb Lindquist; professional cyclist Tom Schuler; YMCA swim director Dave Anderson; high school swim coach Blaine Carlson; track coach Eric Lehmann; and swim friends Craig and Larry Lanza. To pay her fortune forward, Gwen and Patrick designed the Gwen Jorgensen Scholarship for under-19 draft-legal triathletes.

"Mom, could you proofread our application? And maybe fill out the online form? I want to know if the links work."

"So, you and Patrick are offering $5,000?"

"Yup, but we got matching funds from sport brand ROKA, the New York Athletic Club, and USA Triathlon. The total is up to $23,000."

"I saw online that companies are donating product too?"

"Oakley, Ceramic Speed, and PROJECT are partnering with us."

Gwen's success already benefited the triathlon world. She gave USA their first WTS women's win. Her success guaranteed three 2016 women's Olympic spots. Her victories inspired other athletes. But she wanted to contribute more than athletic achievement.

In the scholarship's inaugural year, Gwen and Patrick read over 100 applications and awarded 13 scholarships, but before they posted winners, Patrick said, "Gwen, I think you should call each one personally." Gwen demurred, preferring to remain a silent benefactor. But Patrick persuaded her and later told me, "Each of those kids was so excited just to hear Gwen's voice. I think it's part of the process—she has to make it personal for them." Gwen and Patrick publicly committed to continue the scholarship through 2016.

ELIZABETH

One year later, in 2015, Gwen asked for help with her second round of scholarship applications. "Could you read the applications and make two folders? Separate the outstanding ones from the rest?"

"I'll have time tomorrow." Gwen just sent three pairs of ASICS shoes, two tank tops, and 12 pairs of socks. This was the least I could do.

I opened over 100 applications. Where would I begin? Who was I to decide a person worthy? I relied on teacher skills, looking for specifics—and separating the best, proved easier than I anticipated. From my list, Gwen selected winners. She announced five recipients—three individuals and two teams—and the responses made me proud, humbled, and thankful.

Mallory Kell, a 10-year-old member of the winning Z3 team, wrote,

> *I wanted to thank you for being such a good role*
> *model and for sponsoring Z3! You are so inspiring!*

Kyleigh Spearing wrote,

> *Thank you so much for providing the scholarship*
> *opportunity for junior athletes. You are a great*
> *mentor to us, and we all very much look up to you as*
> *a role model on not only how to race, but also how to*
> *act as humble and respectful athletes.*

Emma Agnus wrote,

> *Your inspiration inspires me to keep doing triathlon.*
> *You are a great role model for us kids. I am a youth*

elite athlete so I have lots of time to keep getting better. With your inspiration I will keep trying my best and working very hard. Thanks again for all that you have done.

My sister did more than win championships—she inspired people. I was proud to help.

CHAPTER 7

Domination Station

2015

NANCY

Gwen's primary goal for the 2015 season was automatic qualification for the 2016 Olympic Games. Two USA athletes could qualify at a July test event by finishing top eight. For athletes who didn't automatically qualify, each country established criteria. Some nations used individual races, some relied on discretion, others counted Olympic points accumulated in ITU races. Many competitors would not be chosen until weeks before the Games.

In addition to the Rio test event, Gwen would race the World Triathlon Series in Australia, Asia, South America, and Europe, and the Grand Final in Chicago. Competitors vied for the World Championship using points from five WTS races plus the Grand Final. The mid-season Rio race offered neither points nor prize money.

When the season began in March, I had just returned to work after recovering from surgery. Joel, Elizabeth, and I planned travel to Rio de Janeiro and Chicago. We would watch the remaining events via live streaming.

The first race, on March 6 in Abu Dhabi, spawned speculation. Who achieved early season fitness? Who trained at altitude? Who hired a new coach? Three top Americans, including Gwen, married in the off-season—would life changes affect performance?

As reigning World Champion, Gwen was the favorite, and experts predicted her string of WTS victories (five consecutive, eight total) could inflate her confidence balloon—or explode it.

I wondered how Gwen would perform and about safety in the Middle East, where religious extremism, political turnover, and border wars created unrest.

Calm. That's how I would describe my experience in Abu Dhabi. It was my first time in the Middle East, a surreal place. The buildings were magnificent, the water was clear, but super salty, and [one day], it was so hot, there was a heat haze.

Hummus, baba ganoush, and dates were plentiful and delish. Alcohol, on the other hand, was not common. In fact, our hotel was a "dry" hotel.

As race day approached, I wasn't as nervous as I've been in the past. I was relieved to be relaxed; it was a nice alternative to my last WTS (Edmonton 2014).

During my week in Abu Dhabi, I was invited to a local's house for dinner. Being able to get out of the hotel and eat a home cooked meal when I'm at a race is refreshing. I was able to catch up with an old friend, Omar Nour (who I hadn't seen in over two years) and a few others from the triathlon scene. Our hosts, Marc and Mary Carol, were incredibly generous. They welcomed us with wine, water, cheese, and nuts, followed by a healthy

dinner of chicken, fish, salads, quinoa, and desserts. I
left full, happy, and at peace. Maybe this is the reason I
was so calm leading into the race.

Situated on the Persian Gulf, Abu Dhabi was windy and warm. With air at 26°C (78.8°F) and water at 22°C (71.6°F), swimmers dove in sans wetsuit. Joel and I watched from home while Elizabeth viewed from her house.

"I think I just saw her," Joel said after swimmers entered the water. "Way in the back."

"Are you positive?"

He leaned toward the screen. "Pretty sure—and she looks slow."

In the sprint distance race, with only 750 meters to swim, Gwen exited the water 38 seconds down. I wondered if pressure from the winning streak impinged her performance.

A lead pack of 11 cyclists formed, dropping Gwen to a chase pack 26 seconds behind. Up front, USA's newlyweds Sarah True—formerly Groff—and Katie Zaferes—formerly Hursey—pushed the pace with Bermuda's Flora Duffy (World XTERRA Champion) and Sweden's Lisa Norden (2012 Olympic silver medalist).

As the competitive season reignited, so did my anxiety. I had seen Gwen crash several times, with significant injury at the 2013 Grand Final. Early in Gwen's career, USA Triathlon's Barb Lindquist predicted, "Gwen will crash. All triathletes crash." But commentator Emma Snowsill (2008 Olympic gold medalist) maintained smart racers learn from crashes so an error is not repeated. I hoped Gwen learned quickly.

The leaders increased their advantage to 60 seconds. Of 64 starting athletes, Gwen entered the run in 30th.

I exited transition on a mission to test myself on the
run. By the end of the first (of two) laps, I saw the
current leader: Flora Duffy.

In the first half of the five-kilometer run, Gwen made up 47 seconds, clocking bursts at 18 to 23 kilometers (11 to 14 miles) per hour. She advanced to fourth, 13 seconds behind Duffy. Two USA athletes—Zaferes and Jerdonek—ran second and third.

"So, what do you think?" I asked.

Joel nodded. "For sure. Make up thirteen seconds in one lap? She's got this."

During the second and final lap, Gwen passed Zaferes with an encouraging butt-tap, and I said, "You're right. I think she can catch Duffy." If the pressure of the winning streak troubled Gwen's swim and bike, it didn't seem to hinder her run.

> *I was shocked I was making up so much time on the run, and before I knew it I was in the lead. As I crossed the finish line and looked over my shoulder, I couldn't have been happier to see USA teammate Katie (Hursey) Zaferes cross the line in second for her first ever WTS podium. Team USA had five women [Zaferes, Jerdonek, True and Donner] in the top ten! I'm proud of our country and proud to be a part of triathlon history with the other USA women.*

With the Abu Dhabi victory, Gwen had six consecutive WTS wins and nine career wins. Headlines included "Gwensanity Reigns in Abu Dhabi." On Slowtwitch.com, Timothy Carlson wrote, "Jorgensen's victory was her sixth straight in the prestigious WTS series, a dominance calling to mind the 12 straight World Cup wins...by Portugal's Vanessa Fernandes a decade ago."

Each time Gwen's name appeared online, I received a Google Alert and printed articles for her scrapbook. At work, I mentioned Gwen's Abu Dhabi win to my teaching partner. "Grace, let's show the five-minute recap. The kids enjoyed replays when Wolfgang subbed for you, and they picked up lessons of perseverance."

"Yes. I would love to see it too." Although young enough to be my daughter, Grace played an equal role, accompanying, conducting, teaching. Still, she considered me a mentor and was eager to find new musical—or motivational—ideas.

"It's fascinating to watch the kids' reactions," I said. "The gender differences are so stereotypical." As predicted, the Treble Choir watched politely, and the Baritone Chorale cheered and chanted, begging for details about athletic training, splits, and Olympic glory. And this batch of students seemed to understand Gwen's defeats and setbacks—challenges that often precede success.

Two weeks later, Gwen raced in Auckland, New Zealand. In 2013, cold conditions pulled her from the race, and in 2014, she finished 12th. On March 28,

2015, conditions were humid with air temperature at 22.9°C (73°F) and water at 21.5°C (71°F). The non-wetsuit swim left her 47 seconds behind, allowing nine leaders to get away on the bike. Snowsill offered Gwen's possible thought: "...have game plans up your sleeve...not to dwell on where am I, what haven't I done. It's a matter of where am I right now, and what am I going to do."

Gwen's chase pack worked together and caught the leaders. But Snowsill speculated that riding in a large group would be as challenging as riding in a chase pack—with so many riders, it would be difficult to find a safe position and survive against tactics. Snowsill said contenders would be thinking, "If [Gwen's] further back in the [pack], let's keep putting the pressure on, let's see how much energy we can take out of her." As Gwen persevered, Snowsill said, "She's here to prove that she's an all-around triathlete, and I think that's something she's definitely starting to do." As though to prove the point, Gwen shot to the front—a move she usually reserved for foot racing.

"Wow! Did you see that?" I said.

"That'll get her into transition ahead of the others, and I'm sure she and Jamie worked on that move."

Gwen led the run and finished with a 1:38 advantage. Teammate Zaferes finished second to once again join Gwen on the podium. I thought marriage suited them both.

ELIZABETH

In 2012, after Gwen's first Olympic qualification, her face popped up in magazines, on billboards, and in advertisements. Friends tagged Gwen in Facebook posts, pointing out her presence in *SELF Magazine*, in *O, The Oprah Magazine*, and on the cover of *Milwaukee Magazine*. A former teammate, Kristy Brager, commented, "Well I knew you were getting to be big but right next to Oprah?!? Now that's some serious celeb status!!" Gwen's best friend, Tristine Horner, saw Gwen on a billboard above Chicago's Blarney Stone bar and commented, "Gwen madness...How cool is this, right by my house!"

I wanted a copy of it all and called Mom. "Did you see *Milwaukee Magazine*? Do you have a copy?"

"No, I just saw it on Facebook. If you're getting one, can you pick up an extra for Dad and me?" Mom kept scrapbooks for each of us. Mine ended after college, as expected. But Gwen kept competing, and hers kept growing—Mom buying more and more plastic sleeves and binders, inserting more and more newspaper clippings, internet printouts, and race pamphlets.

At Barnes & Noble, I pointed out Gwen to the cashier. "This is my sister."

Perhaps not believing, or perhaps not familiar with triathlon, he barely smiled. "Okay. That will be $22.34."

Wow, magazines are expensive. I positioned my purchase inside the green bag, careful not to tear the pages, thankful the plastic prevented dousing in the rain. At home, my stack swelled.

In 2015, the media blitz continued, and Gwen emailed me an early proof.

> *Hey all,*
>
> *Haven't read this article, but if you like you can :)*
> *Don't publish as it's not yet in circulation :)*
>
> *Gwen*

I read it and found mention of me: "As a child growing up, [Gwen] Jorgensen's parents asked their children to choose one sport and something musical, and following in the steps of her older sister, Elizabeth, the violin was the instrument of choice, and Jorgensen dedicated herself to swimming."

I responded to Gwen's email.

> *YES! I MADE A MAGAZINEEEE! Which one is this?*
> *I need a copy!*

Gwen said it was *Triathlon & Multi Sport Magazine* (an Australian publication). I stuck to what millennials know—the internet—and emailed customer service.

I stored my magazine collection in a Tupperware bin, opening it for friends and family on special occasions. "Be careful. This is my only copy."—"Please, don't crinkle the pages."—"Wash your hands. They look greasy."

Around that time, I planned a living room makeover. Exploring design ideas, I surveyed my bin. I slipped magazines into frames and arranged them in two rows of four—Gwen's face repeated eight times on covers, advertisements, and brochures. On my shelves, I added a World Champion bike rack ID, Chicago VIP credentials, and Edmonton cowbells. I gave Gwen a FaceTime tour.

"You're acting like I'm dead. It looks like a shrine," Gwen said.

"Seriously? That's not the response I wanted. I love it." I adjusted my phone, showing Gwen how the frames complimented the knickknacks.

"I don't know, Elizabeth. It's a bit much. And in your living room? Don't you think this might be better in the basement?"

My basement rec room featured sports memorabilia: an Aaron Rodgers matted print, Milwaukee Brewers bobbleheads, and my city league dart trophies. "Gwen, no one goes in the basement."

"Yeah, that's my point."

"Did you hear Mom is doing the same thing?"

"What? No!" I heard Gwen panic.

"Yeah, except she's doing it in your bedroom."

Gwen sighed. "I guess that's better."

NANCY

The third race of the season found Gwen in Gold Coast, Australia, on April 11.

> *I was honored to wear #2 for the Gold Coast WTS. The #1 slot was left open to honor the great Jackie Fairweather. The #1 bike rack in transition had Jackie's name, number, and a rose. Jackie passed away in November of 2014. She was a World Champion in triathlon and duathlon, and active in the sport of triathlon after her sporting career ended. Although I never met Jackie, I have a huge respect for what she did for our sport. She was a mentor for my coach, Jamie Turner, and she apparently loved chocolate, which makes her an instant winner. On race morning, I racked my bike in transition across from Jackie's name and got ready for the race.*

With air at 27.3°C (81.1°F) and water at 24.6°C (76.3°F), women entered from the beach without wetsuits. Gwen's solid swim put her in a lead group of cyclists that included teammates Sarah Groff and Katie Zaferes, and Flora Duffy from Bermuda, and Lucy Hall from Great Britain.

After only a few minutes, live streaming showed Spain's Tamara Gomez Garrido sitting on the curb. Commentators mentioned Gomez's other life as a medical student, and I wondered if her split focus prevented adequate training.

The course's 180 degree turns, repeated several times, thwarted more riders: Carolina Routier of Spain, Natalie Van Coevorden of Australia, Margit Vanek of Hungary, Jolanda Annen of Switzerland, Zsófia Kovacs of Hungary, Miriam Casillas García of Spain. With each crash, my chest hammered, knocking loose the optimism instilled by Gwen's solid swim performance.

> *I felt like I took the corners as good as, if not better than, others in our group. After the race was my favorite moment. Flora Duffy came up to me and said, "Your bike skills have really improved. I was riding behind you one lap on the corners, and you were really good...I hope that's not mean." I laughed and thanked her. It means so much to get a compliment from a peer.*

> *There was a crash around the far turn around. I was behind it. I saw it happen, went on my brakes, made it around the crash site, then had to bridge up in the headwind....the rest of the race (after about 2-3 laps) I took my turn and rolled thru and no one attacked me. It was so nice, everyone working together. I never felt in danger of being dropped. There were corners I knew I could do better than others and loved those sections and doing them fast.*

As Gwen remained in the lead pack, commentator Matthew Keenan said, "[She's] very humble about [her] achievements. Jorgensen is almost embarrassed that she's won seven races in a row. She's very quick to try and deflect away and say, 'I don't know what all the fuss is about.' But clearly, she's the one with the target on her back..."

For years, WTS races featured an array of gold medalists from an international field. It was unusual for one athlete to conquer cold water and hilly terrain, then oppressive heat and technical turns, then choppy waves and cobblestone roads. When media asked Gwen how she accomplished so many wins, she credited Jamie, Patrick, and her training partners. Emma Snowsill recognized Jamie's role too: "Jamie...teaches them a lot of things about how to act, how to race, how to behave, and you have to give a lot of credit to him...The two of them have formed a formidable force."

Gwen entered the run with seven athletes. Taking the lead, she gained nine seconds on the next two runners—Zaferes and True—and ran solo up front, eyes hidden by chartreuse-rimmed glasses, bright orange shoes barely skimming the pavement. In world rankings, Gwen, Zaferes and True created a USA powerhouse. Could they sweep the podium? Only once, with the 2011 Australian team, did that happen.

During lap two, Gwen increased her advantage over True and Zaferes to 45 seconds. The rest ran 1:28 back. Then, Gwen glanced at the board under the penalty tent (as athletes are required to do each lap) and saw number 2. She lifted both hands in a gesture Keenan described as, "But why? Like being called up to the principal's office."

"She loses 15 seconds? What for?" I asked. Gwen had explained that swim gear and bike helmet must be deposited in the assigned box after each respective stage, but I had seen no infraction.

"Not sure," Joel said. "The announcer said something about not racking her bike, but I didn't see it."

"Is it littering?" I knew water bottles could only be discarded in designated zones.

Although she could serve the penalty on any lap, Gwen immediately left the course to stand under the tent. Over the official's shoulder, she monitored his stopwatch. At the official's signal, Gwen resumed her run—and led True and Zaferes by 31 seconds.

I wondered why she pushed herself. Given her lead, she could have relaxed her pace, but as Keenan said, "She races like [her] objective is to get to the finish line completely empty." A ribbon of spit streamed from her chin to chest—she told me later, she was too focused to notice it.

At the end of lap three, Gwen led True and Zaferes by over a minute. Further back, Andrea Hewitt of New Zealand challenged Duffy for fourth, trying to close a 10-second gap.

Running toward the finish, Gwen wiped saliva, raised her sunglasses, and recognized fans with high-fives. She grabbed the tape, ran a few more steps, and lifted her arms, smiling for photographers. Dropping the tape, she bent over to redo her sweaty hair into a top knot before turning to congratulate the next finishers. When True and Zaferes came in second and third, USA celebrated the second sweep in WTS history. Hewitt won her battle for fourth, passing Duffy in the final meters.

With a solid performance in all three disciplines, Gwen was asked in a post-race interview if this was a perfect swim-bike-run, regardless of the penalty.

"I don't think you ever have a perfect race, but I was really thrilled to come out of the water and be in the front pack right away, and I mean one-two-three for team USA—it really couldn't get any better, looking over there and seeing three girls on the podium and...to be able to stand up there and hear the national anthem with all three girls."

Once again, Gwen bounced the recognition ball to her country women, sharing the spotlight. When asked about her penalty, Gwen seemed baffled. "Not really sure what happened there...going to have to go back and ask some people." Later, she posted a blog entry:

> *Well, I racked my bike and it fell over, but the front*
> *wheel was still in so I thought I was fine. Guess not...*
> *live and learn.*

Curious about the rules governing ITU races, I downloaded the 176-page *ITU Competition Rules* and was overwhelmed by its detailed technical jargon. I read the section on bike racking:

> *For the second transition: In any direction, with both*
> *sides of the handlebar, both brake levers or the saddle*
> *within 0.5 m of the rack number or name plate. Bike*

must be racked in a way does not block or interfere
with the progress of another athlete.

I remembered Lindquist telling Gwen to learn something from each race and realized the sport could take years to master.

Answering post-race questions about her eighth consecutive victory, Gwen said, "I don't think about that. When you say it, it sounds really weird. I look back at the triathlon legends and it doesn't seem like I'm at that level at all...So I just try to come in here and do my best."

I thought I understood Gwen's reluctance to celebrate her domination. While the world seemed confident about each successive victory, the string of wins became irrelevant when Gwen placed her toe on the start line—each race a new challenge to be conquered.

****

Pressure mounted as Gwen prepared for the May 16 Yokohama race. Could she win Yokohama for the third straight year? Could she extend her year-long winning streak? Could she earn a ninth consecutive victory, her twelfth WTS win?

Two of the strongest American women—True and Zaferes—skipped the race, but USA still brought nine women competitors, demonstrating a growing dominance.

I added Yokohama to my weather app and worried about the predicted rain. On May 16, the 19°C (66.2°F) water temperature put women in wetsuits. On the road, they found air temperatures of 22.6°C (72.7°F) and puddles under light precipitation.

Gwen exited the swim in 12th, 16 seconds adrift. She made up time in transition and joined the lead pack for nine soggy bike laps, each featuring 20 turns. Through the rain-spotted camera lens, I saw white painted lines Shepley described "like ice in wet conditions." When I wasn't too nervous to watch, I searched for Gwen's new helmet—the silver, yellow, and blue images of Wisconsin's Bucky Badger, Minnesota's butterfly, and Red Bull's logo.

I got out of the water and didn't think I had a great
transition, but somehow I got on the road, got in
my shoes, and when I went to the first U-turn, there

were only two girls in front of me! No idea how that happened.

Through several laps, Gwen remained at the front, and I wondered if she was there to avoid potential crashes. Or was it confidence? She led the group with Sarah-Anne Brault, a Wollongong Wizard from Canada.

Gwen's lead pack grew from 10 riders to 22, and eventually 34, indicative of a slow pace, and I was grateful for cautious riding. Still, several athletes crashed, including Japanese favorites Ai Ueda and Juri Ide who both continued in the race.

> *I knew [our lead pack] would get caught as no one really was working together and people were going way too SLOW around all the corners. I hated being behind anyone going into a corner. Girls would be on the brakes while cornering, and all I thought was they were going to crash, and I need to be on the front...I would go around a corner and think, "We can go around this faster, why are they braking so much?!"*

> *One nice distraction was the rain—it kept me alert, and I think this made the bike ride feel shorter than a normal 40km.*

As they approached transition, cyclists jockeyed for position. After leading the entire race, Gwen was pushed back and entered transition in 22nd. "That's not a great transition for Gwen," Shepley said. "Actually, it's terrible. But the reality is she doesn't have to have a great transition."

"It shouldn't matter, should it?" Trevor Harris said.

Shepley responded with Gwen's possible thoughts: "I'll catch you a little further down the road, but I will catch you."

Gwen ran mid-pack, her frame towering above the others, slick dark hair pulled away from her face. Then, she moved to the front with USA's Renee Tomlin on her heels.

Still in the first lap, she surged, and Shepley said, "Gwen is off and gone. The day is over. Victory number nine is in the books. More interesting for me are the subplots." I relaxed too, assured Gwen would win her third consecutive Yokohama race, ninth consecutive victory, and twelfth WTS race.

Shepley commented on Gwen's running: "There's just nobody at this point that has her capacity. And it's going to be interesting. She has to carry the challenge for the next 14 to 15 months until we get to Rio."

He made me think. Could Gwen keep winning for another year and half? Could she dodge injury? Could she win under Olympic pressure?

Harris asked if a runner is born or trained.

Shepley said, "Gwen was born phenomenal, and she has been phenomenally improved upon by the coaching staff. And at this point, she is moving herself into the position of greatest runner to ever do the sport of triathlon. We've talked about this in the past, and it would be a small handful of...Vanessa Fernandes...Carol Montgomery, who went to the Olympics in the 10,000 meters and the triathlon. In the history of 30 plus years, those are the...greatest women I ever saw run in a triathlon who could also swim and bike."

I agreed with Shepley. Gwen possessed natural talent, but coaching and hard work transformed her gifts into championships.

Apparently unaware of her 73-second advantage, Gwen approached the finish line with a glance over her shoulder.

Answering a post-race question on her improved swim, she said, "Coach Jamie Turner. That's it. Simple as that." On her win streak: "Every race, I get really nervous and you never know how it's going to go." On today's race: "The whole race hurt. It hurt a lot."

Harris seemed to search for insight into the win, the winning streak, Gwen's improvement. But there were no magic formulas. Gwen invested in a world-class coach. She trained and suffered. From the outside, she seemed a phenom, a curiosity, a name for the books; inside Gwen's head, there were just measured decisions and persistence.

ELIZABETH

More interviews flooded sports media, and in each one, Gwen credited her sponsors as vital to her success. In addition to monetary patrons like Sleep Number, The Island House, Columbia Threadneedle, USA Triathlon, Red Bull, and 24 Hour Fitness, ASICS supplied Gwen with shoes and apparel, ROKA with swim gear, HED with wheels, Oakley with sunglasses, and PROJECT with compression wear. The support allowed Gwen to train fulltime with an international group and travel for competitions. She was fortunate. Others worked day jobs or were full-time students, their energies fragmented.

I knew about Gwen's sponsors, but wondered about USA support. Team USA's website stated:

> *"Unlike most of its competitors worldwide, the U.S. Olympic Committee does not receive government funding for Olympic programs. Instead, Team USA's athletes are funded by you—fans who believe in our athletes' Olympic dreams. Your donation equips our athletes with what they need to excel on the world stage: state-of-the-art training centers, coaches, trainers, and sports medicine staff who keep our athletes healthy. Your donation also supports the cutting-edge technology and innovation that help our athletes break through to the medal stand."*

But what did this mean for Gwen? In an email, Gwen said there were three levels of funding for USA Triathlon, and she was on the top—Gold Level. She received travel reimbursements, a coaching stipend, and $5,000 quarterly. According to Team USA:

> *"This funding is intended to support athletes' travel domestically and internationally to ITU events. Travel reimbursements in addition to this will be available based on athlete performances at a given event."*

Gwen said:

> *"But Jamie doesn't receive the stipend because he is not USAT Certified. [It's been] a long battle and one that really annoys me and a bit controversial in my mind...anyway...they pay for my flights to approved*

WTS races [but] they do not pay for anything for Patrick and Jamie...I do get a small camp budget to pay for my flights to camps such as training in AUS/Spain. I could get gear from USAT if I wanted, but I have my own sponsorships. I do have a [USA Triathlon] SRM...which is a power meter on the bike."

I considered Gwen's expenses: flights and hotels, Jamie's bonuses, her agent's percentage. Gwen's compensation provided a comfortable income, but I knew she scolded Patrick when he spent too much on coffee or organic eggs. Gwen, arguably the most dominant triathlete in the world, received nothing close to the financial rewards of Michael Phelps, Usain Bolt, or Gabby Douglas. Was it because triathlon wasn't high profile like swimming, or track, or gymnastics? Was it because Gwen's personality didn't command the spotlight? Or was it only a matter of time?

NANCY

To celebrate her achievements, Gwen's sponsor, Specialized, designed a custom bike. Gwen already rode Specialized race, commuter, and mountain bikes. The $9,000 Amira racing bike was one more piece of equipment to enhance her training and competition. The bike was personalized with Gwen's professional and married names, and custom painted with World Champion stripes and the Wollongong Wizards logo.

I didn't understand the technical terms, but assumed it was state of the art: S-Works 170mm, with SRM power meter spider (110bcd). Her cassette was a 11-25t Dura-Ace cs-9000. She had an Oura expert gel 155 saddle. It was tested in the Specialized wind tunnel (win tunnel) where experts analyzed resistance and speed in relation to Gwen's body position and gear ratio. It was a fancy bike for a woman who learned cycling only five years ago.

****

In the spring and summer of 2015, Joel, Elizabeth, and I shared Gwen's preoccupation with the Rio test event. We studied pictures of her new bike. We read articles. We watched YouTube clips. We discussed Gwen's competitors. Life centered around ITU triathlon, Gwen's races dominating our thoughts.

Before Rio, Gwen raced two WTS sprint events, the first on Saturday, May 30, in London. Patrick's parents joined them for the week. Two days before the race, Gwen called from her hotel room where she ate dinner in bed while Patrick, Jane, and Craig enjoyed a restaurant meal. "Is it something you ate? Or an infection maybe?" I asked.

"No. It's just a cold. I'll be fine."

The next day, when Gwen skipped the press conference and media reported she had the flu, I called Elizabeth. "Did you talk to your sister? Is she okay?"

"She sounded congested, but she said it's just a cold."

I relaxed—if anything were serious, Gwen would tell Elizabeth.

On race day, our computer streamed the familiar ITU opening sequence. As cameras focused on athletes, the opening music triggered tension and anticipation. In my classroom, I emphasized the importance of music at momentous events, this race tradition a perfect example. Percussion joined voices—generic vowel sounds repeated in a short rhythmic phrase, again and again, escalating every few seconds. In a building crescendo, 30 seconds of the ceremonious beat intensified suspense.

Water was 15.2°C (59.4°F) with air at 16.2°C (61.2°F) for the 750-meter swim. World rankings placed three Americans in the top five—Gwen number one, Katie Zaferes two, and Sarah True four. Cameras showed fans in scarves, hats, and rain ponchos, while Gwen, one of 64 competitors, wore a wetsuit, thermal cap, and regulation swim cap. She vied for her 10th straight WTS victory.

Music stopped and the customary solo drum, like a booming heartbeat, signaled the imminent start. Along the pontoon, loudspeakers ensured every racer would hear the horn simultaneously, and when it sounded, the line of swimmers dove in unison.

Ten minutes later, women exited. "Where is she?"

"Not sure," Joel said as the timing board refused to reveal her name.

Scary possibilities scrolled in my head. Then the camera spied her removing her wetsuit.

"Maybe she lost her timing chip." Commentators confirmed his guess, and my pulse calmed.

The top three Americans joined a lead pack of seven, and announcers speculated about another USA sweep while chasers pursued, 30 seconds back. In the 30-minute ride, the leaders maintained their advantage.

Dismounting, the Zaferes-True duo led; Gwen soon made it a trio. With stars-and-stripes in concert at the front, Shepley said, "That could be the US Olympic team right there."

By run's midpoint, Gwen manufactured a six-second lead, True and Zaferes defending second and third. Shepley assessed the remaining American athletes, and said with their times, "[They] could be the national champion in one of 20 other countries and not even make [the USA] Olympics team because the depth of the field in the US is just that strong."

Gwen appeared healthy as she ran, arms loose, stride long, while behind, True and Zaferes traded spots. But when Gwen came down the chute, I knew she wasn't herself. Her glasses stayed in place while her arms pumped mechanically—no signature wave or high-fives for the crowd. Her expression remained serious. She grabbed the tape, stumbled, and bent over, hands on her knees. After a long ten seconds, she straightened, raised her sunglasses, and offered a weak smile. As her expression collapsed into a grimace, she bent again for several seconds before pulling upright to hug her teammates—Zaferes, the silver medalist and True, the bronze.

After a typical race, some athletes collapse to the ground or bend at the waist, heaving for breath. For Gwen, those displays were unprecedented; her actions this day suggested illness.

I heard congestion in Gwen's voice as she answered questions. "Yeah, it was really tough, but I know when I race against my competitors, not everyone is one hundred percent. People are sick, they're coming back from injury. You just have to be able to perform under any condition. It was really hard today, but I gave it my all." I was not surprised she minimized her illness, and then segued to the sweep. "USA one-two-three, I really hope they have three flags to fly today when they play the national anthem." I hadn't realized when USA swept the podium in Australia, the camera never focused on the flagpoles; the unanticipated sweep left organizers short on star-spangled banners.

Just as music started the day, a patriotic hymn ended it. Organizers wisely stocked up on USA flags and flew all three to the familiar, *Oh, say can you see.*

Online stories reported Gwen's victory. Only then did I see pictures of her on the bike, mucous streaming from her nose to handlebars.

Gwen mentioned her illness in a post-race blog.

> *Race morning I wrote in my journal that I felt "good enough to compete, but not well enough to be confident...Remember this is good practice for performing under any circumstance. Enjoy the challenge, push yourself, focus on the controllables." I wasn't excited to race like I normally am. I had doubts, and I didn't know what to expect. But, when race time arrived, I dove in, giving it my all.*

When I talked to Gwen, she admitted the race was difficult, and I thought of the many times I refused to take a sick day. It took hospitalization to keep me in bed. Did she learn my habits? Or did genetics bestow this trait along with athletic talent? I thought back to Gwen's final collegiate race in Fayetteville, Arkansas, when she ran on a stress fracture. Although in pain, she refused to see a doctor, fearing he would forbid running. I felt confident she could now discern injury that required attention from mild illness that could be tolerated safely.

Before she left London, Gwen said, "I have my mid-season break so I can rest now—we'll be in San Sebastian for a few days." She talked about Michelin stars and famous chefs. When she tweeted about food, I knew she felt better.

On Monday morning, in my school mailbox, I found a *Milwaukee Journal Sentinel* article, clipped from the sports page. Next to Gwen's name, a colleague wrote in red ink, "Congratulations! You must be so proud." ITU triathlon is not high profile. Not every teacher in my building followed Gwen's career. Many didn't understand Olympic distance triathlon. Some never heard of the sport. When I retired in six weeks, I would miss the cross-country coach who always knew Gwen's latest result, the principal who inquired about each race, and the student who competed in junior triathlons, inspired by Gwen's performances.

On July 18, in Hamburg, Germany, Gwen competed one last time before the Rio test event. She wore number one, Zaferes two, and True four. Also in the top twenty were USA's Renee Tomlin (14th) and Kirsten Kasper (15th).

With dry roads and sun, Shepley pronounced weather conditions perfect for the non-wetsuit swim. Water registered 21.7°C (71.1°F), air 27.9°C (82.2°F). As swimmers concluded the 10-minute swim by stroking through the Alster's 50-meter tunnel, they emerged to Hamburg's famously enthusiastic crowds. Gwen exited fifth, bolted up the concrete ramp, and climbed two flights of stairs. She removed cap and goggles in transition and joined a lead pack of 13 cyclists that included True. Zaferes rode with the chasers.

On the first few laps, as Gwen lingered toward the back, Shepley reminded viewers about the preponderance of accidents for athletes in poor position.

"I'm glad she made the front pack, but why doesn't she move up?" I relieved my anxiety by scrubbing sink stains.

During the third of six laps, Joel said, "She's leading the pack now."

"Really? At the front?" I walked to the television.

"Never mind. A German took over." Each time riders passed the grandstand, a German athlete took the lead, igniting home crowd cheers.

As Shepley mentioned Gwen's bid to win her 11th consecutive race, he said she was "now doing things we have never seen in the history of the sport...Nobody has had ten and looking like there may be an almost impossibility of finding a way to stop them. She's won by an average of 21 seconds in 2014. She's won by an average of 57 seconds in 2015." I hoped for one more win to give her confidence at the Olympic test event in two weeks.

By the end of the bike, two groups merged and 26 riders entered transition. True led the run with Great Britain's Non Stanford and Vicky Holland, but Gwen's feet, in bright yellow race flats, propelled her—controlled and focused behind blue sunglasses—to make it a two-nation quartet that left 20 other countries behind.

After running one lap, Gwen and Holland battled for gold while True and Stanford fought for bronze. Suddenly, prolonged video focused on the back of the field.

"Why aren't they showing the leaders?" Joel asked.

Shepley apologized for technical difficulties. Viewers would rely on stationary cameras until motorcycle video returned. It meant long intervals with the leaders out of sight.

In our next view, Holland led Gwen by a step. True and Stanford ran side by side, and Zaferes ran herself into the top eight.

"The camera's gone again!" We waited, monitoring the back of the field.

As a finish line camera picked up coverage, we saw Gwen initiate a surge toward the blue carpet. Holland moved to match her pace. With no time to think about photos, Gwen left her sunglasses in place, worked her arms, asserted her long, insistent stride and took first, only five seconds better than Holland. Stanford finished one second ahead of True to claim third, and Zaferes came in 18 seconds later in sixth. Gwen had two weeks to prepare for Rio, and her narrow margin of victory worried me.

ELIZABETH

"Mom, I want to design something for the Olympics." Three years ago, my London shirts were in demand with family and friends, and now I envisioned our group traveling to Rio in matching tees. "What do you think?"

"Sure. Whatever you want. But she hasn't qualified yet."

"I know, but she will. And then people can wear them in Chicago too. How about something with her name? And USA colors?" Gwen was uncomfortable with the 2012 design featuring her face.

"You should ask Gwen what she thinks."

But Gwen was no help. She didn't want the attention, and she said she had Olympic qualification to worry about. So, I worked with a local company, Will Enterprises, who partially sponsored the shirts, bringing the cost to $5 each. After surveying friends via Facebook and email, I ordered 200.

NANCY

While Elizabeth designed t-shirts, so did Joel's sister, Mary Beth. Her red shirts read *Gwensanity Runs In Our Family* on the back.

In late July, Joel, Elizabeth, and I packed both shirts, swimsuits, and sunscreen for a week in Brazil. Rio de Janeiro's beaches, mountains, and samba attract thousands each year, but we traveled for one reason—to watch Gwen race for Olympic qualification.

After a 13-hour overnight flight, we arrived five days before the race. We hadn't seen Gwen and Patrick since Christmas Day in the hospital. During a hurried lunch, we shared plates and discussed itineraries—a bicycle tour and samba for us; training and meetings for Gwen and Patrick.

Some days, we met for breakfast. Then, Gwen swam in the pool, biked hills, and ran roads while we explored Rio. I understood Gwen's limited family time. Like an accountant on a business trip, she committed her time to professional pursuits.

In our hotel room, Elizabeth stashed her suitcase behind the door. With only a narrow path around three beds, Joel's suitcase rested on his nightstand, and mine perched atop a table. It would be a long week without a closet or anywhere to sit, and one tiny bathroom.

"This is terrible," Elizabeth said. "The Wi-Fi doesn't work, and the smell is awful." Only half of Rio's sewage was treated before entering the ocean, its telltale odor permeating our room.

"Let's do the walking tour. People say Rio is a beautiful city." I hoped to pull Elizabeth out of her bad mood with a free three-hour walk around Lapa and Centro. After the tour, I said, "What did you like best about the city?"

"Well, now we know where to find the samba clubs, and I did like climbing the stairs with the mosaic tiles."

"What about the cathedral that looked like a pyramid? And the aqueduct?"

"I think I'll be happy if we spend time at the beach." While Gwen swam in chlorinated pools to avoid Rio's contaminated shores, Elizabeth seemed unconcerned with water-borne viruses. And she heard the beach breeze dispelled the city's odor.

ELIZABETH

I anticipated Copacabana like the song, but media reported foul water and a failing economy. We heard of crime, a corrupt government, and sewage dumping. And the stink assaulted us. A gag reflex taunted my tongue when we walked the streets.

Stress surrounds every race trip Mom, Dad, and I take. Competition anxiety looms like a fog, clouding each meal, conversation, and activity. But our Rio trip passed quickly with Gwen's sponsors filling some time. One lunch, we joined Gwen, Patrick, and the Specialized crew. In addition to maintaining bikes and creating videos, Specialized was there to produce a simulation. When Gwen returned home, she would use it to mentally ride the Rio 2016 course via virtual reality headset.

After the meal, the Specialized guys invited us to trek with them to Brazil's Cristo Redentor, the Art Deco 100-foot tall statue on Corcovado Mountain. In every Olympic promotion it was featured prominently, the site renowned for spectacular city views. Arriving in taxis, we took selfies and admired the views, but after fifteen minutes we looked at each other and said, "Ready to go?"

The next day, Mom scheduled a bike tour. Walking along Copacabana Beach, we searched for the shop. "It says Street Ronald de Carvalho, 21." Mom checked her printout. "Do you see it?"

"There!" I pointed to a metal garage door across the street from a workout park. "But it's not open. What do you think?"

"I think it's Brazil," Dad said. "They'll be late."

We plopped on a bench in the park where elderly women and men pedaled stationary bikes and lifted weights. I wondered how long the stench would park in my nose. Had it stuck like the odor of campfire does to my hair?

Ten minutes past our appointment time, a short, chubby Brazilian scooted by on a bike. He unlocked the metal door as I walked to him. "Is this where we start the bike tour?"

He introduced himself as Bruno, the owner. "Yes. Others are signed up too. I'll find a bike for you." I was impressed with his English and wondered where his accent was.

When the others never showed, the four of us pedaled through the city, to the beach under Sugarloaf Mountain and through Flamengo Park. Bruno stopped several times to explain historical figures, beaches, and sights. "Rio has an outstanding college education system—I was admitted, but only after a rigorous test. It's government funded but only available to a select, high-performing set of students."

As a teacher, I wondered about a public school system that flourished amid political malfeasance.

"I went to private school first. My school and my parents really prepared me for the university test." We biked, sometimes in a straight line, other times with Bruno and me leading, Mom and Dad trailing. "And Rio is hoping to improve public transportation for the Olympics, but we doubt it will be finished in time."

"We hope to be back next year and would love to take the airport shuttle, if it's ready."

"I wouldn't count on it." His tone reminded me Brazil was a third world country. "Rio struggles with poverty. See there?" He pointed to a hill overflowing with stacked shacks. "Those are the favelas. The poorest people live there and deal with the worst crime and violence." He told stories of gunshots, armed militia, police brutality, and drug trafficking.

The next day, we relaxed on Copacabana Beach where chairs and umbrellas rented for the day at $1.50. I was surprised there was no offending odor.

Vendors walked amid beachgoers, hawking chips, grilled blocks of cheese, açaí, shrimp, tea, bags, jewelry, sunglasses, hats. I wanted everything, allowing Dad to pull out his wallet for a selfie stick, hammock, bikini top, and henna tattoos. "Mom, they have paddle boards. We should do it. YOLO!" I had never been on a paddleboard and called it my bucket list item of the trip.

"No, the doctor says I should be careful with my incision." Eight months since her surgery, the skin on Mom's stomach still tore easily.

As Dad floated, I stood, maneuvering around other paddlers, swimmers, and garbage. Dad, struggling with balance and flexibility, couldn't stay upright. After each fall, he chased his board, and then launched himself, only to fall over the other side. Neither of us could stop laughing—a welcome distraction from race nerves.

We returned our boards and joined Mom in the sand. While we rested, triathletes practiced beach starts, coaches making notes on clipboards. Although Gwen wouldn't brave the virus-filled waters until race day, she didn't seem overly concerned.

> *The ITU and the USOC conducted water quality tests,*
> *like before every race. The results met the standards*
> *in order to race. Our health is a priority and the ITU*
> *and USOC conduct tests to make sure the standards*
> *are met. I don't waste energy wondering what if.*

As I sipped a caipirinha in my beach chair, I hoped for another YOLO experience. "Are you up for samba music tonight?"

"Fine with me," Dad said, and Mom agreed.

Much of Rio's samba spills from bars into the streets, but a family friend recommended Rio Scenarium where we found a club atmosphere, complete with dress code and mandatory passports. I decided it was a tamer version of music in the streets, and suggested we return another night to mingle with the locals.

While we snapped selfies with Cristo Redentor, bought Olympic rings tattoos on the beach, and clapped to a samba beat, I wished Gwen was with us. But she needed sleep, coaching, massage, and time to lie backwards on the bed, feet pressed against the hotel walls. Gwen said elevating her legs flushes toxins and lactic acid, but more than that, she said, "It's just my habit. And I don't know why I started it, but now it's my ritual and I have to do it before each race."

NANCY

On Saturday, we watched the paratriathlon—athletes vying in five categories for qualification—on the same course Gwen would use the next day. Since organizers did not erect a grandstand or jumbotron, we watched from the beach and street where temperatures climbed to 32°C (89.6°F). We celebrated the eight USA triathletes who qualified and mentally marked the best places to watch Gwen compete.

On Sunday, August 2, we staked our place behind a security fence, first to arrive for the 9 a.m. start. Our sunscreen and visored hats shielded a blazing sun. Elizabeth toted bottled water in a sling pack. Already the temperature was 28°C (82.4°F). As we pressed against the fence, a crowd of photographers assembled on the other side, blocking our view. When the horn sounded and 65 women bolted toward the 22.5°C (72.5°F) water for a one-lap swim, we jostled to see around cameras.

Two women could earn a USA Olympic berth by finishing top eight. With USA's recent successes, the top three world-ranked athletes were all Americans—Gwen, Sarah True, and Katie Zaferes. At least one of them would leave disappointed.

> *I didn't hear the starting horn. I think a lot of people on the left had a hard time hearing it. I was around fast swimmers (Oliveira was to my right, True to my left a few over)...Around the first can it got rough/ physical and I think I lost focus and places there...I tried to make a move up a little and got belted in the head. My mouth was bleeding and I really lost focus— wondering if my teeth were chipped, etc. By the time I was able to regain my focus and be in the moment of*

*swimming, I think I'd moved back...I would try to put
in surges to get on someone's feet, but then I'd get an
elbow here or a kick there. I was not happy with my
swim result.*

Nineteen minutes later, as swimmers exited up the beach, we again peered around cameras. "Do you see Gwen?"

"No. One, two, three...seven, eight." Joel counted swimmers as they exited. "Twelve, thirteen, fourteen... "

"Where is she?"

"Seventeen, eighteen...there! She's nineteenth."

We sprinted to the road where Gwen transitioned to a lead pack of 30 that included True and Zaferes. On Rio's city streets, riders completed eight laps, each one bedeviled by an arduous climb, then a dangerous, twisting descent. When they rode past us, we had only seconds to see the pack.

When the action sped out of view, we stayed close to the street barricade to maintain our vantage point. The loudspeaker—fuzzy, indistinct—shouted unintelligible updates. The crowd multiplied with locals attracted by fast cycling and cheering fans.

ELIZABETH

Our shouts for Gwen and our custom red shirts from Aunt Mary Beth—*Gwensanity Runs In Our Family*—drew attention and a twenty-something Brazilian tapped me on the shoulder.

"This Gwen's family? I love her! She is best!"

"Yes. I'm her sister. And these are our parents."

"I'm Matheus." Dark and fit with neatly trimmed hair, he practiced his English between laps.

I hoped he wouldn't talk too much. "Tell me if I scream too loud in your ear—I really want Gwen to do well today."

"She number one. She so good. She win. For sure." Matheus offered his Facebook information and I promised to add him when we got within our hotel's Wi-Fi range.

NANCY

Each time cyclists approached, I searched for Gwen. "Can you see her?"

"There! Middle of the pack." Joel recognized her helmet.

"Does she look strong to you? Is that a good position?"

Matheus listened and laughed. "She number one! She get win."

"I hate the biking," I said, hand at my neck, fingering the fabric of my shirt.

"You no worry. She doing great." On each lap, after riders zoomed out of view, Matheus leaned toward me. "How Mom's heart?" Even this stranger sensed my anxiety. And, away from home, I had no chores to distract me from the most dangerous parts of the course.

The lead cycling group, including three Americans, maintained their advantage and entered transition with a one-minute lead.

"Why is Gwen carrying her bike?" Elizabeth asked.

"No idea." Other riders glided bikes along the carpet while Gwen toted hers in the air.

> *[In transition two] something bad happened. I entered in top three and something happened, and my wheel came loose. I couldn't roll my bike because the rear wheel was out so I had to run with my bike all the way to my transition rack. This scared me, and I was just so thankful it didn't happen while riding the bike! Yikes.*

Top contenders quickly took the run lead—Zaferes, True, Gwen, and Great Britain's Vicky Holland and Non Stanford.

> *I started the run and just thought, "Ok, you only need top eight," so I didn't push it. I was scared and didn't want to risk anything, especially in the heat. I ran the two laps with the top girls, but it was starting to get painfully slow.*

Gwen looked strong. I shouted at her and hoped she could hear her name. On lap three,

I put in a surge and Non went with me.

Gwen and Stanford ran together. But as they completed the lap, Gwen took the lead.

I never put in another move—Non just got tired and fell off.

It appeared Gwen would win as she disappeared into the streets for lap four.

ELIZABETH

With no way to see both the final meters and the finish line, we settled on the chute in case someone challenged Gwen in a sprint. Leaning against a street barricade, I applied more sunscreen where the sun burned my face and shoulders. Matheus followed us and asked for a selfie. I felt relieved and happy, confident Gwen just needed to run—and then we could celebrate.

NANCY

I watched Gwen head toward us, in the lead, 19 seconds ahead of Stanford. "Good job, Gwenevere!"—"Yeah! Go, Gwen!"—"GOOOOOOOOOO, GWEEEEEEEN!" With her considerable advantage, she didn't need our shouts as much as we needed to participate in her victory.

When Gwen crossed the finish line, she said, "Oh...oh...oh..," with a little cry after each. Perhaps she released three years of self-imposed pressure—this the culmination of her pursuit to qualify for 2016. Or perhaps she expressed frustration at the bloody swim and mechanical bike mishap.

I felt relief too—knowing Gwen qualified, knowing we had 12 months to plan our 2016 return. Some families would book flights and hotels based on hope and aspiration. Gwen had the luxury of deliberation and planning. So did we.

Stanford came in second, and Holland finished third. True finished fourth, securing her place at the 2016 Olympics. Zaferes came in sixth and missed automatic qualification.

Neither Holland nor Stanford qualified automatically because Great Britain established a two-stage policy. British athletes needed both this podium and a Chicago Grand Final podium to guarantee a spot.

ELIZABETH

Sweaty and out of breath, we hugged each other and high-fived Matheus. "Now what?" I asked.

Dad said, "Let's see the medal ceremony."

We walked along the sidewalk and through an open-air cafe. At a beachside kiosk, I saw the Rio Olympic mascot, Olympic ring glasses, and homemade Olympic torches. Around us stood media crews and Brazilians in yellow and green. One woman wore a fruit hat like Carmen Miranda. A gate separated us from the awards platform. I spotted Gwen behind the podium and screamed, "GOOD JOB, GWEN!" She waved, blew a kiss, and then I screamed again—hoping the cameramen would see our matching shirts and feature us in footage or request an interview.

NANCY

The awards area sat behind a fence, far from spectators. Peering from the side, I looked at Gwen in profile as she accepted her medal. I wondered about setup for 2016. Would there be a grandstand? A jumbotron? Would water quality improve? Gwen told us the re-paved roads were in excellent condition, and I hoped organizers would upgrade other components. I wondered what Bruno would say about the chance for that.

After the ceremony, we wandered outside the cordoned area and found Patrick. He pointed to Gwen behind a chain-link fence. "I've got drug testing now," she shouted. "Wanna get a drink when I'm done?"

In 45 minutes, Gwen joined us at an outdoor table. "Can I try your beer, Mom?" She sipped it. "We don't have a lot of time. I want to see the men's race."

"I do too," Elizabeth said as we paid and exited the veranda.

Patrick led us through narrow streets made narrower by barricades. With the men's race in progress, we walked up a steep hill, positioning ourselves to watch cyclists attack the climb. From across the street, someone shouted, "Hey! Patrick—Gwen—great race today." They both waved.

A group of young women walked behind us and slowed. "Excuse me. Are you Gwen? Could I get a picture with you?" Gwen put her arm around one young woman while another snapped photos. More in the group asked for selfies, and Gwen agreed. The scene repeated itself as spectators recognized the female winner.

ELIZABETH

With a break from requests, Gwen asked, "EJ, can you help me take these off?" She pointed to the 1 on her arms and legs.

"What do I do?"

"Just scrape." They looked like faded window clings, stuck to her body with glue.

"I don't want to hurt you."

"You're ridiculous." Gwen shook her head. "Just scrape."

I dug my fingernails into her legs and arms, pulling back the clear coating. I rubbed and scratched and as each black 1 faded, residue stuck to my palms and fingertips. "What are these things?"

"They're temporary tattoos we get along with stickers for our bike and helmet."

Gwen didn't flinch, though I knew it had to hurt, her skin folding and wrinkling with my efforts. "Maybe people won't recognize you as much now? Is that what you're thinking?"

"No, they'll still recognize me. I'm just too tired to do it myself. And I don't want to work at it in the shower tonight."

NANCY

As men stood out of the saddle to power up the hill, Gwen and Patrick cheered for USA teammates, "Go, Greg! Yeah, Joe Maloy!" and Wollongong Wizards, "Bugs! Good job!" and international friends, "Javi, you got this!" When the men transitioned to the run, we moved to the beachside finish.

I found an open section of barricade and stood next to a young woman who looked familiar. "Non?"

Slight and fair, she smiled, her face shaded by a visor.

"I'm Gwen's mom. Great job today—congratulations."

"Oh, thank you. It's a start," she said in her Welsh lilt. "Now the Brits just have to win again in Chicago." She explained her country's qualification process as Gwen joined us. "Can you understand me? I hope my accent is not so strong as it used to be."

"I understand you perfectly," I said, thinking this accomplished athlete showed humility and grace. Self-deprecating about her accent, she emphasized work she still needed to do.

ELIZABETH

Later that evening, we walked through Rio's Ipanema neighborhood to a Red Bull celebration. On the second floor, sponsors, athletes, friends, family, and coaches gathered at the bar or sat around fireplaces, snacking on appetizers in dim light. Gwen and Patrick roamed, laughing and hugging partygoers. I followed Jamie, wishing he'd make fun of my headband like he usually did and introduce me to the Red Bull athletes. About my age, they exuded coolness, confidence, and swagger—they spoke with exotic accents, their flat-brimmed hats perched above sandy hair and toned bodies.

When no introductions came, I joined Mom and Dad on the deck where white lights twinkled on the balcony railing. We sat with the Specialized and Red Bull crews, and triathlete Flora Duffy and her boyfriend. On TV, I assumed Flora about my size, but she came to my shoulder, her stature especially small in comparison to Gwen.

"I grew up in Bermuda." Her accent made her beautiful. "But I went to school in the US." Her boyfriend leaned in, touching her leg, holding her shoulder. "It's cool because I understand both cultures, and I grew up in the most serene place, with the most beautiful biking trails."

Gwen joined us for a few minutes, nibbling Mom's appetizers. "I'd like to see you guys tomorrow, but my schedule isn't set. Maybe grab lunch after my photo session?"

I looked forward to family time with just the five of us.

NANCY

The next day, we squeezed lunch—communal platters of Brazilian steak, chicken, pork, deviled eggs, vegetables—between Gwen's media commitments.

At 10 p.m., we boarded our respective flights, Gwen and Patrick returning to the Basque Region for six weeks before the Chicago Grand Final where Gwen would vie for a second World Championship.

Twelve consecutive victories. A world championship. Olympic qualification. These were the makings of a legend. But Gwen was still Gwen—cranky when hungry, impatient with my questions, forever focused on her next goal, but also craving family time, sharing secrets with Elizabeth, acknowledging our support. So much had changed, but everything was so much the same.

Gwen said she felt no different. She was still the same person, working hard for her next challenge. Nothing changed about her—it was others' perceptions that shifted. She posted on Snapchat a page from Andre Agassi's memoir, *Open, An Autobiography*, bolding for emphasis.

> I'm supposed to be a different person now that I've won a slam. Everyone says so. No more *Image is Everything*. Now, sportswriters assert, for Andre Agassi, winning is everything. After two years of calling me a fraud, a choke artist, a rebel without a cause, they lionize me. They declare that I'm a winner, a player of substance, the real deal. They say my victory at Wimbledon forces them to reassess me, to reconsider who I really am.
>
> But I don't feel that Wimbledon has changed me. I feel, in fact, as if I've been let in on a dirty little secret: **winning changes nothing.** Now that I've won a slam I know something that very few people on earth are permitted to know. **A win doesn't feel as good as a loss feels bad, and the good feeling doesn't last as long as the bad. Not even close.**

Twenty-seven months ago, we bragged about a top-10 finish and raved when Gwen earned a podium. But her new standard made anything less than gold inadequate. I knew Gwen tried to ignore statistics and focus only on each race.

And I knew I shouldn't be disappointed if she didn't win—that the magical string would eventually snap—but still, I wished for a victory every time.

****

Gwen's next event was the Chicago Grand Final where 2015's World Champion would be crowned. In 2014, Gwen raced the Grand Final with a sizeable point margin, needing top-16 to secure the title. But in 2015, there were four possible winners. Gwen had a perfect 4,000 points, Zaferes 3,700, True 3,322, and Kiwi Andrea Hewitt 3,131. Fans talked of another USA podium sweep. With 1,200 points awarded to the race winner (a sliding scale awarded fewer points to each successive place), experts calculated possibilities.

The week of the race, much of Joel's family—Kenny, Christine, Mary Beth— flew with their spouses and children to reunite with those in Wisconsin—Joel, Charlene, Colleen, Greg, Randie, Bill. We hosted dinner—two slow cookers of Italian sausages, salad, corn on the cob, and Mary Beth's Better Than Sex Cake— for the Chicago-bound crowd and Joel's 95-year-old mother, who would follow the race from Waukesha.

Joel and I arrived in Chicago a day early while the rest would arrive on Friday, September 18, for the 5 p.m. start. We checked in at the Chicago Hilton. Gwen and Patrick lodged a few miles away at the Loews where there would be fewer requests for autographs and selfies, less noise in the halls, and more privacy in the lobby. Gwen restricted her appearances to two events: a one-hour Wednesday morning Q&A and the traditional press conference.

The night before the race, I dreaded waiting for a 5 p.m. start. Race day morning, I couldn't sleep and at 6 a.m., checked my phone. Gwen had sent a text.

Race time moved to 1 p.m. Can you call family?

Changing race time was unprecedented in my experience, but the official website confirmed a four-hour change. With severe thunderstorms predicted— high winds, lightning, heavy downpours—organizers acted to avoid danger.

"Hello, Liz?" I said when my sister-in-law answered her phone at 6:30 a.m.

"Yes..." I heard fear or panic in her voice.

"Don't worry—everything is fine. Gwen just told me the race is moved up four hours. Can you let Steve and your boys know?"

"Yes, of course. I guess we better find an earlier train."

> *Race time was changed, but we were warned. I handled it really well. I ended up waking up and was pleasantly surprised with the new start time. I ate at 9 a.m., swam at hotel pool, biked to course, and did efforts on the lake shore drive (got new 5 sec and 30 sec max powers for the year). Got to venue, did run warm up with Pat as 'body guard,' waited for transition to open, set up transition, went to race start, and did swim bands.*

Joel and I walked to a Michigan Avenue cafe for breakfast, but my stomach fluttered and I ordered only tea, pinching small bites from Joel's plate. "Will your family make it on time?" I asked after Joel slipped his phone in a pocket.

"Mary Beth is checking Amtrak times." Their entourage of 12 needed special arrangements to get to the station, but Joel seemed unconcerned. "They have the information." Growing up with nine siblings, he grew accustomed to every-man-for-himself.

ELIZABETH

Work kept me from arriving with Mom and Dad on Thursday, so my boyfriend Josh and I drove to Chicago on Friday morning. Midway there, my phone dinged with Twitter notifications, text messages, and calls. I dialed Gwen. "What's going on?"

"Race time is moved. Will you make it?"

"Thankfully, we left early and traffic isn't bad. Who should I call?"

"Mom's calling family, so you call friends. But if they're checking social media, they'll see it."

"You going to be okay?"

"Yeah, I had a feeling this might happen after our meetings last night. Patrick and I prepared for both scenarios and I'm ready to go."

Several friends, with the opportunity to see a domestic race, purchased grandstand tickets. They were especially excited when I said, "After the race, Red Bull is hosting a party at the ROOF on theWit." It was Chicago's newest and hottest nightclub. I spent the rest of the drive calling, posting to social media, and texting, nervous now for my friends and for the potential World Champion.

When Josh and I arrived, Mom and Dad joined us to pick up 200 water bottles donated by Specialized. Back in Wisconsin, we would distribute them.

Dad wheeled a dolly through downtown Chicago to their promotional booth where the crew loaded our bottles. One of the Specialized guys approached me. "Can we get a picture of your family?"

Each race, I wore USA apparel. In London, it was a headband and red and white pants; in Chicago, I amped up the theme with flag tights and shorts.

We dragged the bottles to the hotel and returned to the grandstand. I didn't want to miss a minute of the race.

NANCY

When the swim started, a few family members were absent. But while athletes were in the water, most of our group joined us. The washing machine of arms and legs—75 women from 64 countries—stroked through Lake Michigan's 18°C (64.4°F) current. More like an ocean, Lake Michigan's 22,500 square miles and 1,000-foot depth tossed swimmers in its chop. Orange-capped heads bobbed above wetsuited bodies.

With a four-second deficit, Gwen exited to humid 21°C (69.8°F) air and clouds that augured storms. She yanked her wetsuit zipper and peeled off goggles and cap as she ran across the blocked road into transition. She mounted her bike in sixth, and our group shouted: "She's doing good, Joel."—"Woo-hoo! Goooooo, Gweeennnnn!"—"You can relax now, Nancy. She made the front pack."

ELIZABETH

A group of 40 Gwen fans congregated in the bleachers. Family sported *Gwensanity Runs in Our Family* shirts while friends wore gray TEAM GWEN shirts. I put one over the other depending on the pictures we took. Aunt Chinchi passed out noisemakers and miniature American flags. Each time Gwen flew by,

I stood on the metal bench and increased the volume on my screeches. "There! Right there! See her? GOOOOOOOO, GWEN!"

NANCY

In the front pack of eight, Gwen rode with two of her toughest competitors—USA teammates Katie Zaferes and Sarah True.

Announcing the race, Emma Snowsill said, "I have truly seen [Gwen] become an all-around, amazing triathlete. Her bike at times...she clearly stated was not particularly her strongest. She had somewhat of a fear and we have seen in races this year, she has taken charge on the bike. She has gone to the front of the pack. She has dominated...She takes this confidence with her."

During lap one, under raindrops, a chase pack caught the leaders, forming a 20-plus group. With the dominant runners all in one pack, Trevor Harris speculated. "We haven't really seen a fit Non Stanford racing against Gwen Jorgensen off a level start. We might see that today. Because you'd have to think, Stanford is about as close as there is in women's triathlon at the moment, in terms of the run, to Gwen."

Also in the pack was Great Britain's Vicky Holland—both she and Stanford vied for a podium to secure Rio 2016 qualification. I hoped Gwen could match their determination.

I counted down laps—eight, seven. Each time, riders circled Buckingham Fountain's tiers of arcing water. Six, five. As riders pedaled out of view, I watched the jumbotron where Gwen hovered mid-pack, occasionally venturing to the front.

Bermuda's Flora Duffy accelerated, attempting a breakaway. "Gwen should be closer so she can go with her," I said.

"That's the second time Duffy tried that," Joel said. "But she needs at least one other person to go with her." As he spoke, Duffy fell back into the pack.

The camera focused on Stanford as her tires slipped and she lost momentary control before righting herself. Those three seconds shot panic through me, a reminder that cyclists must be deft and swift, responding to surprise hazards.

ELIZABETH

Josh's best friend Mike—late forties, muscular, tattooed—turned to me. "I had no idea this was such a big deal."

I smiled at him, happy to introduce triathlon. "It's pretty cool, hey? Feels like a Bucks or Brewers game, right?"

"Unbelievable and really cool to see this in person. These are awesome athletes."

The lead pack approached the grandstand. "Now, get ready for some real excitement. Watch her rack her bike." I pointed to transition. "It's important her helmet gets into the bucket. If not, she'll go to a penalty tent. Here...here they come." The crowd stood, clapping, cheering, monitoring the screen and riders simultaneously.

NANCY

As cyclists approached transition, Harris mentioned Gwen's 2015 splits—she recorded the fastest run in every race, and in Auckland, Gold Coast, and Yokohama, she won races by over a minute. He guessed she might set another record by winning this World Championship with the maximum points possible—a perfect 5,200.

The leaders entered transition with Gwen in 17th, five seconds back. As the run began, Stanford and Holland asserted themselves at the front, and within minutes Gwen ran herself into third. During the first two kilometers the trio separated from the field, and announcers predicted the podium. At the end of lap one, Stanford led the threesome.

True and Kiwi Andrea Hewitt staged their own contest in fourth and fifth. If Hewitt earned a race podium spot, True needed fifth or better to claim a place on the World Championship podium. If Hewitt bested True, she could take the World Championship silver. Announcers augmented the suspense, posing possibilities, as Gwen and Stanford exchanged the lead a few times, Stanford returning most often to the front.

At the end of lap three, Stanford led the trio past the grandstand.

Joel's brother, Kenny, a white-bearded professional paraglider, sat in front of us and turned around. "This is my favorite part. I love to watch Gwen run." A free spirit, 1960's commune dweller, Kenny wore his own version of our family t-shirt. Instead of *Gwensanity Runs In Our Family*, his read:

GWENNESS

Is a State of Being That I Enjoy Being In

Stanford, Holland, and Gwen exited the stadium and turned left onto the streets.

"Look! There she goes!" Kenny said as Gwen stepped ahead of Stanford. Our group stood on the bleachers.

Within seconds, Gwen manufactured a decisive gap, and our 40-strong entourage shook flags and noisemakers. "I knew she'd take the lead!"—"GOOOOOO, GWEENNNN!"—"You've got this, Gwen!" The crowd—in the grandstand, on streets, and sidewalks—exploded, clamoring for a USA victory.

Speaking as though Gwen would surely retain the lead, Snowsill said, "Her ability to be on top on such a consistent basis for so long is a huge testament to the planning with her coach. I think it's one thing to keep an athlete healthy and uninjured for that amount of time, but to have them winning as well over that period...It definitely takes a very, very, very unique athlete to be able to handle that and the composure that she has shown...particularly in the last 18 months is quite extraordinary."

I wondered if fans perceived Jamie's importance. Snowsill clearly understood, and I assumed she recognized Patrick's role too.

As Gwen finished the final lap, Snowsill said, "A bit of home crowd support as well out there would certainly be something spurring her on all that little bit more. Not that she needed it...To be honest, this is probably the hardest I've seen her mouth move in terms of breathing hard. I think she's probably looking forward to this race being done and won."

ELIZABETH

Uncle Steve and my cousins went back and forth from the stands to the course. "I love how close I can get," he said. "We were cheering for her by the lake too."

I was too afraid to miss commentary or live footage and stayed in the bleachers.

Aunt Chinchi snapped photos and as Aunt Colleen befriended fans in the next section, I saw her point to me. A woman rushed over. "Can I buy one of those Gwen shirts? How much are they?"

"Sure." I gave her my email address between shouts for Gwen.

"Can I buy ten?"

I didn't have that many, but I wanted to get back to the race. "Just email me, and I'll let you know when I'm home."

NANCY

Fans crowded the barricades as Gwen approached the grandstand for the final time. She raised her sunglasses and checked over her shoulder. USA Triathlon's Andy Schmitz reached over the fence, handed her the USA flag, and Gwen smiled, raising the stars and stripes with both hands above her shoulders. With perfect coordination, she held the flag behind her and grabbed the tape in front as she earned her second Grand Final win.

Twenty-nine seconds later, Stanford pumped the air with her palms as she took silver. She and Gwen wrapped arms around each other. Fifteen seconds after that, Holland finished third, and elation spawned a three-woman hug. The Brits appeared unusually ecstatic for athletes in second and third—but both earned Olympic qualification with their podium spots.

Hewitt won her battle against True, finishing fourth in the race and second on the World Championship podium. True finished seventh and claimed the World Championship bronze.

As the clock ticked out finishing times for the rest of the field, Gwen hugged Patrick. She kissed him and grabbed him again, a 10-second acknowledgement of his victory too.

ELIZABETH

Our group hugged and high-fived while fans and the announcer recognized competitors still finishing. "I knew she would do it."—"That was so awesome."—"A two-time World Champion!" I was thankful friends and family joined us—the celebration livelier, more intense. As some cried, others hurried to the podium for photos of Gwen, her hand on her heart, the national anthem playing, a medal around her neck.

After awards, we waited for Gwen as she signed autographs, starred in selfies, and maneuvered toward her hometown crew. We circled around her as cameras and phones snapped photographs. Sweaty, relieved, feeling the rain roll in, I hoped for a repeat in Rio in 2016.

NANCY

In post-race interviews, Gwen acknowledged the Brits: "They're pretty tough. I was really hurting today, and I had no idea what was going to happen. Non was leading a lot of the run and I was just trying to stick with her." On her Rio 2016 qualification, she said, "Jamie Turner has just been incredible to help me along this journey. I'm just really fortunate to have him, and the Wollongong Wizards, and my husband, Pat."

Counting the Rio test event, Gwen finished her season a two-time World Champion with 13 consecutive wins and 16 overall victories. Was this a dream? A vision? Was I really celebrating a two-time World Champion daughter? Thousands of athletes aspire to professional sports careers, to be the best in the world. This day, Gwen was the first woman ITU triathlete to complete her season with a perfect score. The reality seemed chimerical.

ELIZABETH

Gwen wanted a quiet dinner that evening. "Let's just do family this time, okay?"

I agreed and told Josh to join his friends. After a shower, I began my walk, thinking I understood the restaurant's location. Dusk approached as Google Maps rerouted, sending me beneath a highway and through a tunnel. Car horns blared and wind swirled. Two-way traffic sped by as the bowels of Chicago swooped me up. Construction barrels blocked my view.

Google Maps said, "Proceed to the route" when a man—matted hair, dirty clothes, relentless stench—asked me for money. He twirled and said, "Look out for snakes." He pointed to a construction barrel. "Spare change?"

I gripped my phone and scolded myself. Why hadn't I taken a taxi or met Mom and Dad? Thunderstorms crashed above the tunnel, pounding rush-hour traffic. Rain seeped through cracks and pooled. I willed my tears under control. I saw a police officer and ran toward him, umbrella at my side. Within meters, I realized he was not police, but parking authority. "Excuse me, sir, I'm lost."

"Ma'am, you shouldn't be here. Keep walking."

Now I was crying. "But I don't know where I'm going."

"Where are you headed?" Cars zipped inches from his feet.

I told him, and he said, "You're about two miles away. Go that way." He pointed to where the man alerted me to snakes.

"Can you please give me a ride?"

He laughed. "I don't have a car. And good luck getting a taxi in this rain."

I called Gwen, but she was doing media and told me to call Patrick. I didn't let her know I was crying, but when Patrick picked up, I couldn't hold back.

"Elizabeth, what's wrong?"

"This man wants money. I'm lost. My GPS. He wouldn't help. I'm scared." Gasps and tears interrupted my words.

"Elizabeth, ping me your location."

I knew I worried Patrick, but I was too frightened to care. I reminded myself, *You're over thirty. Your sister is the World Champion. You have a phone and GPS. You can do this.*

"Go to someplace that's lit. Go to a restaurant. I see one nearby," Patrick said. He must have been watching my pinged location. "I don't know why you're out there alone. I would have walked with you, had I known. Just stay put. I'll run to you."

I stood near the restaurant, looking for Patrick. His tall frame, moments later, sprinted past the traffic light—I must have been closer than the parking guy said. We embraced, and I felt my body relax and my tears stop. "Patrick, I feel like you saved my life." I feigned composure, trying to relieve my distress with humor. "Let's take a selfie so we can always remember this moment."

"Elizabeth, don't be crazy. I'm just glad I could help." He, confident, calm, undisturbed by my tears offered to hold my purse and hand, all the way back to the restaurant.

Never envious of Gwen's life, her world travel, her media obligations, her fame, her success, or her toned body, I longed for a Patrick. I wanted my own Prince Charming who supported my career, traveled with me, cooked for me, and loved me till I was old and wrinkly. Gwen was lucky. And I was lucky too; Patrick was a brother-in-law who would rush to my side, calm irrational fears, and wipe my tears.

Patrick and I walked into the restaurant where Gwen and Mom and Dad sipped wine.

Gwen scolded me. "EJ, why were you out there alone?"

"You said only family. And I thought I could do it on my own. I am over 30!"

"I meant just not too many more people than family. You could have brought Josh."

"Oh." I tried to laugh off the anxiety that still made my knees shake. "Well, I guess it was a misunderstanding. I'm just so happy Patrick saved me." Gwen placed her trophy on the table and, tired of the panic, I asked if I could take a selfie with it. Struggling to hold its weight, I wasn't sure if it was really that heavy or if I was that exhausted.

"Patrick is amazing," Gwen said, caressing his leg and kissing him on the cheek.

I never saw Patrick envious, frustrated, irritated. I admired him, knowing my sister (like I) could quickly produce impatience and unrealistic expectations. "Yes, I agree."

While in Chicago, NBC Nightly News requested a family interview. Red Bull's Ilana Taub coordinated the arrangements. When we discussed our schedule, I mentioned Dad's family celebration on Saturday—a surprise birthday party for Aunt Christine at Tavern at the Park.

"Sounds like it could be a good opportunity for them to catch up with a few of you, get your thoughts on Gwen's amazing rise, and some fun background stories too." Ilana called the restaurant, alerting them to an NBC camera crew in addition to the Jorgensen party of 14.

We arrived at Tavern at the Park to find Ilana, petite, face framed by red curls. Casual and unobtrusive, she introduced the NBC crew as they microphoned Gwen, Mom, Dad, and me. Filming an NBC Olympics special reminded me that if I weren't a teacher, I would like to work for Bravo. Some show featuring my friends, like *The Young Professionals of Waukesha* would suit me.

The crew asked us to re-enter the restaurant—a take-two. I checked my hair and underarm sweat. Excitement bubbled, and I played an exaggerated form of myself. "Gwen, this is so cool. Don't you think?"

Gwen, no different from the first entrance, ignored the camera. "Let's just do this take. Then you can talk to the camera as much as you want."

NANCY

Our rectangular table was situated among unsuspecting diners who pointed and whispered. Elizabeth sat up straighter. I felt self-conscious as the cameraman leaned over my shoulder. While he lingered, I made uninteresting small talk and thought about how terrible I look in video.

The camera followed Gwen as she circled the table, greeting each family member with a hug or kiss. She hated photographic attention as much as I did but looked natural and beautiful.

After dinner, Elizabeth, Joel, and I excused ourselves to go upstairs for individual interviews.

ELIZABETH

I told stories, asked for second takes, and wiped sweat from my nose. Animating anecdotes, I attempted to make the editor's final cut.

"You look so natural," Ilana said. Not exactly what I was going for, but I was thankful she thought my performance satisfactory.

Mom and Dad took their turns, and then said they wished they'd been more clever.

Gwen's microphone remained on for the rest of the day as the crew followed her to the men's triathlon, an informal Q&A, and then her party at the ROOF on theWit.

At the men's race, I asked her drama-producing questions, typical of a reality star: "Who do you think will win today?"—"I really like Mario Mola. Who's your favorite?"—"What happened to that athlete? Why is he running like that?" The camera hovered inches from our faces.

Gwen pointed to her mic. "Elizabeth, I'm not talking about any of this."

I admired Gwen's presence, her poise, her maturity. I wanted to play, but this was Gwen's job. She had no time for manufactured drama; her focused eyes and pointing finger reminded me she was working.

We used our passes to enter a VIP tent stocked with complimentary appetizers, beer, and wine. Gwen sat at the front with a handheld microphone in addition to the NBC wireless mic, answering questions. "What motivates you?"—"How do you have a successful transition?"—"What's your pre-race routine?"

I was bored with triathlon questions. So, when the moderator said, "Any other questions for Gwen before we wrap up?" I raised my hand.

Gwen shook her head and mouthed, "No."

An assistant handed me the microphone. "What is something that people don't know about you—something you wish they knew, but don't?"

Without pause, Gwen said, "I want them to know I have a sister who asks really difficult questions." The room chuckled, and then checked out Gwen's sister—no doubt surprised at her much shorter height and much rounder figure.

I waved to the crowd and said, "You're right! You do." Laughter and chatter continued as the moderator ended the Q&A. "Thank you so much, Gwen, for your candor and time..."

Before Gwen's next media event, Josh and I met her and Patrick in their hotel room. We walked in as she opened a FedEx box.

"The designer, Gabriela Hearst, sent these," she said. "What do you think? Which one for my interview?"

"OMG. The Hearst family? Gwen, you are so legit."

She held up the samples: a tweed skirt, a dress, a collared top. She tried on each, the designs lengthening her slender figure, exuding elegance, class, prestige.

"Do you guys have to do this right here?" Josh turned to face the window. "She's in her underwear."

"Yeah? So?" Gwen, accustomed to changing in a locker room or competing in a singlet, hadn't noticed she stripped in front of the open window and Josh's modesty.

"I'll just stand here." He looked out the window, his breath clouding the glass. "And you guys let me know when everyone is dressed."

Gwen tried each outfit and chose one for her interview.

"Okay," I said to Josh, "we're headed to the bathroom to do Gwen's hair."

Gwen sat in a sports bra. Her chair faced the sink and mirror as I moved around her, careful not to burn her ears with the straightener. "Where's your brush?"

"I told you I don't have one."

"Well, whatever, Gwen, you know what I mean. Where's your comb?"

"I don't have that either."

"What?" I thought she was playing with me. "How can that be? What do you do?"

"Nothing. I typically do nothing." She scrunched her curls. She said a brush created frizz in her chlorine-damaged hair so she let it dry naturally.

I tried to imagine a scenario where snarled hair and ponytails sufficed until a makeup artist, photo shoot director, or big sister brought a brush, straightener, and pins. This day, Josh offered to get a comb from the front desk.

Later, Gwen said her favorite part of the trip was our makeshift salon. I tried to recall what made it special. Was it comforting, the presence of family? Was it the humor of pushing Josh's discomfort? Was it living in a moment where she didn't think or talk about triathlon?

NANCY

That evening, our group met in the lobby of theWit hotel and took a 27-floor elevator ride to the ROOF where Red Bull staff attached plastic bracelets to verified guests.

A waitress approached, high-heeled steps stretching her abbreviated skirt, and suggested a fruity drink from the bar's punch bowl. While she assembled stemmed martinis and rocks glasses, Joel and I palmed our plates to the outdoor patio where we gazed at toy cars creeping by, skyscrapers standing guard.

ELIZABETH

I wore a cardigan and khaki capris, strikingly different from the four-inch heels and bottom-exposing dresses on—or nearly on—the waitresses. Red Bull provided snacks, sliders, and energy drinks. Family, friends, sponsors, and staff shifted between the outdoor patio—glass on three sides, the twinkle of the city below—and the lounge, hip hop beats shaking the floorboards. Gwen moved among guests, thanking them for their support, for coming to the event, for rearranging schedules last minute.

Around 11 p.m., as Gwen said goodbyes and left for her hotel, a different party began in the adjacent space—theatrical lights swathed a catwalk where dancers shook cleavage and stomped thigh-high boots. My friends and I stayed. We danced and screamed over the Vegas-like atmosphere, and I asked for a picture with two of the dancers, laughing at the dichotomy of teacher and club performer. Slamming $10 drinks, we exited only when the venue closed well after 2 a.m. Continuing the party, we took a taxi for gyros and made drunk conversation in our hotel lobby.

NANCY

The next day, Joel and I returned home on Amtrak, but Gwen and Patrick scheduled one more celebration. When Gwen won the championship, Red Bull contacted Alinea, Chicago's only restaurant to retain a three-star Michelin rating, and made reservations for four. Gwen and Patrick invited Elizabeth and Josh for the $300 per person tasting menu—18 courses of experimental flavors and design. Gwen said it was the perfect reward for her perfect season.

2015 Race Results

1st: ITU WTS Abu Dhabi, United Arab Emirates (6 March)
1st: ITU WTS Auckland, New Zealand (29 March)
1st: ITU WTS Gold Coast, Australia (11 April)
1st: ITU WTS Yokohama, Japan (16 May)
1st: ITU WTS London, United Kingdom (31 May)
1st: ITU WTS Hamburg, Germany (18 July)
1st: Rio Test Event and USA Olympic Trials in Rio de Janeiro, Brazil (1 August)
1st: ITU WTS Grand Final Chicago, United States of America (18 September)

CHAPTER 8

Travel, Tires, and Trying Times

2015 OFF-SEASON

NANCY

After the September 18, 2015, Grand Final, Gwen and Patrick flew to St. Paul. I asked about her schedule, and Gwen said she would sit for photo shoots in California, volunteer at camps in Colorado, and record interviews in Florida. "It will be a relief to start training again. We go to Australia on January 2 and stay there until March." She booked one more triathlon at The Island House in the Bahamas. Despite the time away from home, she said this race, hosted by her sponsor, was her favorite. She enjoyed its idyllic setting and unconventional three-day format.

As Gwen fulfilled her off-season responsibilities, NBC visited our Waukesha home, Elizabeth celebrated a birthday, and we followed Gwen and Patrick's "eatcation."

ELIZABETH

In September, an NBC Olympics producer and her cameraman arrived at Mom and Dad's house. The scent of fresh cranberry bread filled the air. Mom set out apples from the local orchard and arranged brie and cheddar on a Dad-crafted board.

The cameraman walked no further than the foyer before asking, "Someone's repping ASICS, hey?"

Gwen and her agent requested we dress in ASICS. To make that possible, Gwen gave me her August allowance. I didn't care what TV viewers thought. If Gwen needed us to do promotion in return for sponsorship, I was happy to help.

Mom blushed. "I hope this doesn't look weird."

The Chicago-based producer smiled. "I'm sure people will get what's going on." She directed the cameraman as he set up a tripod and lights in front of the snack buffet.

The producer wanted childhood photos of Gwen and natural shots of us. So, after a Q&A at the kitchen table, Mom, Dad, and I—and my cockapoo Branji—piled on the couch. We never got out Gwen's scrapbooks. But for the camera, we laughed at old photos of Gwen, at her braces, at her acne, and at her gangly legs. We told stories of her love affair with Patrick and her obsession with punctuality. Dad handed over family VHS tapes, the producer promising to transfer content to a hard drive in return for permission to use the footage.

As the producer thanked us and packed, Mom offered water bottles and snacks for the road. I took off my ASICS hoodie, hot from the attention and videographer's light. I put on my sunglasses, clasped the leash on Branji, and turned back to Mom and Dad. "When they have the VHS on hard drive, let me know."

NANCY

A few days after the photo shoot, I chatted on the phone with Gwen. "Where are you going this time?" For several years, she and Patrick took an eatcation, exploring cuisine in San Francisco, Croatia, and San Sebastian.

"Nowhere. We're doing eatcation in St. Paul." I was on speakerphone as she and Patrick prepared dinner.

"And we have rules," Patrick said. "No cooking!" Pans clanked in the background.

"Right. For three days, we have to eat out. And every meal has to be in a restaurant we've never been to. It's actually hard. Sometimes, I just want a banana, but our rule is we can't eat at home."

"Gwen gets a ton of people following her on Twitter when we do it. I think they like food pictures more than triathlon."

I thought how lucky Gwen and Patrick were to share a passion, to have time and money to pursue it—and to consume all those calories. In a September 2015, Team USA interview, Gwen told Peggy Shinn, "I am constantly trying to put on weight, so I don't count calories. I just try to eat as much as I can."

I didn't need to read an interview to know that. Gwen loved food and the adventure of new ingredients, preparations, and flavors. For three days, just like Gwen's 20,000 Twitter fans, I followed as she documented each meal, snack, and dessert stop.

ELIZABETH

As sisters, Gwen and I share mundane information, and, in 2015, we chatted about my car. "Gwen, you're so lucky you don't have to deal with cars."

"Yeah, Patrick is really good with that stuff." Gwen upgraded her sponsored Honda Fit to an Odyssey van. While Patrick managed upkeep, Gwen's sponsor (David Hobbs Honda) covered routine maintenance.

"My tires are shot. I need new ones," I said, "but they're so expensive."

"Elizabeth, that's important. You shouldn't put it off."

At Gwen's urging, I enlisted my boyfriend's help. Weeks later, after watching sales, Josh made his recommendation and called Tires Plus. Blindly trusting him, I pulled in, parked the car, and stared at my Discover card, dreading the purchase.

The long-haired teenager at the counter greeted us as the door chimed. "Welcome to Tires Plus. How may I help you today?" The store smelled like grease.

"I'm Elizabeth Jorgensen with the Honda Civic for tires."

"Give me one second to pull up your information." He clicked a keyboard as the printer shot out an invoice. "Here's your receipt. Looks like you've already paid."

"Oh, it does?"

"Your car will be done in a few hours. We'll call when it's ready."

I turned to Josh. "What just happened? Did you pay for the tires?"

"You need to call your sister."

What? Why? What does Gwen have to do with this?

"Just call her."

When we got to Josh's car, I dialed Gwen on speakerphone. "Hi, Gwen. What is going on? Josh said to call you about my tires?"

"HAPPY BIRTHDAY, EJ! I wanted to surprise you!"

"What?! You didn't have to. You shouldn't have."

"Yes, but you read my blog, you edit my interviews. You help with the scholarship. I wanted to do something nice for you. I wanted to surprise you."

I started to cry. "Gwen, thank you, that's the nicest gift—the nicest thing— anyone has ever done for me."

"Elizabeth, it's really okay." She sounded shocked I was so emotional. "Josh helped me, and it wasn't that big of a deal."

I didn't know what else to say—and I was still crying—so we hung up the phone. Thankful and humbled—and now worried about the pressure of Gwen's upcoming birthday—I hugged Josh. "This was the best birthday present ever."

NANCY

A few days after Elizabeth received new tires, Gwen and Patrick hauled suitcases to our spare room. They came for Thanksgiving, bringing mountain bikes and skis.

On Thanksgiving Day, Joel sautéed fennel sausage and onions. I rolled pie crusts and added sugar to 10 cups of apple slices. Elizabeth arrived early to help.

"Mom, can you teach me how to make bread?" Gwen, towering over me in bare feet and athletic clothes, snuck Granny Smiths and licked sugar from her fingers. "Mine always fail."

"If you're teaching Gwen, I want to know too," Elizabeth said.

"Okay, let's get a bowl for each of you and heat up water."

As I read the directions aloud, I realized how much information was missing: to add the last bit of flour gradually; to knead until you have a firm, elastic ball, just a little sticky; to speed rising by setting dough over a bowl of hot water.

Elizabeth added too much flour and had to start over. "Yeah, Gwen, we know yours will be flawless." She teased her sister about champion-style perfection.

At dinnertime, Gwen and Elizabeth set their rustic loaves—brown crusts around a chewy white interior—on our burlap tablecloth next to turkey, Joel's stuffing, side dishes prepared by family, and my pies. I treasured this gathering with both daughters and extended family.

The day after Thanksgiving, we hosted Comcast Sports from Chicago in another Olympic video production. The producer interviewed Gwen at the kitchen table, our family room rigged as a backdrop.

Gwen finished and the producer said, "Let's move to a different space for Patrick." The crew emptied succulents from my bay window, and Patrick spoke in front of a blurred landscape framed by our living room panes.

Patrick answered questions about Gwen's work ethic. "I've been a professional athlete, and I know how hard it is. Gwen has this ability to always bring her best. And when I watch her work that hard as a world class triathlete..." A few tears caught Patrick's voice. "...then I'm inspired to be a world class house husband."

I stirred tomato soup and arranged turkey leftovers for the camera crew, grateful to cook rather than appear on camera.

ELIZABETH

A few days before Christmas, Gwen sent an email with the subject, "Any interest or NO WAY!?" Inside, the email was blank, save for a link to the 10th annual Christmas Day Joyful 5K.

Mimicking her succinctness, I replied, "Interested."

Christmas brought us to Patrick's grandparents' home in Minneapolis. While they vacationed in Florida, we moved in. Taxidermied animals hung on the walls. Bear rugs lay on wooden floors. Tchotchkes sat in glass showcases, on shelves, and atop a grand piano.

Craig emptied his car, box after box (stamped from the grocery store where he worked) of gourmet crackers, artisan cheeses, bread, condiments, beer, and produce. Jane brought her three small dogs, and each entered the house marking his territory in pee and poop. Jane, unbothered, scooped the turds in napkins and returned to coddling, cuddling, and caressing. Patrick's sister, Paige, carried her suitcase across the cul de sac where she would stay with cousins.

Sleeping accommodations left me on an air mattress in Mom and Dad's room. Always a restless sleeper, I regularly wake in the middle of the night with blankets, like vines, gripping my calves. But on the first night, as I pulled the blankets over my chest, I sensed my shoulders connect with the wood floor and realized the air mattress had deflated. In the darkness of past-midnight, frustration rose. As tiredness produced tears, I dragged my blankets and pillow over the dog-marked rugs, trying not to send knickknacks flying. On the living room couch, I surrendered to sobs. That's when Mom found me.

"Honey, what's wrong?"

"I'm going to a hotel." I knew I overreacted, but everything built up— Christmas in a stranger's home, Jane's dogs here while Branji was boarded, and now a deflated mattress.

Mom rubbed my back. "Are you sleepwalking? What are you doing out here?"

As a child, I was known for erratic sleep, sleep-talking, sleep-walking. "I am not!" *Just because I'm sleeping in your room doesn't mean I'm 12 again.*

"Honey, come back to bed."

Why didn't she get it? "That thing has a hole. I'm sleeping on the couch."

"Okay." I knew she wanted to appease and quiet me. "We'll figure something out in the morning."

The next day—the day before the holiday 5K—Patrick fit in last minute shopping for Gwen's Christmas presents (espresso cups, earrings, and a travel mug). He added a new air mattress for me.

Christmas morning, better rested, I wanted to play. "Let's do something to make this 5K interesting," I said as we sat at the kitchen table.

"What do you have in mind?" Patrick seemed cautious but willing to go along.

"How about a bet on who wins?" Gwen said.

"Ummm...so you want to take our money?"

Ever the accountant, she said, "Well, let's do some math." I shoved breakfast into my mouth. Gwen couldn't believe I wanted toast and egg—she said they wouldn't digest well during the race. Best to eat oats. "Everyone come up with a goal time. Anyone who is one minute outside of their goal time is disqualified."

Does she think I have a goal time? Does she think I (or Paige or Patrick) can predict a 5K time? Can non-Olympians do that?

Jane said she'd stay home to snooze with the dogs, while Craig offered to drive us. Mom and Dad would walk 3K, and then cheer.

After a 30-minute drive, we arrived at Claddagh Irish Pub & Restaurant in Maple Grove. Dressed in Santa hats, we joined the sign-up line. Gwen remained anonymous among the leisurely runners and moms with strollers. While I sipped hot chocolate, Gwen did a pre-race run. "There are some spots that are straight ice. I had to walk. Be careful."

Craig found a race official and requested salt on the course. I hoped he wouldn't add any, welcoming the walking sections. Gwen continued her warm up, testing the salt's effect while nerves sent me to the bathroom.

As the countdown began, Gwen positioned herself with the mostly male frontline. Patrick fell in behind, and Paige and I decided to run together.

The looped course, stretched atop a crevasse, allowed me to see almost the entire 5K as I ran. I kept my eye on Gwen, watching her pass a Santa, a man in a tutu, and another without a shirt. Gwen lapped me early on, patting my butt as she went. "Good job, EJ."

I screamed between deep breaths, "I'm trying to draft! TAKE ME WITH YOU," but she sprinted past my nine-minute mile jog.

Gwen (18:19) and Patrick (23:35) cheered as Paige (30:26) and I (29:25) crossed the finish line. Exhausted, spit dripped from my mouth, and snot hung from my nose. I put my hands on my knees and tried to relax my breathing.

Gwen's winning time drew attention, runners figuring out the registered Gwen Lemieux was Gwen Jorgensen. She posed for selfies and signed t-shirts. I asked to stay and drink a beer, but Gwen wanted to get home for another run.

In the van, we applauded each other and never paid out. Later that day, we collaborated on a Christmas meal—lasagna, salads, sweets. We attended an evening movie—*Concussion*—at the local theater. A depressing holiday choice, I imagined Mom calculating how many concussions professional cyclists accrue.

After the movie, Gwen and Patrick set up the bike trainer in the living room where Gwen pedaled, sweat raining onto the towel-protected floor. It was the third time that day I saw her work out.

I retreated to my air mattress in Mom and Dad's room. And the greatest win for me? When Gwen said, "Elizabeth, you actually looked like a runner today."

Where did she think I got my genes?

NANCY

We squeezed a year's worth of family time into Gwen's brief off-season. When together, we played cards, watched home movies, watched theater movies, cooked, baked, laughed. Elizabeth and Gwen told secrets. Joel and I strained to hear their hushed words. We road-tripped to the Twin Cities. To the St. Paul farmer's market. To Minneapolis restaurants. When Gwen and Patrick drove to Waukesha, we stretched fresh sheets over Gwen's childhood bed. When Gwen and Patrick drove to Fargo, we shared them with her in-laws. We celebrated Christmas minus gifts, enjoying each other instead.

Swirling beneath my consciousness was Gwen's upcoming season. Her Olympic race. Her aspiration to win Olympic gold. Anxiety threatened, lurking, pricking at my brain. I tried to ignore it.

ELIZABETH

What would I say to Gwen if she didn't win? What if she got a bronze or silver and should be thrilled, but wasn't? My mind skipped between nervousness and awe. I called her one day after work. "You know, I don't like talk radio, but lots of people are telling me you were all over it today."

"Ugh, oh. What about?"

"Apparently, Mark Belling said you should be getting more publicity and be much more famous than you are."

"Elizabeth, we can't talk about this." Her words, short, cutting, stung me.

"Why?"

"It makes me too nervous. I don't want to think about it."

Think about what? I wanted to ask. But afraid of more stings, I assumed she referred to what would happen when she won gold. But then I wondered if she referred to what would happen if she didn't.

Her directive stopped the conversation, like a dial-tone gone dead, and carried over for the next two months. During that time, we didn't talk about the Olympics. Instead, we talked about her training, her schedule, her friends, her aches and pains, about my life, my dog, my work. We talked about everything but her fame and the race that could make her as acclaimed as Missy Franklin, Serena Williams, and Kerri Walsh Jennings. When NBC Olympic commercials aired, I turned away. The once exciting promos produced anxiety. For weeks, I woke to dreams of Rio (never actually making it to the race's outcome) and one day, I allowed myself to wonder. *What if she does it?* What if she *is* the US Olympic gold medalist, the first American in the history of triathlon? What if that American is my little sister?

CHAPTER 9

Final Preparations

2016

NANCY

Since Gwen's flat tire in London 2012, her single focus was August 20, 2016. Every swim in pool, ocean current, crashing waves. Every run on track, park path, forest trail. Every bike ride on mountains, over cobblestones, at the velodrome. Every session with race car drivers, motorcycle riders, virtual reality headsets. Every go with exercise bands, stationary trainers, free weights. Every appointment for massage, physiotherapy, blood work. Every urine sample in Spain, Australia, Germany, Sweden, Japan, Canada, United States. Every protein-rich meal and organic vegetable. Every sleep, monitored for heart rate and analyzed for recovery. Every journal entry, race report, blog post. All executed in a quest for Olympic gold.

Gwen and Patrick flew to Australia on January 1, 2016, with Gwen's target race eight months away. She would take her mark on Rio's start line as a two-time World Champion. She would dive into Copacabana Beach owning records for most WTS wins, most consecutive wins, and a 2015 perfect, undefeated season. As

Gwen collected victories, we collected memorabilia—*Sports Illustrated* features, *Us Weekly* covers, triathlete magazine articles. In my scrapbook, Gwen was a phenom—the best triathlete on the planet. But the important things never changed. Holiday dinners, birthday celebrations, phone calls about nothing, goofy Snapchats, sisters teasing, daughters asking Mom for a recipe, or Dad to build a table.

****

After two months of training in Australia, Gwen entered a March 5 Continental Cup in Wollongong—her Australian home away from home. She followed with a World Cup on April 3 in New Plymouth, New Zealand. Victories in both complicated her win count. Since these were not part of the WTS, should they be included? Did they contribute to the tally, making it 15 consecutive? Reporters failed to find consensus, each expert determining his own total.

Gwen's first WTS race was in Gold Coast, Australia, on April 9. Elizabeth watched from her house with a few friends, and as Joel and I set up streaming, I considered the field of motivated competitors. Gwen had not lost a race since April 2014, but before the streak began, Britain's Jodie Stimpson and Helen Jenkins each beat her. Both were on Gold Coast's start list where a superior performance could earn one of them an Olympic spot. Several Australians sought Olympic qualification through a top-10 finish. Sweden's Lisa Norden (2012 London silver medalist) also vied for qualification.

After a two-lap swim in 25°C (77°F) water, Gwen exited in 10th to 28°C (82.4°F) air, down by 10 seconds. Eighteen riders converged, and for three laps they enjoyed a one-minute lead, Gwen riding middle of the lead pack.

In lap four, Flora Duffy of Bermuda initiated a breakaway, and Jenkins and New Zealand's Hewitt joined her. "Why doesn't Gwen get up there and go with them?" I asked as the trio manufactured a 10-second lead.

"She wasn't in front when they took off." The three leaders increased their margin to 26-seconds. "It's too late now."

ELIZABETH

Kassie and her infant daughter Opal, Josh and a few other friends crowded around my television, eating taco dip and pizza, drinking beer and sauvignon blanc. The room buzzed with conversation, the baby passed arm to arm. Josh turned up the TV, signaling us to hush, but we ignored him and raised our own volume, making Shepley's commentary inaudible.

A few days before, I asked Mom and Dad to join us, warning, "Everyone talks through the race, but it's fun."

"What? No," Mom said. "I need to hear the announcers." She paused. "Why do you want to watch that way?"

"It's more exciting with the group. And if you're nervous, my kitchen always needs cleaning. Plus, you re-watch the races anyway."

"No, I can't handle the talking."

NANCY

As the ride progressed, the breakaway expanded their margin. By the end of lap six, they were 47 seconds ahead; on lap seven, 1:17; and at the end of the bike, 1:37.

"Gwen's beaten Jenkins on the run before," Joel said. His optimism is hard to break.

Commentators discussed statistics. "Gwen Jorgensen, as we said, has run two minutes faster in the splits than Helen Jenkins in the past. She's going to have to run a similar pace here."

At the end of run-lap one, Jenkins led Hewitt and Duffy by 20 seconds, with Gwen 1:29 back. I wondered if this race would end Gwen's streak.

"She'll go faster soon," Joel said.

At the end of lap two, Jenkins had a 45-second advantage on Hewitt and Duffy, and 1:27 on Gwen. As Jenkins's performance told British Olympic selectors to "look at me," I worried Gwen wouldn't make the podium.

"Gwen will pick it up in the third lap," Joel said.

But completing lap three, Jenkins ran 1:00 ahead of Hewitt and Duffy, and 1:17 ahead of Gwen. I knew, with only one lap left, Gwen could not make up 77 seconds. She might recover 17 seconds to catch Hewitt or Duffy, but she couldn't win. Silence filled the air, Joel's confident predictions absent.

Commentator Emma Snowsill remarked on Gwen's imminent loss—her first in two years. "I honestly think, as scary as this sounds, it can be a blessing in disguise for Gwen. I mean, at some point...it can be a point of just taking that pressure off and for her...she doesn't need to prove herself now. She doesn't need to show that she can win a race here...I really honestly think that this could be probably the best thing that could happen to her. Unfortunate to say for the other athletes."

ELIZABETH

Now, as the race end neared, I wondered if Mom made the right decision. Wouldn't a loss be easier surrounded by Gwen's supporters?

Kassie, observing the uncharacteristic gap, asked, "What will happen if she loses? Will she be okay?"

"She'll have to be, right?"

It was clear Gwen wouldn't win this one, so we sent her Snapchats. I held baby Opal's fist, pumping it as I made her mouth move, adding my screams: "GO, GW! GO, GW!"

NANCY

Jenkins finished with a 41-second margin while Gwen ran with Hewitt and Duffy. Nearing the chute, Gwen and Hewitt sprinted. Considering the grit on my daughter's face, I hoped her thrusting, fibrous arms would send strength to her legs. Hewitt glanced to the right where Gwen squeezed an extra inch into each step. Gwen crossed the line one second ahead of Hewitt, who had to settle for bronze. Duffy, who ran in third the entire race, missed the podium and took fourth.

I searched for Gwen on the screen. She looked fatigued, and I wanted reassurance about her condition. But the camera focused on Jenkins and each successive finisher. Why did Gwen disappear? Why wasn't she congratulating the finishers?

I knew the streak would end someday, but still I questioned the loss. Was Gwen in a training block that produced fatigue? Was Jenkins tapered? Why didn't Gwen join the breakaway?

Instead of celebrating her podium, I grappled with the let down—the end of an era. For two years, the pattern repeated: pre-race jitters...cycling anxiety... celebrating the run...gold medal. Reality struck: Gwen was not infallible. But I was grateful the defeat happened now, allowing her time to repair fractures in her bedrock of training.

The optimist said, "She'll be fine. The important race is in August." But I knew he was disappointed too.

I wondered how Gwen felt about the end of her streak. And I wondered why she wasn't on the screen.

ELIZABETH

"Let's send her another Snapchat." I panned the group with my phone, capturing TEAM GWEN and London 2012 shirts. "We love you, Gwen!"— "Great job, Gwen."—"We're so proud of you."—"Awesome job!"—"Congrats!" Smiles and cheers continued as the Snap timed out. I sent it, hoping Gwen would find the celebration and happy faces reassuring, comforting.

We made no mention of her loss or that I cried (only a little) when she placed second. The tears surprised me, forcing me to wonder what happened and how Gwen felt.

NANCY

Gwen stepped to the interview platform, exhibiting sportsmanship—and exhaustion. "Helen was really strong today. She was the better athlete. Helen, and Andrea, and um, um, oh, I'm so tired right now." [Long pause.] "Who was the third one?" Her depletion evident, Gwen's brain obviously scrambled for information.

"Flora," the interviewer said.

"Flora, yes. They were riding really, really strong and yeah, you know they had a great race. I missed that pack. I wasn't up far enough and made a mistake, wasn't strong enough, and that was the race."

I was proud of her grace in defeat, but still worried about her potential over-exertion. *She was too exhausted to think of Flora Duffy's name.* I also wondered how she felt about second place. I sent an email.

> *Hi Gwenevere,*
>
> *So proud of you—as always. It looked like you worked really hard out there today. We were a little worried*

*when you came across the line, and then the camera
didn't follow you—waited and waited, and then we
were glad to see you were OK when you did the
interview. Even though you looked tired, you said all
the right things again!*

Are you going right to Spain?

Love you,

M & D

After I sent the email, Patrick's dad called. "What did you guys think?"

"Emma Snowsill was right. You hate to see the streak end, but this'll take some pressure off. It would be hard to enter Rio with that winning streak unbroken."

"I agree. She did great today. And we're spoiled—we think second place is a loss. Most of those women would be thrilled with silver."

Often, while waiting for drug testing, Gwen checked her email. I hoped she would do that today and reassure me she was healthy. I saw her response in a few minutes.

when I sprint I get tired. :)

*wish I was more upset about the race, but no tears
from me*

*I was super tired on that bike, and just wasn't as good
as the others today.*

I did fight for 2nd tho so that's good

*we head to Wollongong until Yoko then to spain
after yoko*

Gwen

Two weeks later, Specialized posted additional race footage and only then did I see Gwen at the finish line, bent at the waist, spit and mucus hanging from her mouth. Two officials held her up, one on each side. I wondered how many other details she hid from me.

ELIZABETH

I called Gwen. "We watched you today. Did you get the Snaps?"

"Yes! They were great." She sounded upbeat and like she did when she won. "Looks like you had a big group and lots of great food too. Was it fun?"

"Yes, very. Wish you were here with us." We both laughed. "How do you feel? What's it like not finishing first?"

"Fine." And she really sounded fine. "You know, winning today wasn't the plan. I didn't want to win today—"

"Well, let's be honest, you want to win every day." We both giggled, a giggle only we share, short and choppy and syncopated.

"Well, of course." She paused, apparently formulating an answer her non-athlete sister could understand. "But the plan is for me to win on August 20. It *really* wasn't about winning today. It was about executing the processes. And I learned a lot from this."

She sounded like she believed it, so I did too. "Well, no matter what, you know we're proud of you."

"Oh, EJ." She sighed a little, reminding me it was such a big sister thing to say. "What? I am!"

NANCY

Gwen's next race, on May 14, took her to Japan. She won the Yokohama event in 2013, 2014, and 2015, and analysts speculated about a four-peat. Stakes were high for others too, this the final opportunity to accrue Olympic points. Announcer Barrie Shepley predicted that by day's end, 30 more women would qualify for Rio. Point totals for each country would also be determined—the top eight nations would earn three Olympic spots, others only two. We watched from home as Shepley said, "Many times, athletes have said it was more stressful to make their Olympic team than it was at the actual Olympic Games, and I think this is going to be one of those days."

Katie Zaferes, a proven contender, vied for the third Team USA spot, but she needed a podium finish that beat USA's Renee Tomlin, Summer Cook, Kirsten Kasper, Lindsey Jerdonek, and Erin Jones. Shepley explained: "For her not to make the third spot for the United States, the US athlete has to get on the podium today, and they have to be ahead of [Zaferes]...If [Zaferes] gets on the podium today, it's done."

Temperatures were ideal—air at 25°C (77°F), water at 20.8°C (69.4°F)—but promotional banners whipped as choppy waves produced white-bubbled crests. Gwen later reviewed the conditions in her blog:

> There was a strong current coming from the left that hit the shore and then pushed the water back to the right (making it appear like the current was pushing athletes from right to left)...It was extremely choppy, making it difficult to move up and break away on the swim. This caused a massive pack to exit the water together.

"Oh, wow! Cook is first out of the water!" She was one of USA's newest talents.

"There's Gwen...twentieth," Joel said. "She's okay, though. Only thirteen seconds off."

Forty-two women formed a pack that remained intact throughout the bike. It included Gwen, Zaferes, Cook, Tomlin, and Kasper.

On the run, Japan's Ai Ueda went to the front, with Tomlin and Kasper close behind. Gwen quickly usurped their lead, putting 10 seconds between herself and the field.

"What do you think about so many USA women ahead of Zaferes?" I asked.

"I think Zaferes runs like Gwen—faster in the second 5K." At the end of lap two, Gwen increased her advantage to 43 seconds. Cook and Kasper led Zaferes by 10 seconds. Meanwhile, Ashleigh Gentle, seeking Australian qualification, surged to lead the chasers.

At the end of lap three, Gwen ran 1:02 ahead of Gentle. Ueda, the hometown favorite, ran in third. As my anxiety quelled, I contemplated Zaferes's race. "You were right. Zaferes caught Kasper." The two Americans ran side by side. "But they're still in ninth. Zaferes needs a podium to get to Rio."

At the tape, Gwen finished with a 1:08 advantage. Although she said her solitary goal was to win in Rio, I assumed every victory gave her confidence.

When Gentle came in second, Joel said, "Bet Australia picks her for Rio."

Ueda claimed bronze. Zaferes, with a final sprint, took sixth. She bested the remaining Americans, but did not earn a podium—once again missing automatic qualification. Discretion by committee would determine USA's third Rio spot.

I questioned USA's policy of automatic qualification. Of the American triathletes, Zaferes owned the strongest resume, with multiple WTS podiums. But if another woman had executed a rare stand-out performance in Yokohama, Zaferes would have been eliminated. I reminded myself Gwen did just that in London 2011. In the third WTS race of her career, she ran the race of her life and earned automatic qualification, taking a berth from competitors who spent years on the circuit.

The committee followed prescribed USA procedure. It was a protracted process, allowing fans time to comment. On social media, some accused Gwen of requesting a domestique. She remained silent as the committee deliberated.

More than a week later, USA named Zaferes to the team. The message was clear: USA would send three podium contenders, no one working as a domestique.

ELIZABETH

Dad's sister Colleen is the first to like an @gwenjorgensen tweet and never misses an opportunity to share an ITU Facebook post. Her newsfeed scrolls race-viewing parties and selfies with Gwen. Typically, she watches races at her house, Mom and Dad watch at theirs, and I watch at mine, each with our own rituals, company, and livestream. But before the Leeds race, Aunt Colleen sent me a text.

This time, let's watch the race at your house.

She invited herself, while Josh invited his dad. I envisioned the foursome: Josh and his dad, Aunt Colleen and me—and began mass texting Mom, Dad, Kassie, Uncle Greg, Aunt Chinchi, and Aunt Charlene. "Viewing party. My house. 6 a.m. I will have breakfast."

Mom hesitated—"I won't be able to hear the commentary"—but eventually agreed to join.

NANCY

On June 11, perched on Elizabeth's white leather couch, I monitored the 33 swimmers in Waterloo Lake. In Leeds, where the water registered 18.5°C (65.3°F) and the air 18.9°C (66°F), the Brits enjoyed hometown advantage.

With Elizabeth's morning crowd still quiet, I heard Trevor Harris and Barrie Shepley discuss the field—and the absence of Switzerland's Nicola Spirig (London 2012 gold medalist).

"She was originally on the start list, wasn't she?" Harris asked.

"Uh, you know," Shepley said. I heard hesitation in his words. "Her coach has not had her race very often against Gwen Jorgensen in the last years. We've seen [her] only two or three times."

"I was going to ask if it was kind of Gwen avoidance." Harris must have read the online articles I did, where analysts said Spirig's coach devised a mental game, saving his athlete's secret winning formula for August 20.

At the end of the swim, Bermudian Flora Duffy and two Brits—Lucy Hall and Jessica Learmonth—led a pack of nine, including Gwen, out of the water with a 45-second lead. I stood to do my bike-portion pacing.

ELIZABETH

Waiting through 20 minutes of splashes and kicks, I strained to see cap numbers, rarely able to identify a swimmer without Shepley's or Harris's help. We filled plates with breakfast and waited for the women to transition.

Kassie bounced Opal and asked, "How will Gwen do today? How's she feeling?" Aunt Charlene, ignoring the question, stuck a sausage in the five-month-old's mouth.

"I guess she's not a vegetarian anymore," I said, grabbing the sausage so Opal wouldn't choke.

Mom paced between living room and kitchen, circling back to hear the commentary we talked over.

NANCY

Duffy, still not in her bike shoes, surged and Britain's Learmonth and Hall responded, forming a lead trio. Gwen dropped into a chase pack, and within minutes the three leaders created a 15-second gap. When Harris asked the question in my head—*How much time can Gwen afford to give Duffy?*—Shepley said, "Sixty or seventy seconds and it could definitely be [Duffy's] win here today."

The Duffy-Learmonth-Hall train roared through the long first lap that traversed several West Yorkshire communities. Fans stood within inches, cheering the leaders to a 49-second advantage, and Shepley said, "The superior riders got away."

"Is that a concern for team Jorgensen ahead of Rio?" Harris voiced what we all thought.

"Huge! Huge!" Shepley said. "I would be very concerned if I'm Jamie Turner and the US program."

To me, as raindrops appeared on the camera lens, Leeds seemed a repeat of Gold Coast—Gwen defeated by a cycling breakaway.

As the crowd returned to the kitchen for second helpings, Harris recalled Duffy's comments on creating a multi-country breakaway. "She said to me, 'Of course we are, because it's the only way we can beat Gwen. We know we can't outrun her. We have to out-bike her and out-think her.'"

Still in the first lap, the leaders increased their advantage to 1:30, a successful execution of Duffy's strategy. Then the camera focused on them—gesturing, shouting. Although common, communication between riders is usually brief. This conversation extended over a minute.

Joel's brother Greg said, "What are they doing?"

"Looks like they're making a plan," Joel said.

Shepley questioned whether the Brits were instructed to slow the pace—with Great Britain's medal contenders in the chase pack, perhaps Learmonth and Hall worked to gain advantage for Jodie Stimpson, Vicky Holland, and Non Stanford.

ELIZABETH

We oscillated between our conversations and the race. We cheered, clapped, and hollered. "Dad, can Gwen make up this much time on the run?" I worried Duffy might hold her off.

"I'm calling it. It's in the bag. She's got this."

"Mom! Come in here. You're missing it. We're making predictions..."

NANCY

As I walked a circle around Elizabeth's first floor, Duffy's trio transitioned to the run, 1:30 ahead of Gwen's pack. Once off the bikes, Duffy ran ahead of Learmonth and Hall, prompting Harris to predict Duffy the victor.

At the end of lap one, Duffy led Learmonth and Hall by 24 seconds—and Gwen by 1:17.

During the second lap, Gwen advanced. Like a car speeding on the freeway, she approached. While the others motored steadily, Gwen stepped on the gas and placed herself in second, 38 seconds behind Duffy.

Shepley said, "Ahh, this is scary. That might be the most impressive first five kilometers off the bike I have ever seen. She still has to keep going for another five and there is absolutely no reason she will not be able to keep that pace. Wow! That is insane running by Gwen Jorgensen...I mean, I just don't see Duffy being able to hold her off."

The camera followed Gwen as she held her head and upper body still and erect. Her loose-swinging arms radiated a ripple through her shoulder muscles. In a circle of motion, her yellow race flats flashed their red soles—tap, tap, tap—in rhythm.

With one lap to go, Gwen and Duffy ran shoulder to shoulder past the grandstand. Gwen turned her head toward Duffy, and I read her lips say, "Great job." Then, mimicking Duffy's dominance on the bike, Gwen dominated on foot, accelerating into the distance.

Gwen not only erased her 1:30 deficit, she gained a 51-second lead. As she finished the race, she high-fived fans, at one point reaching into the crowd to brush a child's palm. Duffy, almost a minute later, claimed silver with more high fives. Holland earned bronze. Two other Brits finished in the top ten—Stimpson in fourth, Stanford in ninth. Learmonth and Hall, part of Duffy's three-woman breakaway, took 10th and 13th.

ELIZABETH

"Here, grab some leftovers. I packed containers for everyone," I said. "Mom, you should eat now."

"I knew it," Dad said. "I knew she would win."

The crowd dispersed, retreating home for a nap or chores, and the morning was over before 10 a.m.

NANCY

As Joel and I loaded our slow cooker in the car, I said, "Do you want to watch that again? I'd like to actually hear the announcers."

"I'll set it up after lunch."

We watched the replay, absorbing comments about Gwen, Rio, and triathlon strategy. I was familiar with domestiques and group tactics but learned more. In the one-minute cycling conversation, the Brits apparently informed Duffy about coaches' directives: slow the pace to allow Britain's superior runners (Stanford, Stimpson, and Holland) to stay close to the lead. Harris said, "It is quite a controversial thing this kind of team orders...There's no kind of hard and fast rule in triathlon. It just depends on how an individual federation sees things."

Shepley explained tactics can be motivated by "hundreds of thousands of dollars to your federation from the...governing bodies that fund them...For example, in Canada...the difference in your sport getting a medal in the Olympics and not are hundreds of thousands of dollars a year, so you're going to do everything in your power to be able to do that and have a great performance. In that case, if somebody has to dedicate their day to help your best athlete have a chance of winning a medal, guess what? All of us will share in the finances for the next four years."

We listened to post-race interviews Elizabeth's crowd ignored. Gwen once more voiced her plan: "Rio's the focus for the year, as you know, so it's great to come into these races and get exposed a little and see where I can improve." It occurred to me that while Gwen revealed weaknesses in order to fix them, Spirig wouldn't have that opportunity if she avoided Gwen in competition.

Duffy commented with parsed, yet blunt, words: "The British girls weren't working with me. They had some team tactics that they were...um...using...They were just told they had to [long pause] ride a certain way and so therefore I was the only one who could do work..."

The race raised questions. What if the Brits had worked with Duffy? What if Duffy executed a more successful breakaway in Rio? Gwen erased a 1:30 deficit and won by another 51 seconds—could she repeat that on August 20?

Leeds marked her schedule's midpoint and even with the Olympic race eight weeks away, Gwen and Patrick took a break.

> *Every year in the middle of the season, I take a few days to relax, recharge, and get away from triathlon. We did an amazing drive around Norway, immersed ourselves in fjords, mountains, and glacial lakes, and enjoyed the beauty of Norway and the delicious seafood. Also, I now have a new favorite food: brown cheese.*

When Gwen returned from Norway to prepare for Hamburg—one final event before the Olympic race—she continued broadcasting her intent to win Olympic gold. In Nancy Armour's *USA TODAY Sports* interview, Gwen said, "My only focus this year is Rio. It's been my goal to go to Rio and win the gold for four years."

I read reports that proclaimed Gwen the gold medal pick. I also read about previous favorites who didn't fulfill the prophecies. What would happen if Gwen didn't win gold? What would she say? Did she think about that? Was her strategy say-it-and-it-will-come-true? Was she convincing herself? Her competitors? Fate?

> *Leading into Hamburg, the Wizards were in the middle of a Rio training block. Smashed legs and struggles getting out of bed were common. Hamburg was on the backburner and two weeks before the race, I had doubts. I told Jamie, "We haven't done Hamburg prep, and we know what happened last time I didn't do specific prep for a race." I began to calm down after a small chat with Coach [Jamie] and realized my fitness was on point. Part of being a professional is being able to stand up and perform under any circumstance.*

As Joel and I planned our July 16 viewing, Elizabeth said, "I'm camping that week with Josh and Kassie, but Josh thinks he can set up a computer. What time does the race start?"

I sent Saturday's race time, ignoring Sunday's relay. In 2015, Gwen declined to participate, avoiding dangerous, rainy conditions. With the imminent Olympic race, I assumed she would not risk injury in the fast pace of tags and exchange zones.

The next day, Joel said, "Colleen wants the family to watch at our house. Is that okay?"

Gwen's success brought us together. I appreciated that and reminded myself if they talked too much, we could watch the race again after they left.

On race day, Joel's family joined us at the television in time for the swim start. Trevor Harris mentioned Gwen had not faced Britain's Helen Jenkins since Jenkins beat her in Gold Coast. Completing the 10-minute sprint distance swim, USA's Katie Zaferes exited sixth. She looked strong, proving her worth as an Olympian. Gwen completed the swim in 14th, six seconds ahead of Jenkins.

A lead pack of eight cyclists formed. "Is Gwen in that pack?" I asked, my voice obscured by Joel's sister, Colleen, quoting stats and Joel's brother, Greg, shouting at the television. "Joel!" I said. "JOEL! Is Gwen in the front pack?"

"Uh...no, I don't think so." I couldn't believe he was listening to the blather and not concentrating on the race.

ELIZABETH

After an early morning jog, Kassie and I returned to the campsite to find Josh at the picnic table. "I got the Wi-Fi hotspot to work."

Kassie and I grabbed breakfast. "What's happening? Anything exciting?" I didn't realize the race was a sprint and we missed the shortened swim.

"They're just getting on the bike. It doesn't look like Gwen will make the first pack."

I squinted to see his laptop's screen. "Can you tilt that?" The sun's glare masked the video. "And I can't hear it."

"Yeah, I know. I'm working on that." While fiddling with his portable speaker, he minimized the picture, leaving only muffled commentary.

"Oh, I guess it's fine if we just watch."

NANCY

Gwen's chase pack rode 15 seconds behind, with Jenkins in a group that trailed by another 15. As Colleen read aloud from Twitter, I avoided the cycling.

I walked to my dining room, poked a thumb in plant pots, straightened pillows, and cleaned dust from my piano. When I heard an update from Shepley, I said, "So Jenkins joined Gwen's chase pack?" No one heard me.

Venturing a peek, I inventoried the lead bike group. Two excellent runners lurked, gaining time: Zaferes and Rachel Klamer of the Netherlands. When the leaders increased their advantage to 38 seconds, I heard Harris say, "And if it does get somewhere near a minute, and that's perfectly possible...that will make it fascinating to see whether Gwen can haul back that kind of a deficit. Also Jenkins, too...but can they run through from a [one] minute deficit over just 5,000 meters? We'll see."

Shepley said, "As we get closer to the Olympic games, you have to think Katie Zaferes, you have to think Rachel Klamer—both fantastic runners—are putting themselves in a good position for a podium and maybe a victory...There aren't a lot of chances to win one of these things, so when you get yourself in that position, why not take a risk and go for it?"

What if Gwen lost her last race before the Olympics? What would a defeat do to her confidence? What about the Olympic race—how would Gwen respond to a breakaway like this in Rio?

I tuned out chatter and caught Harris saying, "If this gets to somewhere near 50 seconds, Barrie, my question to you is, can someone like Katie Zaferes—if we think she's somewhere back to her best—can she stave off Jorgensen with a 50-second start over a 5K?"

I wondered too.

With one lap remaining, the front pack led by 46 seconds. Shepley said, "They are moving into the 50-second window and that is still possible for Gwen Jorgensen...So the question is, how hard does Gwen Jorgensen want to run?"

On the bike, I saw a few close calls of people almost crashing. My mind and body switched to protection mode. Six weeks out from the biggest race of my life, I started to play defense. I knew coming into transition I needed to be on the front, but chose to be cautious and safe, entering T2 almost last.

Gwen and Jenkins entered transition in the same pack. Jenkins, moving adroitly, started the run 50 seconds behind. Gwen lost 20 seconds and ran

70 seconds behind. I reminded myself that Gwen's goal was August 20 in Rio, not July 16 in Hamburg.

ELIZABETH

"What was going on with Gwen on the bike?" Josh asked.

Gwen looked stiff, strained. "She said she's in the middle of really hard training. Maybe her muscles can't get going?"

"I'm used to her more confident, more in charge. She doesn't look like Gwen."

Kassie said, "I remember hell week in swimming." She referred to the hardest training block she and Gwen did each year on Waukesha South High School's swim team. "I just didn't want to do anything. And even in competition, I couldn't get my body to go. Everything was tight and heavy."

"I hope that's it," I said. "I'm shocked at how far back she is."

NANCY

Zaferes and Klamer ran confidently, heads steady, arms efficiently reinforcing their strides. Greg and Colleen shouted at the screen. Joel, the peacemaker, said nothing to quiet them.

Gwen quickly passed several competitors. Joel turned up the volume as Shepley said, "Look at Gwen, just destroying...look at this! It looks like a 1,500 meter run. She just needs a blocker in front of her to knock down some other people as she's trying to get through." Shepley named competitors as she passed them. "Backhouse, BOOM, gone. Philippin, BOOM, gone. Aileen Reid, BOOM, gone."

At the end of lap one, Gwen reduced her deficit to 32 seconds and positioned herself in third. Up front, Zaferes created a margin on Klamer. Behind, Jenkins ran in the middle of the chase pack.

With 800 meters to go, I hoped the camera angle deceived me and that Gwen was closer to Zaferes than she appeared. Shepley said, "Here comes Gwen Jorgensen, but I think she's going to run out of geography."

Coverage switched to Zaferes sprinting. Glasses up, she relaxed and released a smile as she took gold. Eleven seconds later, Klamer claimed silver. Fifteen seconds after that, Shepley said, "And it will be Gwen Jorgensen who will be coming [in] third across the line."

Gwen smiled and hugged Zaferes. I read Gwen's lips say, "Good job."

"And it is...the great Gwen Jorgensen," Shepley said, "and a very classy Jorgensen showing appreciation for another countrywoman, her Olympic teammate. Wow! What an Olympic team the United States has heading off to the Games."

In the post-race interview, Gwen said, "Obviously, I'm disappointed, a little bit gutted with my race, but to have Katie cross the line first, definitely bittersweet today...[I] just didn't have it today...I'm not thrilled, but again, you know Katie came across the line first and that's just incredible for her first win and keeping it in the USA family."

Patrick told me Gwen hates to lose more than she loves to win. I wondered how she had the presence after an exhausting race to express humility. I worried about this second loss. And in Gwen's last race before Rio.

ELIZABETH

Now there were two losses. And we tried to figure out why.

Commentary continued online, but Josh's computer refused connection with the wireless speaker. Josh, who would travel with us to the Olympics, said what haunted me: "With the Olympics coming up, are these girls getting an edge on Gwen? Are they figuring out how to beat her?"

"I hope not!" I couldn't believe he said it. I didn't want him putting negativity into the universe. "I'm sure she and Jamie have a plan." Zaferes stood atop the first-place step, waving to the crowd, and I wondered what Gwen thought.

"Well, Gwen needs to do something to adapt to these girls getting stronger. And she has to get with that first bike pack, no matter what."

Two years ago, Josh didn't know what a WTS race was—and now he knew the magic formula. "Obviously, that's a better strategy. And clearly, she was trying to make that first pack."

Kassie asked, "Do you think she's in trouble?" Her unspoken words: Will she be able to win when it's for Olympic gold?

"I think she's fine. The goal is August 20 in Rio. Let's send her a Snapchat."

Later, Olympic.org would write that "chinks in [Jorgensen's] armour started to appear in the build-up to Rio, as she suffered two defeats in short succession."

NANCY

I knew my role was family support—not coach, or mentor, or interviewer—so I dismissed questions and emailed positive words, asking about the charter flight Gwen enjoyed, courtesy of a sponsor.

> *Hi Gwen,*
>
> *So glad the rain held off and everyone had a safe race! We had a group here watching—Greg, Chinchi, Colleen, Charlene—and breakfast during the race. (I was too nervous to eat...hahaha)*
>
> *GREAT interview, complimenting Katie. And you looked genuinely happy for her in your finish line hug. So proud of you! And good job on a podium too!*
>
> *Looking forward to seeing you in Rio - say hi to Pat and Jamie (and Charlotte and Sarah-Anne, and all the rest)*
>
> *Is your return flight a charter again? If so, enjoy it!*
>
> *Love you,*
>
> *Mom & Dad*

I waited all day for a reply and when none appeared, I wondered if Gwen was busy with drug testing, or media, or the men's race, or dinner with Patrick. Or was she upset? Finally, the next morning, when I checked my email at 5 a.m., I saw her reply. No salutation. No valediction.

so sad after that race. and thanks for reminding me -
yes charter flight home but not like i deserve it

I'm racing relay today. :)

So she was upset. But racing the relay? What was she thinking? She could crash and break a collarbone. She could pull a hamstring. She could trip in transition. She could ruin her quest for Olympic gold. Considering the fast tempo and risks, few countries entered their Olympians. Monetary prizes were minimal and neither ITU nor Olympic points were awarded. But Gwen said she was racing. With a smiley face.

I thought I knew her reasons: Redemption. Team.

In a few hours, when Joel and I streamed computer to television, I heard Harris say, "It's the fastest and most frenetic form of triathlon there is." As Gwen and 17 competitors stood at the swim start, I was glad she led—she avoided at least one tag-off.

Harris mentioned outstanding performances that often result from relay format. "You don't want to let your teammates down, do you?"

Shepley agreed. "Often, we've seen people's best performances at the relay race. You know, better than they raced the day before." I hoped their comments foreshadowed Gwen's results.

A good swim and transition placed Gwen in the lead cycling group. She rode at the front, holding off chasers, and then transitioned to the run.

"Well, that's a much better transition zone today for Gwen Jorgensen," Shepley said. "Terrible yesterday. She was dead last out of the transition zone. She's third here and zooming immediately."

In the one-mile run, Gwen created a 10-second advantage for Ben Kanute.

Kanute built on Gwen's lead with a solo breakaway on the bike, increasing USA's advantage to over 45 seconds.

Kirsten Kasper took over, swimming, riding, and running solo, again holding off competitors, and tagged Joe Maloy.

Maloy, starting with a 33-second advantage, increased the lead to 50 seconds, and Shepley said, "There's no question that the combo of Gwen Jorgensen and Ben Kanute have given this lead so that Kasper was able to hold on and Joe Maloy has had the luxury of just being able to race stress free."

Maloy, who never won a WTS medal, headed for the finish holding both arms aloft, forefingers pointing straight up. He grabbed the tape and ran into the arms of Gwen, Kanute, and Kasper.

"I'm so proud of them," Gwen said in a post-race interview. "It was amazing, you know, they all had to do it the tough way—solo—which is really hard. I'm just so proud, and yeah, it was incredible today."

In her tweet about the weekend, Gwen posted three pictures. All celebrated the USA relay team with not one of her bronze podium.

In six weeks, Gwen would compete in the Rio 2016 Olympic race.

CHAPTER 10

Rio de Janeiro

2016

NANCY

As Olympic publicity exploded, I shopped weekly at Barnes & Noble, alerted by Gwen, or her agent, or Snapchat that she graced a magazine cover—or hid inside. "Elizabeth, I'm going to the bookstore," I said. "Did you see *Us Weekly* with Gwen and her doppelgänger? It's Kate Middleton."

"No. Can you get me one?"

"How about *Marie Claire* too? It has her picture and fun facts like her guilty pleasures and beauty routine."

"That should be short—she doesn't have a beauty routine."

Gwen occupied pages in *Outside Magazine*, *Oxygen*, *Self*, and *Popular Science*. I already collected triathlon periodicals that featured her. Suddenly, she circulated in glossy magazines that real people read.

I talked with Gwen about the publicity. "Should I get copies for you, too?"

"Usually, I don't care about that stuff, but I really want the *Us* Collector's Edition—I can't believe I share a cover with Serena Williams and Gabby Douglas."

Two weeks before the August 20 race, I dove into a *Sports Illustrated* piece by Austin Murphy. His perspective seemed hyperbolic—"...Jorgensen has emerged as the International Triathlon Union's equivalent of Usain Bolt"—but reassuring. Didn't Usain Bolt win every race? Murphy discussed Gwen's fear of biking speed and the "twisting, narrow and steep road plunging to Copacabana Beach, site of the upcoming Olympic triathlon." He wrote, "Jorgensen has hit the pavement before and will again." Not reassuring.

The article detailed Gwen's training for descents and the fear that accompanies them. First, as a motorcycle passenger, she rode five miles fraught with blind corners. It familiarized her with speed and the techniques needed to navigate safely. Then, she duplicated the descent on her bike, side by side with coaches. But even those coaches had a history of fractures, cracked vertebra, and emergency airlift. The article diverged into diving heights that terrified David Boudia and cycling accidents that resulted in surgeries for Taylor Phinney. "Elizabeth, I bought *Sports Illustrated* for you. But don't read it. There are things you don't want to know."

We watched the first week of Olympic competition from home. "Is this road cycling? In the rain?" I asked. Joel was fascinated by the breakaways, pelotons, and tortuous descents. "At least triathlon has shorter downhills." I avoided the television.

"Don't look. There's a crash."

I approached anyway—a mistake. By the time I got there, more riders ripped skin on pavement before splatting against a barrier that prevented a cliff-side tumble.

"I'll mute the sound," Joel said.

But producers rehashed each crash. And when we switched channels, the images replayed in my head.

ELIZABETH

On Tuesday, August 16, Mom checked passports as Josh loaded suitcases in his Jeep. We were en route to Chicago's O'Hare airport for a three-hour trip to Miami, a layover, and finally a nine-hour overnight flight to Rio de Janeiro,

Brazil. I felt nervous and uneasy. This is where the end of the story began. I anticipated leaving Rio elated or regretful. The sister of an Olympic gold medalist who fulfilled expectations and proclamations or the sister of the favorite who crashed or suffered a flat tire, just like in London. I prepared to cry either way.

We arrived hours before our flight and agreed on lunch outside the terminal. In matching TEAM GWEN shirts, we looked for LongHorn's hostess. A woman waiting for her table asked, "What are those shirts?" She looked unathletic in her silk blouse and employer's ID badge.

Dad said, "We're going to the Olympics to watch our daughter."

She opened her eyes wider. "Oh, really? That's so cool. I love the Olympics. What sport?"

"Triathlon." Dad turned to show the back of his shirt: #GWENSANITY.

"Oh, it sounds awesome. I'll have to watch. What's her name?"

Talking over each other, we said, "Gwen."—"Gwen Jorgensen."

The hostess interrupted. "I can take you to your table. Four of you?"

From our booth, we ordered a round of beers to calm our pre-flight and race anxiety when the woman returned. "Oh, my goodness. I'm sorry to interrupt." Her eyes watered. "I Googled your daughter." She looked at Dad. "She's the Olympic favorite? For the gold? I can't believe it."

I said, "You're crying? Don't cry. You'll make me cry too."

She touched my arm as she got out her phone. "Can we take a picture? I'm going to watch the race. I'll be cheering the whole time. I can't wait to go back to work—I'm going to tell my co-workers I met the family of the soon-to-be gold medalist."

Our waiter offered to take the picture. The woman crouched in front of us, her enthusiasm prickling the hair on my arms as I fought her contagious tears.

NANCY

We arrived in Rio on Wednesday, four days before the race. Our goals: attend an Olympic event each day, reserve time for Gwen's inevitable errands, and enjoy our second Olympic experience. I lectured myself: *This should be fun. You are the mother of the Olympic favorite. It should be the most exciting week of your life.* And it was. But it was also the most unsettling. I used Gwen's visualization techniques and sketched images of her on the podium, accepting the gold. I imagined the grandstand celebration. I envisioned a life without what-ifs and relied on our busy schedule to deflect anxiety.

We checked in at the JW Marriott on Copacabana Beach—an Americanized hotel with grand lobby, conference halls, and concierge. Rooms were spacious and air-conditioned. Personnel spoke fluent English. In the bathroom, we tossed toilet paper into the bowl—anathema in every other facility where placards read, "Please no paper in the toilet" and a wastebasket kept Charmin from the ocean. Turn-down service and evening chocolates erased any thought of favelas (slums, ruled by drug lords, that sprawled across the hillsides). A dignified contrast to the cramped local hotel we booked in 2015, this JW Marriott once housed President Obama.

After checking in, we inquired about a Brazilian steakhouse.

"My friends eat here," the concierge said while on hold for reservations. After trilling Portuguese into the phone, she smiled. "They're holding a table for you. It's only a 10-minute walk."

Following her directions, we found the restaurant under a red awning. We gorged on a buffet of sushi, pickled fish, and salads—and then mounds of grilled meat carved directly onto our plates. Later, I was glad we enjoyed this authentic lunch because most future meals were in hospitality houses or the hotel breakfast room.

"We could see track and field this evening," I said between courses. "We should be able to order tickets online. They're about $150 each." For finals, best prices were $370. Finding $150 tickets seemed a bargain.

"Let's do it," Elizabeth said. "But I think they call it athletics."

At the hotel, I accessed the ticket website on my iPhone, but twice my credit card was refused.

"I'm sorry your card was denied," the Capital One agent said in a phone call. "You are approved, but the Rio website is not working."

With only hours before athletics started, we checked with the concierge who described a beachside ticket booth. Elizabeth, Josh, and I set off on foot while Joel rested.

"Liz, I just got a whiff of the smell you warned me about." Josh put his hand over his nose.

"Yeah, and it's worse when you don't have the ocean breeze."

At the kiosk, we waited 15 minutes for an agent to appear. Working slowly, she placed our order and swiped my card. Success! To save time, we hailed a taxi to the hotel and met Joel.

"What a mess, Dad. Even at the kiosk, ticket sales were disorganized. It's just like reporters say—Rio is not ready for the Games. You good? I'll get a taxi." We piled in and Elizabeth showed our driver the stadium address.

In the evening heat of the open-air stadium, rows and rows sat unoccupied. Instead of climbing to our nosebleed section, I pointed to seats closer to the track. "Is this okay? We can always move."

"This railing is perfect," Elizabeth said as she unfurled our three- by five-foot American flag.

As the men's decathlon began, we followed USA's Ashton Eaton in high jump. Then activity escalated as long jump started. Soon, javelin throwers made it a three-ring spectacle, launching their eight-foot spears into a grassy field. Officials noted each throw and loaded the javelins, straight up, into toy-sized remote-controlled cars that returned them to the athletes.

When a woman next to me smiled and asked where we were from, I continued the conversation. "Are you from Brazil? Do you know why the stadium is so empty?"

She seemed offended. "Everyone is waiting for Usain Bolt. It will be filled when he runs."

Crowds increased slightly for Bolt's appearance, but media reported low turnout at other venues too. I assumed inefficient ticket sales affected attendance.

By evening's end, we cheered Eaton's progress, got on our feet for Bolt, and waved our flag for a USA podium sweep of the women's 100-meter hurdles.

ELIZABETH

The next morning, at the hotel breakfast buffet, we heaped our table with coffee, tea, juice, and plates of cheese, meat, eggs, and fruit. Next to us, a wall of windows framed billowing waves on Copacabana Beach where early-morning joggers dotted the oceanfront.

As I rubbed bleary eyes and faked enthusiasm, I focused on three people a few tables over. They reminded me of us. The daughter—tall, slender, in athletic gear—ate slowly and attended to her parents' questions. "You see her?" I whispered.

"Who?" Dad ignored my quiet cue. "Where?"

"Shhhh. That one." I pointed across my coffee cup. "Do you know who that is?"

Mom turned to look. "No, who?"

"That has to be Kristi Castlin." I searched on my phone, comparing an online image to the woman across the room.

"Who?" Mom asked.

"The hurdler. She took bronze last night." I spent days watching NBC Olympic coverage, observing athlete personalities and performances. Castlin wore a bindi between her eyebrows, and I recalled her elation as she qualified, surprisingly beating Keni Harrison. "Do you think it would be weird if I asked for a selfie?" Gwen, frequently approached, obliged fans, and I hoped Castlin would do the same.

"You sure it's her?" Josh asked.

"No. But I'm doing it now before I lose my confidence." Cell phone in hand, I approached Castlin. "I'm so sorry to interrupt. We were just enjoying breakfast and I...I...hope you find this a compliment. I think you look a lot like Kristi Castlin."

She looked up from her plate and smiled. "That's because that's me."

"Oh! You did so great in the hurdles. We were there. To see USA go one-two-three...What a race! Would you mind if we take a selfie?" I held my phone out long and upwards, finding the best light.

"I can take it," Kristi's mom said as she took the phone from my hands.

Kristi put her arm around me. "Who else are you cheering for?"

I told her about Gwen and the triathlon, encouraging her to attend. She was on her way home but wished Gwen and our family luck. I was reminded that athletes, like Gwen, were in Rio fulfilling a goal and a dream. They squeezed family time between commitments and fan requests.

Throughout the trip, my confidence grew as more athletes agreed to selfies. Olympians, magnificent on television, shrank to life-size as they welcomed a fangirl. By week's end, my portfolio featured a far-away Usain Bolt, the Olympic rings, and cardboard cutouts of Allyson Felix and Simone Biles. Even more impressive were my photos with Richard Murray, Andrea Salvisberg, and Greg Billington (4th, 16th and 37th respectively in the Rio men's triathlon); Nicola Spirig (2012 triathlon gold medalist); David Boudia (bronze medal in the Rio 10-meter platform diving); Dan Patrick and Tony Dungy (American sportscasters);

the Olympic Torch; Mo Farah (double Rio gold medalist in the 5,000 and 10,000 meters); Sven Riederer (bronze medalist in the 2004 Athens men's triathlon); and Meb Keflezighi (33rd in the Rio marathon). I posted my collection to Facebook, challenging friends and family to identify each.

NANCY

The next day, Thursday, Gwen called. "Hi, Mom. You guys stopping by our hotel? I'm free from nine to eleven."

"With all of Jamie's travel, ASICS sent his gear to us. Can we bring you anything else?"

"Just bring Jamie's stuff. But is it too far to walk?"

"It's only eight blocks. We'll be fine."

We arrived, flushed from the 80-degree morning, and hugged Gwen and Patrick. Then, Gwen lounged on the bed while Elizabeth examined Gwen's closing ceremony outfit.

"Is this Jamie's?" Patrick poked through the bag. Although Jamie coached athletes from several countries, ASICS provided USA gear for race day. They sent free apparel for us too. Olympic rules banned athletes from wearing sponsored clothing, so outfitting family or coach advertised support.

Joel admired Gwen's race bike. "This is new—an orange bike."

"Touch it," Patrick said. "It changes color with the heat." When Joel clasped the frame with his hand, a palm-shaped section turned from orange to yellow. He snapped a photo for his brothers and sisters.

"I have some errands for you," Gwen said. "I think it'll be fun, though. Your names are on pass lists at the Red Bull House and the Oakley House." Sponsors hosted hospitality houses where athletes and guests could relax, graze at a buffet, or watch the Games. "Just pick up my packages and then everything will be free."

"Tomorrow maybe? Men's triathlon is today," Joel said.

"Yeah, of course. We want to watch that too." Pre-race, Gwen didn't attend events in person but followed online coverage. "EJ, will you be in the grandstand?"

"Mom and Dad have tickets. Josh and I are watching from the street."

Later that day, inside the triathlon venue, Joel and I met Gwen's agent, Heather, and found seats in the nearly full grandstand—a ticket was no guarantee of a seat and hundreds of fans paid $75 to stand. I tried to memorize my internal calm so

I could channel it on Saturday—but already my stomach fluttered thinking about Gwen on this course.

ELIZABETH

During the men's triathlon, Heather told Mom about an Ernst & Young gift to be presented that evening. Mom agreed the family would accept it for Gwen. So, after dinner, we met in Marriott's second floor hospitality room where Ernst & Young employees clutched wine goblets and caipirinhas next to an Olympic torch.

Addressing the crowd, executive Steve Howe said, "We asked our people... to contribute our best wishes to Gwen. That's what's in this book. Maybe a last minute extra piece of inspiration. We give you this book to pass along to Gwen."

Heather and I took turns at the microphone, thanking the crowd, commending Ernst & Young's sponsorship of both Gwen and the Olympic Games. After the presentation, in a Q&A, Benita Fitzgerald Mosley (1984 Olympic champion) said, "We just won our 1,000th summer Olympic medal a few days ago...That's it... There are 300 million people in the United States today...Think about the rarified air that one is in, not only if you win a gold medal, but just to make an Olympic team...It's a terrific honor."

The interviewer interrupted. "There are 100,000 Olympians living in the world today. It's a very small club."

I felt pride in my sister's accomplishment. She lived in rarified air. And I hoped she would add to the American gold medal total. But my vibrating phone interrupted the daydream with a text from her.

> *Huge favor! I need two yellow edition Red Bulls. Tropical/yellow edition. If you see and can grab [them] that'd be awesome. Pat can meet you or you can drop off at our hotel? ;)*

I promised to do my best tomorrow.

The next afternoon, we arrived at the Red Bull House, set in a paddle board club on the water. A hostess greeted us. We gave Gwen's name and received her bag of shoes, apparel, backpack, and Red Bull. I submitted her request for the yellow cans, but they had none on site. I assumed Gwen wanted the cans for her traditional race day water bottle: half water, half Red Bull. Recently, she insisted on the tropical flavor—an exclusive edition not easily found.

We lounged on the patio when I spied a jet ski, two Red Bull decals charging its fiberglass nose. The adrenaline machine screamed pre-race distraction. "Josh, will you go with me?"

He analyzed the choppy, unclean waters. "No, I don't think so."

"Dad?"

"Maybe."

I walked to the jet ski when our waitress said, "You can't actually drive it. Some girls took off yesterday and nearly killed themselves. Someone will take you."

Lifejacket clasped, I put my arms around a Brazilian who spoke no English. Tanned, in his early twenties, he used hand signals to communicate as we glided through a channel to the ocean. Fishermen and swimmers dotted the path. The 15-minute ride ended with me at the helm, waving at Mom, Dad, and Josh, the driver holding my waist. When I got off, a full box of yellow Red Bull had appeared. Apparently, to keep Olympians happy, sponsors granted impossible requests.

NANCY

A posh club atmosphere welcomed us at our next stop—the Oakley House. Low-slung leather couches circled a giant screen playing live Olympic action. Beyond, at the outdoor patio, we spooned açai under a pergola, and then wandered a manicured lawn, filled with hammocks that overlooked a horse track.

Back inside, Elizabeth approached the desk. "Hi. I'm here for a package— Gwen Jorgensen."

Oakley's Greg Welch, fit and trim at 52, offered his hand. He approved our pickup and pointed us toward the buffet of grilled meats, seafood, and salads. We overindulged on the gourmet fare and headed back to our hotel.

ELIZABETH

While Craig, Jane, and Paige used the subway, we preferred taxis and Ubers, chatting with drivers who shared Rio's culture and hospitality. One driver, chubby and smiley, transported us from the Oakley House to our hotel.

"English not good," he said as he confirmed our route on his app.

"That's okay. Hablas Español?" During our 2015 trip to Rio, I used my high school Spanish.

Putting his phone to his face and speak activating its translation app, Portuguese spilled from his mouth—nasal vowels and strong Rs. The app deciphered his words: "We can communicate this way. It will be fun." For 45 minutes, he made jokes and asked questions, all translated by his phone.

As we exited the car, Patrick pedaled toward us, a backpack hunching his shoulders. "Hi, guys! You got the goods?"

I offered the bag of swag, and Patrick looked through it. Josh stood by, holding the box of Red Bull.

"How is Gwen feeling?" Mom asked.

"Yeah, good. She's ready to race tomorrow." Patrick pulled out shoes and a top. "And she just needs two of the Red Bulls." He remounted his bike and said, "Gwen's waiting. Gotta run."

NANCY

As anticipation built, I was grateful for the diversion of errands and Friday evening's futebol (soccer) tickets. Late in the afternoon, we hitched a ride on Ernst & Young's chartered bus. Our destination: Maracana Stadium for the gold medal women's match between Sweden and Germany. We arrived at the venue with tickets purchased online several weeks earlier.

"Mom! How did you get these tickets? Only 12 rows from the goal?"

I wondered too—we were close enough to see the athletes' defined muscles as they warmed up. In contrast to athletics, this arena filled fast with tourists and Brazilian families. Perhaps attendance reflected Rio's well-known love affair with futebol.

As the match started, I turned to Josh. "Where is the scoreboard? And game clock?"

A knowledgeable sports fan, Josh explained. "Each half is forty-five minutes, but the official has discretion in adding time."

"And we don't know how many minutes have passed or the score?" I didn't understand, considering my familiarity with the NBA shot clock or the dramatic final seconds of an NFL fourth quarter.

"The players don't see a clock either." Josh defined free kicks, offsides, and shootouts. It would take years to absorb the rules—aspects of cycling and triathlon still mystified me—and I decided to just enjoy the action.

A close score spawned raucous shouts, repeated rounds of the wave, and chants sung to recorded music. After Germany won, we lingered, waiting for the awards ceremony as officials hauled podiums, lined up players, and assembled a platter of medals. When Germany's national anthem played, a group across the aisle waved miniature flags—black, red, and yellow stripes. I hoped tomorrow's anthem would be celebrated with red, white, and blue and my daughter on the top step.

ELIZABETH

The Ernst & Young bus left at halftime, so after the game we searched for a ride to the JW Marriott. But barricades blocked traffic—even buses and taxis were prohibited in the area—as streets overflowed with the stadium's 78,000 fans.

Perched in chairs similar to lifeguard stands, staff and volunteers wore 361 Degrees brand track pants and matching shirts. They pointed, directing the crowds.

We looped the stadium. Through dark streets, punctuated by camera flashes and streetlights, we arrived at our only option: three flights of steep, rickety metal steps. I looked to Dad. "Can you make this? Should we turn around?"

"I can do it," Dad said. "Not much choice."

I clung to the railing, uneasy with its swaying, exposed risers. I grabbed Josh's hand and hustled to the top. "Where are we going? How do we know what to do?" I asked questions, but Mom, Dad, and Josh followed the crowd, failing to answer. Josh covered his nose each time sewage stench belched from a manhole.

A concrete path led to the train station. The crowds overwhelmed me, and I was apprehensive—we hadn't used public transportation. I found another person in 361 Degrees. "Do you speak English?"

He shook his head.

"Copacabana?" I signaled the question with my hands, asking left or right. People pushed past as Mom studied a map. "Mom, Dad, Josh! He pointed right."

The crowds driving our pace, we rode the escalator below ground and boarded without tickets—the subway turnstiles spun free rides in the post-game celebration. "Does anyone know where we're going? When will we get off?"

We stood, crammed on the train, jockeying for a view of the map. "I'm not sure," Mom said as she and I studied the stops: Riocentro, Alvorada, Sambodromo, Marina da Gloria. None looked familiar.

Continuing their festive mood, fans laughed and conversed, one hand anchored to a pole or strap as they swayed with the moving train. Yellow and green Brazilian costumes populated the cars, but it was our American accents and fair complexions that prompted stares. I just wanted to get off and find a taxi.

Mom, struggling with motion sickness, turned to me. "Well, I'm not nervous about the race—now, I'm worried I might throw up."

A tall Brazilian in his early twenties tapped me on the shoulder. "Do you need help?"

"Yes! We do."

"Where are you going?" At 6'4", with dark hair and a beard still growing in, he comforted me with his confident English.

"Copacabana Beach. Are we on the right train?"

"Yes, this will take you there...at least, it *should*." He paused to laugh and introduce his dad. "When there are games, sometimes the conductors are nice. They'll probably keep the lines open to the beach. If not, you'll transfer."

I hesitated, uneasy with Brazilian customs of should, and sometimes, and probably. "How will we know?"

"I will help. We're going to the same place."

Through the 45-minute ride, the subway train lurched, hesitated, and stalled. My Brazilian hero conversed about his dad's education in America and his own studies in Australia. I told him about Gwen, and he jotted "Jorgensen" in his phone, promising to follow her after they watched canoeing, kayaking, and water polo. When the line ended near Copacabana Beach as he predicted, we said goodbye, and he wished Gwen luck. Climbing subway stairs to dark skies and familiar surroundings—we walked these streets in 2015—we bought gelato and rehashed our adventure.

Arriving at the JW Marriott, we found Craig in the Ernst & Young hospitality room snacking on beer and chips. We compared our best selfies, Craig most pleased with his Kerri Walsh Jennings shot. "I have a good feeling about tomorrow," he said.

Mom nodded. "Me too."

Dad, Josh, and I agreed.

NANCY

On Saturday, at 8:30 a.m., our group of 17 met in the JW Marriott lobby—Joel, Elizabeth, Josh, me; Heather; Red Bull's Ilana Taub; Joel's brothers Greg and Bill; Craig, Jane, and Paige; Gwen's high school friends; and Gwen's college friends. Through online purchases, complimentary tickets for Olympic families, and Heather's efforts, everyone held a ticket for the 11 a.m. race.

Wearing TEAM GWEN shirts, stars-and-stripes tights, and USA hats, our group walked along Copacabana Beach to the grandstand where we claimed a block of seats four rows deep by five seats wide.

"Nancy, can I use your sunscreen?" Ilana ran a hand through her ginger curls as others draped USA flags over their seats.

"Absolutely. And can you tell me what time it is?"

"9:30." She put down her phone to squeeze white lotion on even whiter skin.

I held a water bottle to my neck, dreading the next 90 minutes of tension and anticipation. I tracked a rainstorm for several days, but it disappeared from my weather app, and now I worried about strong winds.

NBC's Al Trautwig explained the race to viewers at home. "To me, it's one of the most compelling things in sports. What do you do when you're supposed to win? Like Usain Bolt, or Simone Biles, or the men's basketball team from the United States? That's the story here with Gwen Jorgensen of the United States."

Trautwig's television partner, Julie Swail, agreed. "[Jorgensen] has a target so big on her back, you're gonna be able to see it from the bottom of the hill all the way to the top."

Greg Welch announced live in the Rio booth. "That's Welchy," I said. "We met him at the Oakley House." In his Aussie accent, Welch inventoried athletes—Switzerland's Nicola Spirig (2012 gold medalist); Sweden's Lisa Norden (2012 silver medalist); Australia's Emma Moffat (2008 bronze medalist). In the past weeks, I felt positive about Gwen's chance for gold. Now, hearing this litany of talent, the feeling hid.

Between announcements, white-clad Brazilian dancers gathered in front of the grandstand and performed acrobatics—handstands, cartwheels, breakdance moves. Behind them, in gold caftans and multi-colored turbans, three brass players and four percussionists provided open harmonies and a throbbing pulse, step-touching to their own beat.

ELIZABETH

Josh and I walked to the beach leaving Mom and Dad, uncles, and friends in the stands. Our plan: watch the swim and dash back for transition. I spied Patrick, removed my sandals and sprinted to him. "How is she? How are you?"

"She's great. I'm feeling good." He hugged me and tucked back his wavy hair. "All she has to do is have an average day." He stood calm, confident, composed. I knew what he meant. Every day in practice, Gwen executed the required skills. She just had to replicate that today.

"Well, then, let's hope for an average day. I don't know how you guys are so relaxed."

"We're prepped and ready. She's ready."

Patrick and I took a selfie and I wished him luck.

NANCY

First in Portuguese, then in Welch's English, each athlete was announced. At their names, women jogged a ramp to the beach. "Wearing number 20 today, from the United States, 2014 World Champion and reigning 2015 World Champion... GWEN JORGENSEN."

Hearing Gwen's name and seeing her jog to the beach jump-started a tingling in my hands and feet. Our section—"Woo-hoo!"—"Go, Gwen!"—"Let's do this!"—waved flags for the three USA athletes introduced consecutively: Gwen, Sarah True, Katie Zaferes.

Regulation orange swim cap on Gwen's head, a stars-and-stripes suit on her torso, and timing chips on her ankles, she jogged, stopped on the ramp to kiss Patrick, and then took her place. As the athlete with most Olympic points, Gwen was first to select her starting position the day before.

"It's good and bad," she told us earlier. "I got first choice, which is blind for the first ten, but then everyone else knew where I would be when they selected a spot."

Gradually, the line filled with athletes representing Australia, Europe, Asia, Africa, South America, and North America.

ELIZABETH

My toes tight-roped a metal barricade as I peered toward athletes jogging the ramp. I cheered equally for Gwen's training partner from Canada, Sarah-Anne Brault, and her USA teammates, True and Zaferes.

When Gwen sprinted past, she waved, and anxiety tied my throat. *This is it. This is the moment, the day, the next two hours...This is it.* I wondered how Gwen controlled the energy, the anticipation, the expectation.

Josh and I moved closer to the start line. I screamed—and tears surprised me. Time lagged, each second paused, as athletes' rituals played out in slow motion.

NANCY

With swimmers assembled, the crowd quieted. Gwen leaned, left foot forward. An eerie sound from strings and percussion—long drawn out moments of dramatic suspense—emanated from the loudspeakers. From behind me, one of Gwen's friends whispered, "This music is making me nervous."

So much was unpredictable—contact in the water, pack dynamics on the bike, a rider's mistake, a rider's determination, mechanical failure, heat, humidity. The horn sounded, and as sweat dripped down my back, 55 athletes from 31 countries dashed, knees high, from 26°C (78.8°F) beach to 21.6°C (70.9°F) water. Welch mentioned the 17-mile per hour winds. Immediately, two groups formed as women stroked the chop, riding each crest.

I said, "It looks like the left pack is ahead—Gwen must be there, right?"

"That's where she started." Although impossible to identify individual competitors, Joel sounded confident.

Breathing bilaterally, swimmers raised their heads to follow the pack and see the course. Yellow kayaks manned by officials bobbed next to yellow buoys; orange kayaks and buoys identified turns.

At the first buoy, athletes converged into a single pack that resembled a flock of geese. Announcers identified those in front. Carolina Routier from Spain led; Zaferes and Australia's Moffat followed. The remaining swimmers fanned out, four wide. When the pack turned and swam parallel to the beach, swimmers disappeared behind the waves.

With 20 minutes to fill, online commentator Nicole Livingstone considered the history of triathlon. "Triathlon is unpredictable…[and being the] World Champion [doesn't] necessarily mean you're going to come into the Olympic Games and win. So, it's almost like a bit of a World Champion's curse, particularly with triathlon—of being the World Champion in the year prior…and coming here to the Games and not being able to convert. We'll see whether or not that will also be the outcome today."

As the pack swam toward shore, I squinted, searching for Gwen's long arms and legs. Swimmers rose to vertical, bodies tilting forward in the shallow water, toes prodding sand.

> *I was in a good position the entire swim, until about 200m to go when I lost a few places. I'm still not sure how or why, but I exited at the end of the pack in about 24th place after being in the top 10 for most of the swim.*

Gwen ran toward transition, 11 seconds behind the leader.
"GOOOOOO, GWEEEENNNNN!" Elizabeth had returned from the beach.
"You're hurting my ears." Anxiety heightened my sensitivity.
She ignored me. "YEEEAAAHHH, GWEEENNN!"
Gwen passed a few women in transition and joined the 30-strong lead bike pack.
"Nancy." Craig called my attention. "She's doing good. She'll be fine now that she's in that lead pack." I could tell he was as anxious as I was.

ELIZABETH

"How much longer until she's off the bike?" I knew the answer but relied on chatter to accelerate the 60 minutes. Josh and I alternated between sitting in our plastic chairs and standing in the aisle. I grabbed his elbow and squeezed.

"She's fine," he said. "But let's hope the time goes fast."

The screen to our left projected a live feed. The screen to our right—about 100 meters down the blue carpet—scrolled timing results. We struggled to see either in the glare.

Uncle Greg held a video camera, leaning over Uncle Bill's shoulder. "Can you move back, Bill? I can't get the shot."

Gwen's friends waved flags and clapped as Heather and Ilana willed optimism into our group. "She's fine."—"She's got this."—"This is just how it's supposed to go."

But I wasn't sure. London's flat tire and 2013's World Championship crash replayed in my mind. I rolled my t-shirt sleeves and sipped from communal water bottles stashed beneath our seats. Sometimes I put my head in my hands and hoped if I refused to see a crash, it wouldn't happen.

NANCY

Flora Duffy of Bermuda went to the front of the lead pack while Gwen lingered eighth from the back. "She's got to get to the front," I said. "She can't let Flora break away. She knows that! Why doesn't she move up?"

Joel, to my left, said, "She's fine. She needs to get her bike legs."

As riders attacked the hill, the camera zoomed in. Standing on their pedals, women bore down, bikes swaying side to side with the momentum.

Then came the downhill that haunted Gwen, motivating her to spend three days in a speed camp, desensitizing herself to danger. I remembered it from the 2015 qualifying race: narrow—barricades compressed the road to only meters across; steep—riders appeared to fly down the grade; winding—the pavement skewed left, then right, then right again. I turned away and said to Elizabeth, "Tell me when they're past it." I dreaded the seven more times Gwen would descend.

ELIZABETH

When Gwen approached the downhill, I looked at Mom and said, "It's coming." Mom crouched, tilting her head away from the screen, sighing. On the jumbotron, I spied Gwen's helmet and bike, then lost her in the bodies, pedals, and aero bars. Through the camera's lens, the descent appeared moderate. But on each lap,

Gwen lost her uphill gains when she hesitated downhill. I shielded the sun with my hand, analyzing each pedal rotation, each maneuver, each competitor. Gwen's face remained a mask of grit and concentration whizzing past at 40 miles per hour. "Okay, it's over."

Mom turned to the jumbotron and sighed again, another release of anxiety that sounded exactly like how I felt.

NANCY

The lead pack dropped eight riders—now 22 strong. Taking turns at the front were Spirig; Great Britain's Non Stanford and Vicky Holland; and New Zealand's Andrea Hewitt—podium winners, each proficient in breakaways. Gwen continued to hang off the back.

The crowd, wild at the start of the bike, quieted, waiting to see riders circle past the grandstand. The blue carpet stretched in front of us, the ocean beyond—a sequence of ultramarines, each laden with opportunity and danger. Online commentator Mark Tompkins assessed the situation: "These girls will know that if they want to stand a chance of beating Jorgensen to a gold, they have to push it on the bike. They have to try and leave her behind on the bike."

Twice this season, Duffy executed a breakaway. Gwen's back-of-the-pack position offered one more opportunity. But Spirig took the lead, intensified the pace, and the pack decreased to 18 as they approached the grandstand.

ELIZABETH

"We need a cheer!" I shouted to the rows behind us. "Here they come!"

"USA! USA! USA! USA! USA..." Seventeen voices yelled in unison.

I pumped my fist until the pack sped out of view. I studied the jumbotron and saw Gwen riding middle of the pack and sometimes at the front.

Mom turned to Dad. "Is she finding those bike legs?"

He shouted at the screen. "Yeah, Gwenevere! Goooooo!"

> *The first lap of the bike, I was under pressure and in a*
> *bad position at the back of the pack. After a few laps,*
> *I was able to work myself up to the front.*

Again, I stood, gathered attention, and our group chanted, "GO, GWEN, GO! GO, GWEN, GO! GO, GWEN, GO..." On this lap, Gwen led—with Spirig, Stanford, and Holland on her wheel. I hoped Gwen heard us and that Livingstone's observation—"So no US woman has won an Olympic Games gold medal, no US man, in the triathlon..."—would very soon be untrue.

NANCY

On the jumbotron, Gwen reached for her bottle—half water, half tropical edition Red Bull. A few minutes later, she turned her head, smiled, and appeared to laugh as Spirig rode next to her. Did Spirig say something? What was that?

Swail commented, "Nicola Spirig really poses the greatest threat to Gwen's chance at getting the gold medal. She's an extremely good cyclist. We saw [that] four years ago at the Olympics. She can put it together...We haven't seen much of her this year...She did a race earlier this year, broke her wrist and has come back after having a child...and has really proven her fitness so far in this race."

ELIZABETH

The camera switched to True. Fifty seconds behind, True sat on the pavement, massaging her knee. She attempted to remount her bike but couldn't swing her leg over. Eventually, she pedaled again.

In London 2012, True finished fourth. One position short of a medal. One position short of fame. One position short of the history books. I wanted her to catch the lead group and hammer out a USA gold-silver-bronze like in Gold Coast and London.

NANCY

Coverage refocused on the leaders. "There's Flora again," Elizabeth said as Duffy led. "Gwen! Stay up there!"

In an efficient partnership, the women at the front—Duffy, Spirig, Hewitt, Stanford, Gwen—shared the work. But more and more, Spirig pushed the pace. Was she tiring her competitors' legs? Apparently—the pack shrank. Was she putting distance on the chase pack? Yes—they were 1:25 behind. Could she establish a breakaway? Not yet—competitors were unwilling or unable to join her.

Once again, cameras found True. She rode 5:58 behind. Several minutes later, they featured her one last time. Lapped by the leaders, rules forced her to withdraw. I felt a pang for her mother and wondered where she was, watching the end of her daughter's unfinished story.

On several laps, Gwen passed women uphill and appeared at the front on straightaways.

Then, Spirig, in the lead, pedaled abruptly from left to right. "What is happening?" I asked.

"She wants Gwen to lead," Joel said. The pack followed, on Spirig's wheel, to the other side of the road. "Gwen doesn't want to and no one else does either, I guess."

Several times, Spirig waved other cyclists to the fore, but competitors refused, leaving her to do the work.

Livingstone said, "Jorgensen is just like a lion watching prey. Just sitting there, so focused, second wheel."

On the eighth and final lap, 13 nations rode in the lead pack: Switzerland, USA, Bermuda, Great Britain, New Zealand, Australia, Netherlands, Sweden, Chile, Japan, Italy, Mexico, South Africa. For the last time, riders stood out of the saddle as they ascended the hill.

ELIZABETH

"LOOK!" I said. "Gwen's leading on the downhill. GOOOOOOOO, GWEEENNN!" Mom still wouldn't watch. With only a few more minutes on the bike, I hoped when Gwen dismounted, she could establish a lead—and I could relax.

> *I had more fun riding in this race than in any other race. Ever. I felt strong and confident. It felt like a game we were playing. I would go to the front, but then Nicola would attack and I and/or the group would cover the move. Because Nicola was attacking, others were not encouraged to lead (if someone went to the front and took a turn, Nicola would attack and they risked being dropped).*

The pack of 18 racked their bikes and grabbed water, dousing heads and necks, as they exited transition. Within seconds, Gwen moved to the front, Spirig on her shoulder as they approached another water station—sopping sponges, dripping bottles. Already, Gwen and Spirig created a gap on Stanford and Holland—training partners, roommates, best friends—who ran together in third and fourth.

On the first of four laps, Gwen ran into the headwind while Spirig tucked behind.

"She looks great!" I said. "She can do this!" I anticipated a Gwensanity run, negative splitting, spinning a stride that left each competitor at her back. "Go get 'em, GW!"

NANCY

Gwen—smooth, steady, controlled—glided atop the concrete, her focus hidden by bright green Oakley glasses. Spirig—head bobbing, shoulders shifting, a slight jounce—stayed within a step.

On lap two, Gwen still led, her blue shoes a metronome as she reached for another water bottle to soak her dark head, hair pulled into a bun at her nape. Was there more jerk in Spirig's arms? Was her bobble more pronounced? If so, neither slowed her.

At the end of the second lap, as they ran together past the grandstand, Spirig took the lead. "Oh, no..." I said. "I wish Gwen would stay ahead." I longed for the familiar—Gwen dominating the run, destroying the field, creating time others couldn't recoup. Meanwhile, Holland and Stanford, still in third and fourth, ran like twins—two blondes, fair and thin, in matching lime green glasses, navy British tri suits, and white shoes—23 seconds back.

> I planned to build throughout the 10km. I was running strong, ready to put in a surge after two laps, when I noticed Nicola was still with me. I wasn't sure if Nicola was suffering or not, and I wanted her to take the lead so I could get a better read of the situation.

Tompkins said, "Can Nicola Spirig make it two in a row? She'd be the first person to win two [gold] medals in the women's triathlon—to defend the title. But she has the ominous figure of Gwen Jorgensen right on her shoulder."

Livingstone said, "We just get the feeling that Jorgensen's just biding her time at the moment—happy to sit in second leg there."

ELIZABETH

"What's going on? Why can't Gwen pass her?"

Dad turned to me. "She's fine. She's just waiting for the right time."

Uncle Greg balanced his camcorder, recording both the crowd and jumbotron. Josh tried to calm my anxiety. "She's running. It's all fine."

But this didn't feel fine. With Gwen and Spirig side-by-side, I wondered how strong Spirig's fitness was, how quick her sprint, how tough her will. I scolded myself for not checking Spirig's 10K time or her Olympic distance triathlon results.

Spirig's stride hiccupped while Gwen's floated. Spirig's arms crossed her body while Gwen's swayed parallel to the ground. Spirig's feet landed flat while Gwen's sprang. But I wondered if sisterly love clouded my vision. Did everyone else see what I saw?

Gwen's high school and college friends screamed and shouted. Heather turned back from the row in front of me. "She's got this. No need to worry now."

But I did worry. How could Heather predict the effect of Olympic adrenaline? How could Heather know what Gwen needed to do? "I just want her to go NOW!" I said. "She can negative split. She should get faster. I just want it now." I worried that Spirig would match Gwen's surge. I remembered that in London 2012, Spirig out-sprinted Lisa Norden for the gold. Tears welled.

NANCY

At the end of lap three, Spirig darted left across the road and Gwen followed. Then Gwen spurted to the right, and Spirig boomeranged after her.

Tompkins said, "Well, this is unusual. Never seen this before."

Livingstone said, "Mind games out there. Spirig waiting for Jorgensen to take a turn. She didn't want to take a turn. [They] almost stopped."

Tompkins: "Just cut right across the track and then cut back again."

Livingstone: "It's like what [Spirig] was doing on the bike."

When Spirig slowed her pace, Gwen pulled up next to her and said something. For a full minute, the game continued: Spirig spurting. A gesture. A word. A smile. Gwen surging.

ELIZABETH

"Gwen, just run your race! Quit playing her game," I said as though Gwen could hear me.

"She's making me nervous," Mom said.

"She should just RUN. No talking, no playing games. JUST RUN!"

I looked to Josh. He wrinkled his forehead and stared at the screen, clapping, repeating my will: "Run, Gwen!"

The crowd quieted, leaning in to hear the commentary and perhaps catch an explanation.

> *On the third of four laps, Nicola was hesitant to take the lead. We were running into a headwind, and it's easier to sit on in a headwind than take the lead. Nicola...decided to play mental games.*
>
> *Nicola said, "Let's share the lead."*
>
> *"I led last two laps," I responded.*
>
> *"I already have a medal."*
>
> *"I don't care. You also are a mother and that's more impressive!" I responded. I respect Nicola. She is a strong athlete, but she is also someone who proves you can be a mother and an amazing athlete...Anyway, our conversation happened while we were running, and I've been told it looked quite strange on TV. I can tell you that there is no playbook for triathlon and what happened on August 20th has never happened before, and will likely never happen again. It's why athletes train to expect the unexpected.*

Gwen and Spirig exchanged positions a few more times, our group erupting in cheers each time Gwen led.

NANCY

Gwen surged and Spirig responded. Then Spirig led into the final lap as camera coverage reverted to Stanford and Holland—only one of these two best friends could medal. Usually, I relax when Gwen runs. Not this day.

> *Nicola took the lead after our conversation and as we rounded the turnaround, we were in a tailwind. If Nicola was tired, it would be more difficult for her to surge with me in a tailwind (as opposed to a headwind), so I surged and didn't look back. I only focused on getting to that finish line. I couldn't hear Nicola behind me, but to be honest, I didn't hear her the first two laps either (the crowds were too loud – which is a good thing!).*

When video returned to Gwen and Spirig, Gwen led with a sizeable gap.

"GOOOOOOOOO, GWEEEEEENNNN!" Elizabeth jumped and pumped her fist.

I looked at Joel, and he didn't say anything. I thought he was crying.

"You've got this, Gwen!" I said to the air.

> *I came to the final turn with about 1.25km to go and saw I had created a small gap. A white board said I had a 9 second lead. I thought the race was going to come down to a sprint, so I continued to run hard...*

Now, with only minutes remaining in the two-hour race, I allowed myself to believe Gwen could win.

Our entourage stood, yelled, waved flags, and waited for Gwen to jump from jumbotron to blue carpet. "Gooooooooo, Gweeeeeennnn, go!"—"Yeah, yeah, yeah!"—"She's gonna do it!" My focus flitted—searching the road, studying the jumbotron. Finally, in the distance, I spied the motorcycle that foreshadowed the leader's advance. Greg cried. Joel cried. Elizabeth cried.

Closer and closer, Gwen ran toward the blue carpet, her tiny figure growing. Spirig was nowhere in sight. Then, Gwen was in front of us, and we screamed her name, yelled to her, shook our flags. "GOOOOO, GWEEENNN, GOOOO!"— "YEAH!"—"YOU GOT THIS!" She had ample time for celebration, but instead of grabbing a USA flag, she sprinted harder.

Like the swim start, the finish played in slow motion. With only strides remaining, Gwen raised her hand to her mouth, a gesture of amazement. She grabbed the tape, took four steps, and rested her hands on her knees. As she stood up, I said, "Oh, Elizabeth...look...she's crying!" I felt Gwen's tears prompt my own.

Gwen fumbled with the blue and green finish line banner, sobs shaking her shoulders as she raised it—Rio 2016—overhead. Her expression alternated, morphing in half-second increments between cries and elation. She dropped the banner and put both hands to her face, apparently unable to control her emotion. She circled a tight path, hands still covering her mouth, and bent again, head almost touching her knees.

I thought back to Gwen's 2012 Olympic tears. Although heartbreaking then, her disappointment over the flat tire was mingled with astonishment at qualifying. I knew these 2016 tears, more sustained and intense, released a self-imposed four-year encumbrance. Four years of expectation. Four years of focus. Four years of work.

I caught Elizabeth in my arms, then Joel. The two of them, one on each side, sandwiched me and we held each other. "She did it!"—"I can't believe it!"— "I'm so happy for her!" We turned to friends, brothers, fans—slapping hands, congratulating, releasing long-held breaths of anticipation.

"Nancy." Craig held his palm for a high-five. "She did it!"

Forty seconds later, Spirig crossed the line for silver.

Five seconds behind Spirig, Stanford, and Holland sprinted. Holland took bronze by three seconds.

Face still contorted, Gwen hugged Spirig, and on the jumbotron I read her lips say, "I can't stop crying," as she moved to embrace Holland.

Trautwig said, "...the pressure to [win gold] was so extraordinary. But then the moment she did it, unlike her personality, she burst into tears."

ELIZABETH

I couldn't believe it. My sister. The Olympic gold medalist. I checked the jumbotron, nervous for a last-minute penalty or disqualification. But when none showed, I turned to see tears in the eyes of our 17-member entourage.

On the screen, Gwen searched for Jamie and when she saw him, climbed past bikes in transition and sprinted. Head tilted to accommodate Gwen's height, Jamie pulled her close and grinned as he rubbed her back. Face still scrunched, Gwen dropped her head to Jamie's chest and covered her mouth with one hand. Then, she buried her head on his shoulder, both arms circling his neck, Jamie's smile a foil for her contorted face. Finally, she broke away to wipe tears and hug USA Triathlon's Andy Schmitz.

Commentator Swail, a triathlete herself, said, "Just the emotional release. You know, she kept it together—everything—physically, emotionally, mentally, all through the race. There is sure to be a celebration tonight for the Americans, never finding themselves on the top of the podium in triathlon since it was added to the Olympics in 2000."

Wiping her face with a towel, Gwen walked past spectators and I knew she searched for Patrick, but she stopped to hug Chilean Barbara Riveros, the Wollongong Wizard who finished fifth.

Then Gwen jogged across the blue carpet toward our group. Mom, Dad, and I ran to the grandstand's first row. We pushed ourselves against the railing. Gwen held her arms out and we did the same, unable to bridge the five-foot gap separating us. We motioned an embrace. "You did it!" I shouted to her.

"I can't believe it. I'm so happy." Gwen's face buzzed with endorphins.

Mom and Dad shouted over each other. "We're so proud of you."—"We love you!"—"Way to go, Gwenevere!"

I knew drug testing, media, and a medal ceremony came next. "We'll follow you. We'll figure out the plan and join you."

"Where's Patrick? I have to find Patrick." A current coursed beneath her words. She gasped and looked like she might cry again—a tangle of emotions, exhilaration jumbled with relief.

"There." I pointed across the blue carpet. "He's behind that barricade." Patrick pushed his way to the front of the crowd, waving to Gwen. She turned and ran.

NANCY

Gwen sprinted across the blue carpet to embrace Patrick, who invested his life in her dream. Arching over the barricade, Gwen gripped him. Directly above, the jumbotron replayed Gwen's finish line reaction, a conglomeration of awe, and joy, and relief, and triumph that continued in real time.

When they finally broke apart, Gwen turned to a reporter for an interview. "Oh, I'm gonna start crying again." Choked sobs interrupted her words. "I mean it's just...I've had a great support crew." An irrepressible smile performed backup to her creased face and broken voice. "Patrick, my husband, and Jamie, they've just been so great the past four years, and I wish they could stand on that podium for me."

Joel, Elizabeth, and I mingled—relieved, ecstatic, grateful—sharing the moment. Canadian Amelie Kretz's family congratulated us. Matheus, the young Brazilian fan who worried about my heart in 2015, held my hand during congratulations. Phones appeared as our group texted home, bridging thousands of miles from Rio to the USA.

When we saw Gwen again, she stood 100 yards away next to the podium, her back to us. She wore USA's official red-sleeved jacket, blue athletic pants, and chartreuse Nike shoes I saw so many times in Rio 2016 coverage.

First Holland, then Spirig stepped to the podium. After a trilingual introduction in French, English, and Portuguese, Gwen ascended to the top step, turned immediately to her right and waved at us. She rotated further, turning in a circle toward the beach to blow two kisses at Jamie and Patrick. Several more times, from the top step—between handshakes for Holland and Spirig and accepting the gold medal—she gestured to us. She knew exactly where we were.

Although I repeatedly said, "I can't believe it! I can't believe she did it," I did believe it. There is luck in triathlon, and I was grateful for Gwen's luck—no slippery pavement, no crashes, no brutality in the water. But I knew Gwen created her own luck. Her investments reran in my head. Four years far from home in Australia and Spain. Solo morning runs. Team ocean swims. Group bike rides. Mountain descents with Patrick. Shifting lessons with Patrick. Nutrition and recovery with Patrick. Deciphering Jamie's accent. Decoding Jamie's metaphors. Absorbing Jamie's wisdom. Building an image online, in print, on television. Building a schedule of local races, road races, duathlon races, professional races, international races. Crashing in a World Championship race. Winning a World Championship race. Winning a second World Championship race. A perpetual race for time. To be ready for Hamburg, Cape Town, Auckland, London, Yokohama. Ready for Rio.

Gwen created herself, her body, her mind. She created her own luck, and I believed it.

ELIZABETH

The opening instrumental of the Star Spangled Banner—brass, strings, percussion—blared as uniformed military raised the American flag. At the first notes—*Oh, say can you see*—Gwen placed her hand over her heart. I watched her on the jumbotron, singing each word, and tried to join, but tears knotted my voice. Gwen filled the screen, wet hair in a top knot, gold medal draped from a ribbon, dry-eyed during the anthem: she exhausted those reserves earlier. After the final phrase—*and the home of the brave*—she again waved to us, then invited the other winners to the top step, stretching an arm around each.

My sister did it. She won. The Olympic gold medal.

NANCY

As the ceremony concluded and the winners were escorted off the podium, I leaned toward Heather and Ilana. "So, what happens now?"

Already, Heather's thumbs flew across her phone. "Don't plan on seeing her for a while. For the next 24 hours, Gwen belongs to the United States Olympic Committee."

"What does that mean?"

"After drug testing, she'll do media at the IBC—International Broadcast Center—in the city." Ilana would facilitate USOC arrangements. "Your group is registered at the NBC studio, so as soon as everyone is gathered, I'll take you there. Eventually, that's where Gwen will do a domestic broadcast."

I nodded. "We'd like to be there when she gets back."

Like a tour guide, Ilana led our group of 17 to the temporary NBC beachfront studio, walking backward to check on us. Outside a fence, we waited for ID tags as bystanders noticed our TEAM GWEN shirts. "Pleese? Seelfie?"—"Uno mas?"—"Senhora? Thee beeg group?" We formed a semicircle for their shots. When a little girl asked Jane for her autograph, Jane, with a laugh, put her arm around the child and offered to pose for a picture too. Gwen's high school friend and first triathlon partner, Maggie Lach—tall, blonde, athletic—was approached repeatedly for a selfie. They must have thought she was an Olympian.

We walked through NBC's open-air broadcast studio. "Be careful where you step," our guide said as we tiptoed over camera cables and electrical cords. Told to hush, spurts of excitement sprang up anyway, giddy giggles erupting from whispered conversations. The guide pointed to a storage area. "This is where we'll record video of your group. We'd like footage of Gwen's fans."

After the tour, most left for lunch while family and a few friends followed Ilana up scaffolding to the green room. We crowded on the floor, sofa, and chairs, sharing space with a hairdresser and makeup artist. A curtain created a dressing room in the corner.

"It'll be a few hours." Ilana surfed her phone. "Help yourself to water from the cooler and there's fruit there too. Oh, look! Gwen's trending on Twitter." Our group reached for phones to read tweets and Facebook posts. Jane made friends with the hairdresser who offered to give her a blowout before our group video.

Famous television personalities floated in and out, changing clothes, preparing for broadcast. Mike Tirico, ESPN's Monday Night Football announcer, praised the Packers, with a nod to the Vikings when Patrick's family revealed their Minnesota ties. Tony Dungy, former coach of the Tampa Bay Buccaneers and Indianapolis Colts, posed for photos with us.

After a few hours, Elizabeth and I ducked outside and down the scaffolding to a bathroom. "I'm so glad this rain held off until after the race." Gray skies dropped sprinkles.

"Oh, my gosh, here she is!" Gwen and Patrick were only a few steps from us. Gwen, with an unstoppable smile, hugged us both. On a day when I shared Gwen with the world, I treasured these moments with just her, Patrick, and Elizabeth.

"Sorry I have to rush, Mom, we're on a tight schedule."

"I know. We'll follow you."

We hurried up the steps and entered the green room to applause, hugs and, "Congratulations!"—"Can I see the medal?"—"Can I hold it? Is it heavy?" Gwen's friends had returned from lunch and cheered for her.

An NBC escort interrupted. "We only have ten minutes before the taping, Gwen. Let's do hair and makeup."

Gwen plopped in the swivel chair as the hairdresser brushed and dried, and the makeup artist creamed and shadowed.

ELIZABETH

Gwen faced the mirror, head steady for mascara application. "Is there any food? I'm starving. I've only had a banana since the race."

"Here, someone brought this for you." I held out a foam container.

"What is it?"

I opened the box and showed her. "A salad. Steak. Broccoli. It's probably cold."

"I'll eat anything. Elizabeth, can you feed it to me while they do my hair?"

I pulled a chair next to hers and cut with a plastic knife, alternating between vegetable and steak.

"And I feel gross, but there's no time to shower."

"So, what's the plan?"

"Let's meet up later. I don't know exactly when. I have more interviews and media stuff. Check your phone for details."

"Okay. We'll shower and be ready for whatever is next."

While Gwen sat for hair and makeup, she shared the gold medal, passed hand-to-hand as the group remarked on its weight. On one side: the traditional laurel leaf and Rio Olympic logo. On the other: an etching of Nike, the Greek goddess of victory beneath the five Olympic rings and "XXXI Olimpiada Rio 2016." Stamped on the lower edge: "TRIATHLON | Women."

Gwen devoured the cold food. "Do I have broccoli in my teeth?" She leaned toward me as handlers hurried us downstairs to the studio.

"No, you look great. Really natural and pretty."

Gwen answered questions for the recorded TV spot while a cameraman videotaped our group in the storage space, encouraging fist-pumping and cheers. The segment would show during halftime of the gold medal basketball game between USA and Spain. I texted friends who promised to record it.

We returned to the green room, and within 15 minutes Gwen's interview (and our cameo) aired. Gwen looked poised, rested, and calm. Most viewers would be unaware of her hurried preparation, five-minute meal, and postponed shower.

A three-second shot of our group flashed on screen when the interviewer mentioned Gwen's fans. My phone buzzed with messages: "We saw you on TV!"— "Way to go, Gwen!"—"Her interview was awesome!" A family friend, Emily Reddy, took a selfie of herself next to our televised image and texted it to me.

NANCY

Minutes after the TV spot, Ilana approached. "Gwen, you have another interview waiting."

Our short-lived reunion ended with photos of the gold medal around my neck, Joel's, Elizabeth's, Josh's, Craig's, Jane's, Paige's, Greg's, Maggie's, Sarah's, Sara's...

Before Gwen left, she found me. "Mom, do you have any deodorant? I think I smell."

"You smell fine. Really. I guess we'll see you later?"

"Yeah, I'm not sure. You should go to the celebration at USA House. I may get there around nine or ten."

I was surprised that after earning a gold medal, as if the achievement not enough, Gwen faced more demands. I expected drug testing and post-race interviews, but I was astonished at the full-day media blitz. Tired myself from stress, and heat, and cheering, I empathized with Gwen, but she seemed on a natural high.

ELIZABETH

After a hotel shower, we hailed a taxi to the USA House. Our driver swerved around spectators spilling from bars into streets. With the men's futebol match between Brazil and Germany in progress, fans rooted for Brazil's first Olympic soccer title. Cervejas and caipirinhas fueled the celebration. Our driver used his horn and shouts to navigate the streets, dense with fans.

"Wow. Look at that," I said. Behind a white gate, Colégio São Paulo, a local elementary school, sparkled in red-white-and-blue lights. Team USA had renovated the building, adding an upgraded kitchen, air-conditioning, and faster Wi-Fi. Students returning after the Olympic break would benefit from the amenities. We entered under a Team USA awning where a suited security guard checked our names.

Josh and I toured the retail shop while Mom and Dad went to the lounge. Jane accompanied us, cooing over USA Triathlon pins to trade or save for friends. We admired the official gear designed by Ralph Lauren and Nike and calculated prices at over $200 for most items.

Joining Mom and Dad, we settled around a high-top table, sipping wine and beer, sampling appetizers from circular platters. Gwen's college friends and uncles Greg and Bill joined us. Gwen's high school friends opted to attend athletics at the Olympic Stadium and cheer for USA's Matt Centrowitz in the 1,500 meters and USA's 4x400 relay team. Both would win gold.

Athletics coverage played live on one television, the futebol match on another. A third screen scrolled family candids and race photos of Team USA triathletes. "Look! There I am!" I pointed to a wall-sized projection of Gwen and me playing the violin with Grandpa Stanley, Dad's father. "But they cut me off. That's the top of my head at the bottom of the screen."

"There you are again," Mom said when another shot appeared. "At Grandma's pool." The slideshow continued, highlighting each USA triathlete.

We took turns at the buffet, and then the official celebration began. Andy Schmitz, emcee for the evening, recognized staff. Then Olympians Greg Billington, Ben Kanute, and Joe Maloy took turns thanking friends, family, supporters, and Team USA.

Next, Katie Zaferes stood. Only hours since her 18th place finish, sadness and regret colored her voice. "I give a lot of credit to the recruitment program, the training camps, and being inspired by the people who came before me." Katie thanked each person who contributed to her success, but she later told me, "I am so disappointed with the result. I'm trying to think of this kind of like what happened to Gwen in London. It's awful, but it will inspire me to work hard for the next four years." I hoped Katie could resolve her disappointment and return in 2020 to achieve her dream.

Sarah True addressed the crowd next. "I remember being in London with Gwen, and I was amazed at her dedication. And now seeing her, I'm amazed at her growth, her transformation, her level of professionalism, and her ability to heighten the level of USA triathlon."

I admired her ability to speak eloquently of my sister when her own race was forfeited through injury.

"I have just learned so much from Gwen and how she handles her career. Although things were bad for me in this race, Gwen achieved her dream. And what connects us both is the sport of triathlon and the love we share for sport and competing. Gwen always says that things are an investment for her, not a sacrifice, and I have just learned so much from Gwen. And at the end of the day, we are all winners because we are all Olympians."

Graciousness and emotion grounded True's words. Most in the room likely surmised that at age 34, True ended her Olympic career with today's race. I sensed empathy in the crowd as they chanted, "USA! USA! USA!" and applauded.

At 10 p.m., when Gwen still hadn't arrived, I texted her.

Elizabeth: You better get here quick. Everyone is saying amazing things about you.

Gwen: We're en route. Media is taking so long. Traffic is bad. Be there soon.

Although she ate a meal at the Olympic Village, Gwen hadn't showered or brushed her teeth, and she still lamented her body odor and breath.

As the night progressed, the day's excitement drained from my body in waves of exhaustion and jitters. During the athletes' speeches, I wondered how their energy remained, long after mine dissipated.

NANCY

Gwen arrived as the last speech ended, just in time for Schmitz to call her to the front. The space buzzed with conversation, groups standing shoulder to shoulder around high-top tables or squeezed on upholstered benches. Schmitz recalled Gwen's rise through USA Triathlon's recruitment program and her focused approach to training. "And now, I would like Gwen to present the Order of Ikkos medallion." The namesake award honors Ikkos of Tarentum, who competed at the 84th Olympiad in 444 B.C. He later became the first recorded Olympic coach. "Each USA medalist is privileged to present this award to one of their coaches and I am proud to say USA Triathlon is represented by a gold medalist." As Schmitz held out the mic, the crowd—a little drunk at this point—jokingly shouted their choices.

Jamie called out, "Mum."

Several people chanted, "Patrick, Patrick, Patrick."

Gwen took the mic to whistles and screams. Although her job was to confer an award, the crowd applauded Gwen's gold medal. After several minutes, the cheering ebbed, then surged again. I knew Gwen felt uncomfortable with the ovation, but I tried to memorize it, this affirmation of my daughter's achievement.

One hand on her hip, Gwen matter-of-factly said, "Okay." But the noise continued. She ignored it and spoke. "So, I'm not one to love getting up in front of crowds and giving speeches. But before I give this award out, I want to thank some other people who have really made this a success. USA Triathlon...contacted me way back in...I'm so bad with dates...2009, and they said, 'We think you can be an Olympian,' and I laughed at them and said, 'There's no way.' It's kind of funny to look back now that I have a gold medal and it's all because of them. They've been with me every single day. They've helped me out enormously, and I just want to say a big thank you to them as well [as] to my family and friends who are here. And obviously Patrick has been a huge support member. He gave up his career to support me, and everyone who sees me or has been around me has definitely seen Patrick as well. We know how hard he works, and I'd really like to give him a round of applause." The crowd clapped and cheered for Patrick, well known among the triathlon set. "But for this award, I would like to give it to Jamie Turner who's hiding...over there."

I was proud of my daughter, who refused to gloat or boast. Even with an Olympic gold medal, she recognized others. I wanted to remember teaching her that but decided she must have learned it on her own.

Jamie joined Gwen and took the microphone. He made a few jokes I missed in his fast-paced New Zealand accent before he voiced his own thanks. "I've beene really fortunate. So thoinks Mum and Ded, for geeving your daughtah the veelues and atteetudes through the expeeriences ya gave her groiwing up. Because ya set her up for success. Ya gave me a cake and I was able to just put the oicing on the top."

Not expecting the shout-out, I flushed and thought perhaps it was Jamie who taught Gwen to acknowledge others. I admired Jamie, who perfected more than swim strokes, cycling moves, and run strides. I believed him as much philosopher as coach. Gifted in the study of humans, he constructed a world where competitors became the architects of their own careers—and themselves. To convey his expertise, Jamie spoke in riddles, stories, and metaphors and then expected his athletes to translate them into practical use. He empowered them to mine for their best, knowing they would unearth rewards for him as well.

As the formal celebration ended, I hugged Gwen again, relishing this incredible day.

ELIZABETH

Gwen, Patrick, Heather, and Jamie stood around a bar table, each holding a glass of wine. Mom, Dad, Josh, and Craig chatted nearby. The party showed no signs of slowing. When I saw Gwen move to a long pillowed couch, I joined her. I scooted in, emphasizing my next words' importance. "Gwen, before this day is over, I just wanted to make sure I tell you how proud I am." Gwen reached over to hug me, and I rubbed her back. "Seriously, I know you always say this was an investment, but it was a sacrifice too." I wanted my sister to know how huge this accomplishment, how deep my admiration and pride. "You and Patrick have worked incredibly hard, and I am so happy you won. You are the most hard-working, dedicated, persistent person. You have given up so much. But you've given so much too. You are a great role model for little kids—and adults too. Just what you've done for the sport: you've started the scholarship, you've inspired people to be more active, and to achieve their dreams. And now you've won a gold medal."

"It's pretty crazy, hey?"

"I'm just...I just want you to know that I'm really proud to call you my sister. You're an amazing athlete and example. And sister and person too."

"Thanks, EJ. You are too." She patted my knee and then Mom joined us.

NANCY

"We are all so proud of you." Gwen stood and hugged me.

"Thanks, Mom. I have interviews in the morning, but I'll see you at the Oakley House around noon?" Looking tired, she hugged Joel and Elizabeth and said she was headed out. I heard later that she, Patrick, and Jamie stopped at a bar, and Gwen got drunk on caipirinhas. Many times, I watched bartenders mix the Brazilian favorite, muddling lime wedges with sugar, adding crushed ice and Cachaça (rum-type alcohol) to overflowing. It wouldn't take much to inebriate Gwen's slender, exhausted body.

Joel, Elizabeth, Josh, Jane, Craig, Paige, and I wandered the USA House. We ordered one last beer and appetizer from the rooftop cafe, then returned to the JW Marriott.

Just like Gwen's performance-based insomnia, my body resisted sleep. A silent movie of the day flickered and, although I closed my eyes, the story captivated me. I periodically checked the hotel clock and remember seeing 3:00, and 4:00, and 4:15.

We got up early for a Sunday morning at the beach—sun on our backs, sand in our toes, and caipirinhas in our fists. Elizabeth entered our room with Josh, swimsuit in hand. She opened the drapes. "Oh, no. Did anyone check the weather? What's the temperature?"

I stood next to her, looking through our rain-streaked window at the deserted beach. "Not a great day for tanning." I touched my phone's weather app. "This rain isn't stopping. And today's high is 68."

"We have to use our swimsuits at least once," Elizabeth said.

"What about the hotel pool?" Joel was determined too. "It's outside on the rooftop and you can see the beach."

"If the pool's heated, it could be fun," Josh said.

The attendant on the rooftop seemed surprised to see us. "Just checking out the facilities?"

"Actually, we're planning to swim," Elizabeth said.

The attendant smiled. "It's chilly. Stop here on your way out. I have robes for everyone."

I preferred a sunny day in the sand to shivering under gray skies, but still, I floated on a foam noodle for thirty minutes, shoulders submerged in the heated water. "It could be worse. Race day was dry and safe—and Gwen won the gold! We can't complain."

A few hours later, Joel, Elizabeth, Josh, and I met Joel's brothers Greg and Bill, and Gwen's friends at the Oakley House. Behind the two-story white columned facade, rambling spaces were divided into conversation nooks. We strolled past leather-furnished rooms and through open doors to the patio. Under the pergola, our group ordered a round of drinks and admired the mountain view, waiting for Gwen to arrive. When she joined us, Welch's staff presented champagne glasses, popped corks, and poured.

Welch pinched the stem of his glass and raised it. "When I saw Gwen at the London Olympics, I knew she was a special athlete. I knew Oakley had to support her..." Welch, who did the announcing at yesterday's race, spoke with affection and pride. "Incredible. Gwen had to really rise up on the bike, especially. This course was set up to have a twenty percent grade on every lap—eight laps...This was simply amazing to watch. I was just saying that this was my favorite gold medal to watch of this Olympic Games. And yes, I do show some bias...amazing race yesterday, Gwen."

Later, I told Welch I noticed his admiration for Gwen.

"But I tried to be objective in my race commentary. I hope you didn't detect any favoritism there?" I assured him he sounded professional.

After Welch's speech, we filled our plates at the buffet, assisted by waiters serving grilled ribs, sliced-to-order prime rib, and pork fillets. Then we shared cream pies and coconut sweets.

A man with a camera approached our table. "Greg [Welch] would like some photos with Gwen's family and friends, if that's okay?" We gathered on the lawn, posing with Gwen in front of her larger-than-life, USA flag-draped mural image.

As we returned to the pergola, Elizabeth nodded toward a family of three sitting on a garden bench. "Isn't that Spirig?"

Joel turned. "Yeah. I think it is."

Welch called our attention, directing us indoors for a second speech. As the crowd gathered, he praised Spirig and presented her with gifts similar to Gwen's—Oakley sunglasses, wireless earbuds—and toasted the two-time Olympic medalist. When the presentation concluded, Elizabeth asked Spirig for a selfie and offered a high-five to her three-year-old, Yannis.

Gwen and Patrick invited Nicola, her husband, and son to join them. Yannis, a typical toddler, fidgeted, ignored some questions, answered others, and pretended he knew only German. I overheard Gwen's questions to Nicola: "How did you train and breastfeed at the same time?"—"Is it hard traveling with a baby?"—"Do you have any help with childcare?" Gwen and Spirig smiled and laughed, one a mother sharing her experience, the other hoping to follow her example. In the

Olympic tradition, rivals in competition became friends off the course. Gwen fawned over Yannis and said she intended to travel as a trio soon.

I knew Gwen planned to start a family after Rio, but she would postpone immediate attempts because of potential exposure to the Zika virus. Already, I pictured us cuddling a baby, and calling ourselves Grandma and Grandpa.

Mid-afternoon, I said, "Gwen, we need to head to the airport." I didn't want the week to end.

"Okay, Mom. Thank you for everything."

"So, will you be at the Closing Ceremony?" Before the Games, Gwen made no post-race plans.

"There's just no time. Heather organized a round of interviews and media appearances in New York City, so we're flying out tomorrow. I'll send you the schedule—some are online, and some on TV." I wondered how Gwen's life might change, the power of the gold medal to confer celebrity, opportunity, prosperity.

As we exchanged hugs with Gwen, Patrick, Greg, Bill, and Gwen's friends, an Oakley representative approached. "We have a pair of sandals for everyone in your group. Could you tell me your sizes, please?"

We waited for our presents, and then taxied to our hotel before traveling to the airport.

****

Our long, boring wait at international check-in contrasted with the busy, emotional days of Olympic competition. Pre-race anxiety, Olympic events, and USA celebrations were replaced with heavy luggage, long lines, and security checks. In Rio, we played a part in the story, live and in person. Now, Gwen's story continued with interviews and appearances, and we would return to viewing remotely. Although I was ready for home, I wished we could be with her in New York.

After our overnight flight, we retraced our route from Chicago's O'Hare Airport to Waukesha, Josh in the driver's seat. It felt good to be almost home where I could sleep in my own bed and enjoy America's water-and-waste technology. It felt good, too, knowing my suitcase held reminders of Rio, of Gwen's victory, and of friends and family who shared it with us. Most of my souvenirs cost nothing. Ernst & Young gave us a batch of pins we traded, in the Olympic tradition, for others. My collection included pins from Bermuda, the Los Angeles 2024 committee, the United States Olympic Team, Proctor & Gamble, the P&G Thank You, Mom campaign, and swimsuit sponsor ROKA. I saved ticket stubs from athletics, and futebol, and men's and women's triathlon. I packed the ubiquitous yellow beer cup sold at every venue. On my feet, I wore my Oakley sandals. On my wrist, I wore an açai bracelet—brown and ecru seeds—given to me at the Oakley House, a reminder that some Brazilian women string beads to feed their families. I collected lanyards, postcards, and an 82-page Olympic program I can't read because it's in Portuguese. Photos crammed my camera with images of family and friends, the Olympic rings, and Copacabana Beach. Captured in the shots were smiles and tears, worry and celebration, laughter and hugs. The gold medal became a character, close-ups of it next to my favorite people. There are pictures of Gwen alone, Gwen with friends, Gwen with family. There are pictures of Elizabeth taking selfies, Elizabeth posing, Elizabeth laughing and negotiating with Brazilians. And there are pictures of Joel, calm and confident, his optimistic conviction realized.

ELIZABETH

Pulling into my driveway, I spotted red-white-and-blue balloons swaying on my front porch. "What's that?"

"I'm not sure," Josh said.

A sparkling gold poster declared "USA" and "WOW!" in red, white and blue letters. The center: *Milwaukee Journal Sentinel's* front page, Gwen clasping her face. The headline: "Striking gold".

Josh exited the car and approached my front door. "It says, 'Love, Steve, Liz, Pete, and Paul.'"

"Wow! That's so nice of them." My mom's brother and sister-in-law decorated her front porch too. I left the sign and balloons up for the next month.

Josh and I collapsed onto the couch. My cockapoo jumped, and then quickly settled, curling on my chest. I picked up the TV remote. "Want to watch the race?"

"Of course!"

We made it no more than a few minutes before I paused the video, pulled out my phone, and recorded segments to send to Gwen. "GW! We're watching the race! Can't wait to see how it ends." Josh and I searched for TEAM GWEN shirts in the crowd and relived the moment—this time eagerly awaiting the outcome—forgetting how worry once tinged our experience. "Wow. She did it," I said as I cried again.

"Yeah, it was unbelievable." We admired NBC coverage, Copacabana Beach, Sugarloaf Mountain, and spectators dressed in Brazilian colors, cheering next to a kaleidoscope of international fans.

When the race ended, I saved the recording and opened my laptop. I had news alerts set up and the results filled my email. "Gwen Jorgensen Wins First U.S. Olympic Gold Medal in Triathlon"—"Waukesha Native Gwen Jorgensen Wins Gold"— "Unbreakable Gwen Jorgensen wins USA's first gold in triathlon." I was happy. This was the way it was supposed to end.

NANCY

In our post-race tradition, Joel and I watched replays over the next few days—first the NBC version with personal interest stories about Gwen, then online streaming without commercials. "Can you believe it? Gwen is an Olympic gold medalist," I said.

"Yeah, pretty crazy."

A knock interrupted as someone shouted, "Hey! She did it," through the screen door.

I recognized the voice. Waukesha South High School track coach Eric Lehmann, one of the first to recognize Gwen's talent for running, joined us at the kitchen table. He told us about Wisconsin fans who watched the race at home, at bars, and at basement parties. For 15 years, Eric followed Gwen, called her, texted her, and supported her. We were fortunate to have people like Eric—and swim coach Blaine Carlson; university coach Jim Stintzi; USA Triathlon's Barb Lindquist; swim director Dave Anderson; triathlon coach Cindi Bannink; cyclist Tom Schuler; and Patrick, and Jamie, and so many others—to foster and grow our daughter's dream before even she imagined it.

When Eric left, I looked at my email inbox, overflowing with alerts. My email system grouped them, 50 or 100 at a time. I printed each one, read slowly, and filed them along with newspaper clippings neighbors collected. Gwen told me she broke her habit of responding to every email, Facebook message, Twitter post, and Instagram comment. With so many, it would be impossible. But she forwarded some messages, including one from Jim Stintzi, her University of Wisconsin track coach.

I have to share this email from my college running coach—just read the last paragraph...it's so me :)

Subject: CONGRATS OLYMPIC GOLD MEDALIST!

Gwen:

Congratulations on your awesome win! I am really, really proud of you!! I know how hard you've worked for this—and to watch you fulfill what is pretty much the ultimate in sport—was really exciting.

That was the first (and maybe the only) triathlon I've ever watched straight through—and I was yelling at the TV screen (and the announcers) the whole way.

I have to say I laughed when the other woman wanted you to lead during the running part. I kind of said in my head a. It doesn't matter—you aren't going to stay with her and b. Even if you stay with her—you've never seen Gwen really kick before—so you might as well lead!!

(I'm looking at the subject line of my text and it looks like some spam advertisement aimed at Olympic gold medalists!)

Anyway—congrats. Incredibly proud of you as a competitor and as a person!

Last thing—do you remember after one of your first races when I told you you might want to give up

swimming and concentrate on track? You looked me
right in the eye and said "If you ever say that again—
I'm never going to run!" I tell that to people (because
you scared me a little)—because you are so fierce in
everything you do and all of your convictions. I've
always admired that about you.

Sorry to ramble. Really happy for you!

Take care,

Jim

While we spent Monday and Tuesday re-watching the race, Gwen and Patrick flew to New York City. Gwen met with Gabriela Hearst, who provided designer outfits for her appearances. Tory Burch also provided clothing. During the week, Gwen posed for photo shoots, sat for interviews, and appeared live on television and Facebook. Gwen emailed her schedule for one of the busiest days, Wednesday, August 24:

7:40	CNBC Squawk Box Live
9:45	CBSN Josh Elliott Live
10:45	CNN Headline News
11:30	Fox News Facebook Livestream
12:00	*US Weekly* Facebook Livestream
1:30	SI Now (*Sports Illustrated*)
4:35	AOL Build Livestream
5:10	Makers Interview

I set my phone's alarm for each appearance. Some, I recorded while they aired; others, I watched on computer, sharing URLs on Facebook. Gwen appeared genuine and forthright, and I realized she learned more these past four years than triathlon. She learned to be candid, but also to dodge inappropriate questions. She learned to smile when her body cried for rest. She learned, although private by nature, to share herself and her story with the world.

Gwen discussed her training, the race, and her uncharacteristic display of emotion. "I thought Nicola was a lot closer to me, so...I was sprinting as fast as I could. When I actually grabbed the tape, I think it was just so...emotional...I mean and I'm not normally that emotional. I put four years of everything I did [into] that race. And, you know, I had my husband...[who] gave up everything, his career, to support me. And my coach as well. You know, four years ago, I asked [Jamie], 'Do you think I can win gold at the Olympics?' and he told me, 'Well, you need to swim faster, and you need to bike faster. You're probably going to need to run a 32-minute 10K.' And he invested these four years in me, so crossing that finish line was a relief, a celebration for them. It was just so many emotions."

I heard congestion in Gwen's voice, a by-product of whatever she caught after Rio. Perhaps she contracted a virus from the water. Or maybe a bug from people hugging, touching, and congratulating her. Or maybe it was sheer exhaustion—a post-race emotional release that left her vulnerable.

Before we left Brazil, Gwen had said, "I have a secret. I'm going to announce it on Thursday, so you can't say anything until then."

"You know we wouldn't say anything. What is it?"

"So, ASICS sponsors the New York City marathon, right? Well, they want me to do it this year, and it's been on my bucket list for a long time, so I'm announcing on Thursday that I'll be running the marathon on November 6th."

Running the marathon? My only thoughts were questions. Was she exploring new opportunities? Was she fulfilling a sponsor's request? Or was she serious about a new sport? But there was no time to ask.

On Thursday, September 25, my phone lit up with social media and news alerts announcing, "Fresh Off Olympic Gold, Triathlete Will Run NYC Marathon." Gwen, smiling atop the Empire State Building, cradled two sports. In one hand, she held triathlon—a gold medal—and in the other, marathon—her NYC race bib.

Six years ago, in 2010, USA Triathlon recruited Gwen. With opportunity, ambition, and a support team, Gwen transformed herself into the best in the world. One week after she celebrated the ultimate athletic achievement, ASICS dangled a new idea: the chance to realize a bucket list item and explore another sport.

When Gwen returned from her media trip, I called her. "Do you have time to train? For 26.2 miles?" I worried about her.

"I can't train like I should, but it's an LSD experience." It was one of Jamie's trademark expressions. "Look, search, discover."

My questions persisted. Was running Gwen's new career? Would she trade swim laps and bike hills for run miles? Did we just begin another four-year journey? I didn't think even Gwen knew. "Well, you know whatever you do, we're there for you." Already, Joel and I researched hotels and flights to the Big Apple.

ELIZABETH

Each time I phoned Gwen in the weeks post Rio, she brought up Tokyo 2020. Wishfully, longingly—like a lover missed—she talked of the Games, of the excitement, of competition. Finally, I lost my patience. "Gwen, you keep talking about Tokyo, but you haven't mentioned which sport." I didn't know if I was right to assume the triathlon dream fulfilled, and the next goal waiting to be explored.

"Elizabeth, I'm not saying that yet."

"Are you serious?" I thought she would at least tell her sister.

"Yeah, it's too early to tell, but I know I want to be in Tokyo in 2020."

> *Up next for me is the Island House Triathlon and the New York City Marathon. But the big question is what's after that? Charlotte knows, Patrick knows, but not many others know. I've been afraid to say it aloud because I'm scared of failing; but if I've learned anything these past four years, it's that I can condition myself for greatness. So, I'm going to start conditioning myself now for my next life goals: Patrick and I want to have a baby, and I want to go to Tokyo 2020. There, I said it. It's in the universe and there's no taking it back. Thank you all for your support these past four years. It's been a great journey and I can't wait for the next four.*

****

Two weeks after the New York City Marathon, on Tuesday, November 22, Gwen called from the car as she traveled from St. Paul. "Hi, EJ, we should be home in an hour. We need to unload the van and then head to David Hobbs

Honda." The local dealership renewed Gwen's sponsorship with another three-year lease. "Patrick and I need to sign papers for the Odyssey, and there's media and a meet-and-greet."

"Supper when you get back?"

"That sounds great. Just so we have protein plus a carb and a veggie."

"Perfect! Dad bought pork chops for the grill. And Josh is coming too."

During Gwen and Patrick's four-day stay, Gwen would speak to Waukesha Express Swim Team athletes, join high school friends for coffee, ride bike trails at Waukesha's Minooka Park, brave early morning runs, celebrate my birthday, and help host Thanksgiving.

I looked forward to this week, spending time together at Mom and Dad's, everyone singing, "Happy birthday to you, Elizabeth." And I smiled that night at a familiar sight: Gwen's athletic gear clogging the doorway. "I know who is here."

For my birthday, Mom made my requests: homemade pretzels; hand-crafted pizzas with sundried tomato, artichoke and goat cheese; a salad; and lemon crepes with a candle. But the best part was being together. Dad made a fire and talked with Josh about woodworking. At the kitchen table, we played games and giggled. Then, Gwen, Patrick, Josh, and I moved to the family room as Mom and Dad loaded the dishwasher. Gwen told stories, laying on the couch, Patrick rubbing her feet.

Even with the thousands of miles she and Patrick traveled, even after a failed Olympics and a successful one, and even after becoming the winningest woman in the history of triathlon, she was still my little sister. She still flubbed her sayings, she still asked Dad to bring her water, no ice, and she still wanted to be in bed by nine.

"What a year, GW. So where do you go now?"

"Triathlon found me, and I'm glad it did." Gwen shifted, signaling Patrick where to rub. "But, now I'm ready for something new."

Running? A baby? Whatever it was, I wanted her to find it near me. She talked of moving to Portland. "Gwen, you could run and have a baby in Waukesha." The fire crackled and my cheeks turned rosy from wine and heat. "Plus, there would be so much free babysitting."

"You should be happy we're not living in Spain or Australia."

I knew she and Patrick wanted to start their own family, in their own town, in their own way. "Maybe I could visit you on my spring break?"

"Yes! We should have a house by then."

The evening ended, all of us sleepy, and although I longed for more conversation, I was grateful for these days together.

NANCY

Thanksgiving Day, our house filled with Joel's siblings—Colleen, Charlene, Greg and his wife, Chinchi; and my family—my brother Steve, his wife Liz and their sons, Pete and Paul. We squeezed 13 around an L-shaped table. Next to dark red plates on a white tablecloth, Liz placed her cheesy broccoli dish. Chinchi set her onion casserole next to the turkey.

As we sat down, Charlene said, "Thanks for all the pictures, Gwen." Before the meal, Gwen shared her gold medal, allowing each cousin, aunt, and uncle to wear it.

"After dinner, I have some Olympic postcards to sign for you too."

"Oh, goody, Gwen. I was hoping you'd remember." Colleen said she would take hers to work on Monday.

Joel limped around the table, offering his sausage and onion stuffing.

"When are you getting that second hip replaced?" Steve recently had his own hip surgery.

"I didn't want to risk it before the Olympics, so in January." After the stuffing, Joel offered his garlic mashed potatoes. "Maybe we'll get back to a normal life now."

Elizabeth laughed. "Normal? Are you kidding? Remember, Gwen and Patrick want to have a baby. You guys could be grandparents soon."

Patrick put his arm around Gwen.

My sister-in law, Liz, turned to me as I passed the sweet potatoes. "What about you, Nancy? What are your plans?"

"We may visit Gwen and Patrick in Portland." I suggested they move to Madison, or Appleton, or Cable, Wisconsin, but they would settle 3,000 miles west. "I've learned to enjoy traveling, and I would love to see Oregon."

Greg twisted toward Gwen. "So, you win gold at the Olympics, and then take 14th at the New York City Marathon. The coverage was terrible, but we watched anyway. You beat a bunch of really good runners."

"It was really cool," Elizabeth said. "Mom, Dad, Josh, and I were in Central Park watching."

"It was tough for me without the right training. I could barely walk for a week after."

"So, is running the plan now?" Greg asked.

"Well, the plan is to get pregnant, so with running, it's an LSD experience—look, search, discover—while we wait and see what happens. And I hope when Mom and Dad and EJ visit us in Portland, it will be to see a baby." Gwen and Patrick planned a pregnancy as soon as possible, giving Gwen three years to prepare for Tokyo 2020.

I envisioned our roles as Grandma and Grandpa, changing diapers, rocking, babysitting. I remembered Elizabeth and Gwen sleeping and cooing, and even before Gwen and Pat conceived our grandchild, I longed to cuddle it.

Gwen conditioned herself for Olympic greatness, but she couldn't yet comprehend the greatness of motherhood. For that, she needed to hold and nurse her own baby. Thirty-four years after my first, I still marveled. That two girls grew up to play music and sports. That one dedicated herself to teaching, the other to sport. That Joel and I made mistakes and got some things right, and Elizabeth and Gwen survived. That through illness or heartache, a teaching triumph or Olympic gold, our family adapted, but also stayed the same.

Sunday morning as I dressed, I heard Gwen tiptoe down the stairs, run water in the kitchen sink, and then ease the front door closed. I looked out the window and saw her round the curve toward Minooka Park. Tall and thin in leggings, fitted top, gloves, and Red Bull headband, I imagined her the only runner on the trails at that hour. When she returned, the table was set and Elizabeth joined us for breakfast. Joel made bacon while I ladled batter into waffle irons.

"I'll take a shower and be ready in five minutes. Breakfast looks amazing."

With everyone at the table, I laid a waffle on each plate and set the frittata pan on a hot pad. Elizabeth narrated a social media post about the food. Joel poured juice, and Patrick refilled his coffee.

Gwen scooped eggs. "I have news. The doctor gave us the go-ahead to try for a baby right after the marathon. When was that, Patrick? Two weeks ago? And I took a test last night and it's positive." She laid her hand on Patrick's arm, and he kissed her.

"Oh, wow, Gwen! That's so great." Elizabeth put down her phone and got up to hug her.

"Well, I haven't seen a doctor yet, but I think the drug store tests are pretty reliable."

Although obviously delighted, Gwen presented the news in her quiet manner, so we took her cue. Joel and I hugged both Gwen and Patrick. "Gwen, this is so exciting!" I held her a little longer than I usually do. "Have you told anyone yet?"

"Just you guys. We'll call Patrick's parents today."

Elizabeth gave Gwen a teasing look and said, "I guess no matter what you try, you are just always a success. You probably know the name and what college he's going to already."

As we passed butter and syrup, conversation centered on babies. Due dates. Names. Baby shower. A house. Crib. Childcare. Gwen and Patrick planned to buy a home before April. The baby would be due in August. Gwen would continue training with her doctor's supervision, but not compete until after the birth.

"Mom, Dad, I hope you guys can be there when I deliver. I'd feel better if you are with me that first week."

"Of course. We would love to be there!"

After breakfast, Gwen and Patrick loaded their van for the trip to St. Paul. Bikes, skis, and backpacks filled every space. Joel, Elizabeth, and I hugged them once more before they buckled in. Then, we stood at the front window, watching Gwen and Patrick back out of the driveway. Gwen's Olympic quest concluded more than an athletic goal. It capped a life dream. And now, with a baby on the way, our family had a brand new journey.

Epilogue

2017

ELIZABETH

One month before Gwen's due date, I flew to Portland for a week to help prepare her house for the baby. We ran wood-chipped paths in Portland's parks, Gwen's belly supported by a sling. Her pace matched mine, my steps doubling hers.

"Elizabeth, you know I really love running."

I wasn't sure how. She said her Achilles burned, the thirty extra pounds straining muscles accustomed to a lighter load. I ached for water and a bench.

"I called Jerry Schumacher. Remember him from UW-Madison?"

I nodded.

"He thinks I have a shot at the marathon. He didn't count me out, at least." She said other coaches called her crazy; some said she couldn't do it. "I'm making the announcement in November, but I'm not retiring from triathlon. I'm transitioning to marathon." She said it matter-of-factly, as though confident in her analysis, research, and planning. I heard passion and a dream in her voice.

I wasn't surprised. When she and Patrick bought a Portland home, I assumed it was to explore running with Schumacher and the Bowerman Track Club. She said her plan would evolve—she would listen to her body as she regained fitness after the birth. "But don't say anything until after my announcement. I'm still working out contracts."

NANCY

On an 80-degree August Monday, with snow-capped Mount Hood on the horizon, Gwen—two weeks overdue—finished an easy bike ride. She stored her helmet and shoes in the garage and placed her overnight bag in the van. Then she and Patrick drove to the hospital where doctors would induce labor. That same day, Joel and I landed in Portland, ready to meet our first grandchild. From the airport, we went to the hospital where Gwen chatted with us, showing little effect from the first round of drugs. Her doctor expected she would deliver the next day.

On Tuesday morning, we walked from Gwen and Patrick's house to the hospital where Patrick had spent the night. Gwen still displayed no signs of labor. We visited in the morning, and Gwen napped in the afternoon. Patrick stayed overnight again.

On Wednesday morning at 8 a.m., Patrick called. Gwen was in active labor. "It won't be long now."

I invented chores to distract myself. I cleaned Gwen and Patrick's stove, polished their sink, wiped their counters. I checked the time—every 10 minutes. I mopped the floor, swished the toilets, dusted the windowsills.

At noon, my phone rang. I answered immediately. "How is she?"

Gwen had been in active labor for four hours—panting, breathing, pushing— but her body refused to relinquish the baby. Doctors offered two options; Gwen chose vacuum delivery over Cesarean. "I'll call again when the baby is here."

Another slow hour ticked by. Joel suggested we walk to a cafe for lunch where I ordered a sandwich and forced a few bites. We talked about Gwen's birth, and Elizabeth's birth, and tried to remember what it felt like to hold a newborn. My phone buzzed, and Patrick's name flashed on the screen. "Patrick!"

"Well, what do you think? Boy or girl?"

First, I made sure both Gwen and the baby were fine. Then, "Joel thinks boy. I think girl."

"Come on over and meet your grandson."

We paid our bill, hurried to the hospital, and arrived before the baby was an hour old. I had forgotten how tiny a seven-pound baby looks. How wrinkled. How beautiful in his swaddle.

The room smelled of blood. Gwen smelled of sweat. Her pallor matched the white walls and sheets. She endured a long, excruciating labor and avoided surgery—but she sustained internal and external tears that staff monitored throughout the afternoon. Joel and I took turns cradling the baby while Gwen and Patrick called Elizabeth and other family to announce the birth.

Due to fever and complications, Gwen stayed in the hospital until Saturday, a total of six days. When she returned home, Elizabeth had arrived, and Joel and I stayed another week. All three of us cooked, cleaned, and retrieved Stanley from Gwen's arms at 5 a.m. so she and Patrick could sleep another hour. We held and nuzzled him when he napped, when he woke, when he whimpered, when he gazed at the world.

Gwen, meanwhile, endured painful urination and difficulty walking. I cringed at her tentative steps and worried about the exhaustion on her face. On examination, her doctor said she needed additional stitches and scheduled a reconstructive surgery.

Joel returned home for medical appointments, and Elizabeth to begin the school year, but I stayed extra days while Patrick accompanied Gwen to surgery. Gwen's job was to recover—and it seemed more challenging than any triathlon. My job was to help her by caring for Stanley—and it was the best job I ever had. I tried to memorize the scent of his hair, the velvet skin on his cheek, his thin legs tucked inside a cotton sleeper.

Pre-birth, Gwen intended to return to easy runs, or bikes, or swims as soon as possible. But the traumatic delivery made recovery difficult. To regain pre-pregnancy fitness would require months of treatment with a physiotherapist, pelvic floor specialist, and massage therapist.

ELIZABETH

When Stanley was four days old, I returned to Portland for a week. The baby looked healthy and strong. Gwen looked nothing like she did a month earlier. She hobbled from bedroom to kitchen, sighing, willing each step. She could barely shuffle, much less run. Mom and Dad and I helped as much as we could, changing diapers, washing dishes, cooking.

Over the next few months, Gwen prehabbed, rehabbed, massaged, and recovered. She started by walking Stanley around the block. She progressed to a slow jog. To her first mile. Then five. Her ultimate goal was 120 per week. Meanwhile, she breastfed, battled broken sleep, and established a new routine.

As she adjusted, we texted and FaceTimed. She seemed different—lighter, happier, more peaceful. She said she saw other mothers come back to compete. And win. And she wanted to be among them.

On November 7, 2017, Gwen posted a video to Twitter. Her own voice-over announced the plan: "You can say a lot has changed since 2016. We got a new home, in a new city. I achieved my dream of winning and being the best in the world. I achieved my truest dream and had my first child. My beautiful Stanley. Giving birth was amazing. But also very difficult. My body needed time to heal. I always knew I would make a comeback, be a working mom. He would have a bib. And I would have a bib. I would train in this new body and get that feeling back, to grind again, to achieve again. To try again to be the best. I want it all again. Except, entirely new. I am ready to make a comeback to a stage I've never been. Hello, Marathon. It's nice to meet you. My name is Gwen Jorgensen."

Under the video she posted four boxes, the first three checked: World Champion in Triathlon; Olympic gold in Triathlon; Become a mom. The last box, Olympic gold in Marathon, remained blank.

Gwen redesigned her life: new baby, new body, new beginning.

And she redesigned her dream: "I want to go to Tokyo, and I want to win gold."

ACKNOWLEDGMENTS

This is our family story. But without so many others, it would not have been possible. Thank you, Gwen and Patrick, for hours of interviews, for allowing us to tell our story, for trusting us with your emails and conversations. Patrick, your endless empathy continues to amaze. Gwen, we are so proud you are part of our clan. Thank you for providing inspiration in your achievement—and for helping us to follow our own aspirations.

So many believed in Gwen and helped her achieve a dream she didn't even know was possible. To you, we are grateful: Dave Anderson, Cindi Bannink, Blaine Carlson, Craig and Larry Lanza, Eric Lehmann, Patrick Lemieux, Barb Lindquist, Bobby McGee, Andy Schmitz, Tom Schuler, Jim Stintzi, Jamie Turner, Team USA, USA Triathlon, International Olympic Committee. Thank you also to the countless others who were integral to the journey—coaches, fans, training partners, teammates, sponsors.

We are also thankful to the group of highly talented people who worked with us. Thank you to Kathie Giorgio, Allwriters' Workplace & Workshop, and the Tuesday Night Book-Writing Workshop for your feedback, your line-by-line edits, and your honesty. You helped us explain triathlon and sports. Thank you to our beta readers, Kassie Slotty and Terri Carnell. Your positivity, encouragement, and attention to detail gave us confidence and drive.

Thank you to the commentators who etched Gwen's legacy in hours of race footage and are featured in this memoir: Trevor Harris, Matthew Keenan, Nicole Livingstone, Barrie Shepley, Emma Snowsill, Julie Swail, Mark Tompkins, Al Trautwig, Greg Welch.

Thank you, Joel and Josh, for your support and optimism, for listening to us read chapters aloud (for hours at the kitchen table), for supporting our years at the computer, and for believing.

Thank you, Liz Evans and Meyer & Meyer Sport, for your faith in the project and story, and for giving our voice a home. Your ideas and direction transformed our dream into this book.

Bob Babbitt, thank you for your time and foreword.

Thank you to those who generously supplied images: Talbot Cox, Amy Horst, Josh Olson, Emily Reddy, Marsh Smith.

We are deeply grateful to all who asked about the project, who celebrated our progress, and who sought a book about Gwen on social media. Your emails, messages, and texts inspired us.

To our family, we heard your cheers, both in the stands and for this memoir. Thank you for providing years of celebration. Thank you for your love.

This memoir is a labor of love, and we are so thankful to have done this together, mother and two daughters.

Photo courtesy of Talbot Cox.